Ethno-political Conflict in Pakistan

This book critically examines the causes of the increase in insurgent violence in Balochistan and explores the relations between the national government of Pakistan and the province of Balochistan.

Based on historical analysis, the book argues that the national government of Pakistan and the leaders of Balochistan both use a standard narrative when dealing with each other. According to the Baloch narrative, Islamabad exploits Balochistan's natural resources without giving Balochistan its due share and has never accepted and granted Balochistan equal rights. The centre's narrative emphasizes the tribal character of the Baloch society and suggests that the Baloch elite hinder Balochistan's integration with the federation. This book demonstrates that both narratives are inherently flawed and presents a precipitous picture of the problem of insurgent violence. It also shows that the Baloch leadership is divided along tribal lines and lacks a unified voice and proposes that the Baloch elite use the narrative of enduring injustice only as a source of politicization of Baloch ethnicity when an actual or perceived injustice is taking place.

An important addition to the literature on ethno-political conflicts, this unique analysis of the importance of narrative in the imagination of political movements will be of interest to scholars in the fields of South Asian studies, ethnic conflicts, separatist and political movements and Asian politics.

Rizwan Zeb is an Associate Professor and Chair in the Department of Social Sciences at Iqra University, Islamabad, Pakistan.

Routledge Advances in South Asian Studies
Series Editors
Subrata K. Mitra, *Heidelberg University, Germany*
Rani Mullen, *College of William and Mary, USA*

South Asia, with its burgeoning, ethnically diverse population, soaring economies, and nuclear weapons, is an increasingly important region in the global context. The series, which builds on this complex, dynamic and volatile area, features innovative and original research on the region as a whole or on the countries. Its scope extends to scholarly works drawing on history, politics, development studies, sociology and economics of individual countries from the region as well those that take an interdisciplinary and comparative approach to the area as a whole or to a comparison of two or more countries from this region. In terms of theory and method, rather than basing itself on any one orthodoxy, the series draws broadly on the insights germane to area studies, as well as the tool kit of the social sciences in general, emphasizing comparison, the analysis of the structure and processes, and the application of qualitative and quantitative methods. The series welcomes submissions from established authors in the field as well as from young authors who have recently completed their doctoral dissertations.

Indigenous Identity in South Asia
Making Claims in the Colonial Chittagong Hill Tracts
Tamina M. Chowdhury

Gender justice and proportionality in India
Comparative perspectives
Juliette Gregory Duara

Governance and Development in India
A Comparative Study on Andhra Pradesh and Bihar After Liberalization
Seyed Hossein Zarhani

Ethno-political Conflict in Pakistan
The Baloch Movement
Rizwan Zeb

For a full list of titles, please see: www.routledge.com/asianstudies/series/RASAS

Ethno-political Conflict in Pakistan
The Baloch Movement

Rizwan Zeb

LONDON AND NEW YORK

First published 2020
by Routledge
2 Park Square, Milton Park, Abingdon, Oxon OX14 4RN

and by Routledge
52 Vanderbilt Avenue, New York, NY 10017

Routledge is an imprint of the Taylor & Francis Group, an informa business

© 2020 Rizwan Zeb

The right of Rizwan Zeb to be identified as author of this work has been asserted by him in accordance with sections 77 and 78 of the Copyright, Designs and Patents Act 1988.

All rights reserved. No part of this book may be reprinted or reproduced or utilised in any form or by any electronic, mechanical, or other means, now known or hereafter invented, including photocopying and recording, or in any information storage or retrieval system, without permission in writing from the publishers.

Trademark notice: Product or corporate names may be trademarks or registered trademarks, and are used only for identification and explanation without intent to infringe.

British Library Cataloguing-in-Publication Data
A catalogue record for this book is available from the British Library

Library of Congress Cataloging-in-Publication Data
Names: Zeb, Rizwan, author.
Title: Ethno-political conflict in Pakistan : the Baloch movement / Rizwan Zeb.
Description: 1. | New York : Routledge, 2019. | Series: Routledge advances in South Asian studies | Includes bibliographical references and index.
Identifiers: LCCN 2019033098 (print) | LCCN 2019033099 (ebook) | ISBN 9780367331450 (hardback) | ISBN 9780429318139 (ebook) | ISBN 9781000729627 (adobe pdf) | ISBN 9781000729771 (mobi) | ISBN 9781000729924 (epub)
Subjects: LCSH: Balochistān (Pakistan)—Politics and government. | Baluchi (Southwest Asian people)—History—Autonomy and independence movements.| Pakistan—Ethnic relations.
Classification: LCC DS392.B28 Z43 2019 (print) | LCC DS392.B28 (ebook) | DDC 954.91/505–dc23
LC record available at https://lccn.loc.gov/2019033098
LC ebook record available at https://lccn.loc.gov/2019033099

ISBN: 978-0-367-33145-0 (hbk)
ISBN: 978-0-429-31813-9 (ebk)

Typeset in Times New Roman
by Scientific Publishing Services

To Ammi and Abu
This is for you
And
To Bushra, Huzaifa and Maryam

Contents

Acknowledgements	viii
Foreword	x
Introduction	1

PART I 21
Baloch and Balochistan through history

1	Baloch and Balochistan through history	23
2	Balochistan during the British rule in India	39

PART II 61
**Centre–Province (Islamabad–Balochistan) relations
post-independence**

3	Independence of Pakistan, accession of Kalat and centre–Balochistan relations (1947–69)	63
4	Centre–Balochistan relations (1969–77)	93
5	Balochistan and the peace interval (1977–99)	121
6	The return of insurgency in Balochistan	145

Conclusion	180
Epilogue	187
Bibliography	193
Index	202

Acknowledgements

Now that this book is complete, I must confess that this remarkable research journey turned out to be my *Ray Buduick story*. Just like Ray Buduick, I could never have imagined what is in store for me in this journey. During this time, I had a number of experiences good as well as bad. What astonished me the most is that in my naivety, I always believed that in academia, one would never be libelled for questioning something, especially when one tries to do it to the best of one's ability with objectivity and providing detailed sources. Alas, I was proven wrong. My book is a critical analysis of the Baloch nationalist narrative. This implies that in it the flaws in the Baloch narrative will also be highlighted, and this is something that was unacceptable for many within the academic community, be it in Australia, Europe and elsewhere. For them, my research was driven by some ulterior motive. For this, I was accused of holding extremely conservative, derogatory positions and value judgements towards the Baloch society and leadership and that in my work, I was providing unconditional defence of the central state's policies in Balochistan, under a variety of administrations and because of this, my work lacks credibility.

Fortunately for me, there were many who held a different view about me and my work. I was fortunate enough to have found such people who not necessarily agreeing to what I wrote helped, supported and guided me through this journey. First and foremost, I am grateful to Dr. Michael Azeriadis. He was always generous with his time and provided excellent feedback and guidance on how to write, rewrite and/or sharpen my argument.

I also owe a huge debt and gratitude to Professor Emeritus Paul Wallace of University of Missouri and Professor Philip Oldenburg of the Columbia University. They helped me during the early stages of the research and provided helpful comments throughout the research. They were generous with their time and read early drafts and provided helpful comments and suggestions how to improve the drafts. The study benefitted immensely from their insightful comments. Arguably the most prominent and authoritative historian of Pakistan and India, especially the partition of the Indian subcontinent, Professor Ian Talbot (University of Southampton) provided valuable comments and suggestions on how to further improve the research. I was fortunate that Pakistan's leading political scientist Professor

Acknowledgements ix

Hasan Askari Rizvi read the complete draft and provided detailed feedback. I am grateful to all these dons of South Asian studies. I must also acknowledge the continuous support and guidance of Professor Marvin G. Weinbaum. He also read the whole manuscript and provided valuable feedback. Late Professor Pervaiz Iqbal Cheema (one of the C3)[1] was always supportive and inspirational.

I must thank Dr. Chris Smith formerly from the department of war studies at Kings College London, Professor A Foster, then head of the department of Politics and Governance Research Center (GRC), Professor Martin White and Ms. Karine Taylor, then provost and administrator of the Institute for Advance Studies, University of Bristol for providing me an opportunity to join the IAS as a Benjamin Meaker visiting professor. It was at IAS that I first studied about narratives.

My sister-in-law Shehzadday Afzal was my unofficial research assistant throughout my research. She located a number of articles, reports and books. She also ensured that I received all the books I required. I am also grateful to Ms. Areebah Shahid, a former student and good friend, for providing a few important books. During these five years, I was fortunate to always have on my side my mates: Adriaan Wolvaardt and Will Lee. No words can express my gratitude to them. I am confident this friendship is for life.

I was fortunate to find the best editorial team one can hope for. Advances in South Asia Studies series editor Professor Subrata Kumar Mitra and Asian Studies senior editor Dorothea Schaefter not only were supportive throughout but graciously provided me support when I needed it the most. For this, I am indebted to them. I must also thank Alexandra de Brauw, who very patiently worked with me and ignored missed deadlines and repeated delays.

I am grateful to Professor Hafeez Malik, Villanova University, and the editor of the prestigious Journal of South Asian and Middle Eastern Studies, and Nadia Barsoum, assistant editor of the journal for their cooperation, support and permission to incorporate the paper on the NAP government in Balochistan during the 1970s in the book.

For her patience and unstinting support and for her love, I am grateful to Bushra. Words would be completely inadequate to express my true feelings and thanks, so I would not even attempt it. Our kids Huzaifa and Maryam got used to "baba is working on his book."

Last but not least, I must remember my parents late Aziz Shaheen and late Muhammad Bashir Ahmed. It was my mother who inculcated the love of books in me and my father who throughout supported me. It is my regret that he could not witness the fulfilment of perhaps his last wish.

Note

1 Stephen Cohen, Late P. R. Chari, and Late P. I. Cheema.

Foreword

When Henry Kissinger was asked to comment on the Baloch insurgency in Pakistan on a fact-finding mission for President Kennedy in 1962, he replied, "I wouldn't recognize the Balochistan problem if it hit me in the face."

Even though the next decades in the region would be turbulent and attract the attention of the world – the revolution in Iran, the invasion of Afghanistan by the Soviets and their eventual expulsion and the rise of the Taliban – Balochistan remained an isolated island in the midst of the geopolitical storm. This is not to say that there was tranquillity in the Baloch areas of Pakistan; on the contrary, the Baloch increasingly felt marginalized and deprived, especially by what they saw as the arrogant and incompetent central government.

As I discovered when I was Commissioner consecutively of three divisions in the province during the 1980s, the Baloch viewed their identity through an ethnic prism that had been distorted by its interaction with Pakistan. Many elders told me that there was a time when a Baloch woman wearing her entire marriage jewellery could walk alone from one end of the province to the other and not be molested by anyone; she represented the honour of the Baloch tribes. And yet today, they lamented the passing of that time and the loss of honour.

The books and studies on Balochistan were few and far between, and the province was largely inaccessible. Balochistan, its people and their customs, thus remained little known in the rest of Pakistan. Over the decades, Pakistanis increasingly saw the Baloch as backward, illiterate and unsophisticated. My experience was to the contrary. I found the Baloch literate, wise and people of honour. Let me illustrate this through two stories.

Upon my arrival in Makran to take charge as Commissioner of the Makran Division in the mid-1980s, I was faced with an urgent challenge. Local Muslim religious extremists, working with similar-minded zealots in others parts of Pakistan, had been planning a bloodbath of the Zikri sect. Fired by President General Zia-ul-Haq's harsh plans to "Islamize" Pakistan, they declared that they would exterminate the Zikris who they did not consider Muslims. The day this was to happen had been fixed even before my arrival. I had only a few days to diffuse the situation. I was suddenly faced with the greatest crisis of my period in Makran with no time and little resources at hand.

Foreword xi

Fortunately for me, Mir Ghaus Bakhsh Bizenjo, the prominent opposition leader and an elder of the Bizenjo tribe, was visiting Makran to reconnect with his supporters, especially among the Zikri. I had met him earlier and we had hit it off. I realized Bizenjo held the key to the problem. I took a bold step and invited him for dinner at the Commissioner's House. He responded with equal boldness and agreed to come. At dinner, we both chuckled as we contemplated how our respective organizations, without doubt monitoring our meeting with unease, would be outraged. But it allowed me to discuss the Zikri situation in detail and request Bizenjo to travel from household to household calming the situation. I would deal with the religious extremists through the law. It was largely thanks to Bizenjo that the threatened bloodbath did not take place. I had survived my first big crisis in Balochistan.

As anticipated, the intelligence agencies reporting on our supposedly secret dinner sent a negative report which went directly to Zia-ul-Haq. He wrote to the Governor of the Province demanding to know why the Commissioner met a critic as prominent as Bizenjo. The Governor, Lt. General K.K. Afridi, dismissed the President's query by saying he had full faith in the Commissioner and backed his actions.

A few years later, when I was Commissioner of the Sibi Division, Bizenjo arrived to deliver a blistering public speech about the President in the main Sibi bazaar. He also praised me profusely. Immediately after the meeting, a worried-looking intelligence officer called on me to ask how a leading critic of the President could be praising me so lavishly and in public. Hurriedly, I sent a trusted messenger to Bizenjo requesting him not to praise me and certainly not in public. On the contrary, I pointed out some salty abuse directed at the Commissioner would be appropriate. I could almost hear him chuckling when he received my message.

As Commissioner of the Sibi Division, I was aware that Nawab Akbar Bugti was one of the most important Baloch leaders in my division and also that he had many critics and was one of the most difficult leaders to deal with. Fortunately for me, he had read some of my books on the Pukhtun tribes and invited me for dinner in his traditional home of Dera Bugti. His charisma and authority were unchallenged. At the dinner, I was the only guest although the Nawab's cousin, a federal minister, was also present. We were served by the Nawab's son Saleem, then a minister of the provincial cabinet, who did not sit at the table to eat with us as a special gesture to show honour to the guest. We spoke of politics, history, and tribes and their customs late into the night.

I was amazed to hear that not only had he read Ibn Khaldun, when he was in a Pakistani jail, but could apply Khaldun's theories to the situation of the Bugti tribe. I thought to myself which Pakistani politician would have heard the name Ibn Khaldun, let alone read him intelligently. During my time in Sibi, I had no problem with his tribe. The word was out that during my tenure the tribe would cooperate.

That is why when I heard of the brutal manner of the Nawab's killing, I was shocked. It was a tragedy for Pakistan as it not only antagonized the Baloch but

xii *Foreword*

lost one of Pakistan's strongest links to Balochistan. Since his humiliating murder, Balochistan has been in a state of some turmoil and he is seen by nationalists as the first martyr for the independence of Balochistan.

I found the Balochistan society fascinating – on the one hand, here were the Baloch discussing Ibn Khaldun, and on the other, there were also those that still practised the ancient custom of trial by fire ordeal.[1]

The problem for Pakistan is that not only is Balochistan poorly understood but the central structural conundrum in the relationship remains irresolvable: while Balochistan has a population of some 12 million people of the 210 million Pakistanis, its area comprises almost 50% of the land mass. Besides, Balochistan has rich, untapped mineral, oil and gas deposits. It also has a large coast, which gives it access to the sealanes of the Persian Gulf, and has long borders with both Iran and Afghanistan, placing it in one of the most sensitive geopolitical regions of Asia. It is quite clear that while Pakistan will find it difficult to survive without Balochistan, Balochistan could easily survive without Pakistan.

Considering the dearth of literature on Balochistan, Dr. Rizwan's book is a boon. It reflects the structure of a conventional PhD thesis: Chapter 1 is on Balochistan history, Chapter 2 deals with British colonialism, Chapter 3 deals with the independence of Pakistan, Chapter 4 deals with relations between the central government of Pakistan and Balochistan, Chapter 5 is on what the author calls the "Peace Interval," the period between 1977 and 1999, and Chapter 6 is titled "The Return of Insurgency in Balochistan."

The last paragraph of Dr. Rizwan's book sums up its essence while capturing his sense of optimism and underlining the importance of Balochistan itself: "The significance of Balochistan in the future stability of Pakistan cannot be over-emphasized. Its geostrategic location, hard-working and brave people, vast resources and critical projects such as Gwadar Port and the China–Pakistan Economic Corridor (CPEC) are too vital for Pakistan. Due to these factors, Balochistan has become a centre of attention of regional and global players. While this might provide the Baloch insurgents more reasons to fight the state of Pakistan yet, for exactly these factors Islamabad is unlikely to let its guard down. However, it would make sense if Islamabad considers its policy options regarding Balochistan. One way to do this is working out an arrangement like the Alaska Permanent Fund for Balochistan.

Although it is too soon to objectively analyse the prospects and pitfalls of CPEC, especially when the available data are limited yet one can easily infer from what is publicly known that once CPEC is fully operational, it has the potential to transfer Pakistan from just a South Asian state to a West-Central and South Asian state. This would also provide India and Pakistan ample options and choices to revisit their hostile relationship."

I was intrigued by what attracted Dr Rizwan to the study of Balochistan and asked him. He explained, "Honestly, it was not something that I never thought I would work on. At the Institute of Regional Studies, Brookings Institution and the University of Bristol, I researched on Strategic stability in South Asia especially conventional imbalance and nuclear doctrines.

Foreword xiii

When I applied for admission to do a PhD at the University of Western Australia, I submitted a research proposal Risk-Taking and Crisis Behaviour of India and Pakistan: Case studies of Kargil and 2002 Standoff. I was admitted into UWA's PhD in Political Science & International Relations program with this proposal and was awarded full scholarship by UWA to conduct doctoral research on it. I realized that no one has seriously analyzed the Baloch nationalist movement other than in parts and bits and pieces. I decided that if I have to work on Balochistan, I better work on Balochistan Nationalist struggle. From there, I narrowed my research further and eventually wrote my dissertation on Baloch national narrative."

But there were many hurdles along the way:

Lack of research material and accessing what was there was the most important hurdle at the start of the research. Then came the <question of> approval from UWA's research ethics committee to do field research in Pakistan especially Balochistan. The timing coincided with the alarming reports coming for the area. Another issue that I faced was that no one I spoke to was willing to consider the points that went against their position/narrative.

I asked him what the world should know about Balochistan. "The world should know," he said, "Balochistan is much more than just oil, gas, sardars, CPEC, Gwadar. People just like all of us live there; honest, brave and hardworking people. They have a beautiful culture. Their problems are real; their sufferings are real as well as immense. They need a healing touch not an iron fist.

In Islamabad, there is a famous eatery, Bolan Saltish that is renowned for its sajji [roast]. Perhaps other than Gwadar, Sardars Mengal, Marri and Bugti, this Baloch item is the most known Baloch thing in Islamabad, what we don't know is what a common Baloch nomad eats and when he might get to eat sajji."

I wondered what the author hoped to achieve by writing this book. "I hope that this book would help in developing a better understanding of Baloch nationalist narrative. For instance, there is hardly anyone in Pakistani academia who rejects or disputes Ahmedyar Khan's position that Kalat's accession was under duress and without his consent. Most of the Baloch historians insist that the Kalat's elected representatives in the House of Commons and House of Lords rejected accession with Pakistan. No one mentions how these representatives were elected in the first place. For the first time in this book, I am challenging these established facts. For Centre's narratives, I have pointed the flaws in it.

By challenging the Baloch stated position, I am not denying the legitimacy of their demands for the rights promised to them by the constitution of Pakistan. I believe that understanding the Baloch narrative(s) and its drivers is most important for any crisis management and conflict resolution there. Also this is why I think that alarming issues such as missing persons and targeted killings are a means to an end and not an end in itself."

We owe a debt of gratitude to Dr. Rizwan Zeb for dedicating so many years of his life to studying Balochistan with such perseverance and presenting the findings to the world with such empathy. Although it is a labour of love, he has not

xiv *Foreword*

avoided the hard questions and issues. In the end, Dr. Rizwan has provided a much needed "healing touch."

Perhaps if Dr. Rizwan sent his book with compliments to Dr. Kissinger, the good doctor may well be tempted to reassess his perception of Balochistan.

Professor Akbar Ahmed,
Ibn Khaldun Chair of Islamic Studies,
American University, Washington, D.C.
September, 2018

Note

1 See Akbar S. Ahmed, "Trial By Ordeal Among Bugtis: Ritual as a Diacritical Factor in Baloch Ethnicity," in *Marginality and Modernity: Ethnicity and Change in Post-Colonial Balochistan*, ed. Paul Titus (Karachi: Oxford University Press, 1996).

Introduction

In Akira Kurosawa's classic *Rashomon*, different characters narrate their perspective of the story. *Vantage Point* treats the plot and its execution in a similar way. The story of the film is presented through the perspectives of different characters, and just like the classical Indian fable *the blind men and the elephant*, a complete picture emerges only after piecing all the perspectives and views together. By doing this, one gets the whole picture of the story.

What we learn from these examples is that by taking into account all versions of an event or a series of events, one gets the complete picture or *at least* a better understanding of how and why it happened. Can one apply this method to understand real political events? Take for instance the *single shot that shook the world*: the murder of Hapsburg Archduke Franz Ferdinand and his wife Sonia in Sarajevo that resulted in developments that culminated into the First World War.[1] They were murdered by one Gavrilo Princip. Who was he? Was he just a man who happened to be at that street with a gun? Understanding Mr. Princip's narrative of why killing Archduke was important and why he volunteered for this action would be really helpful in understanding the underlying reasons behind this murder. This narrative would bring to our attention the Serb independence struggle. In this narrative, Princip, a Serb nationalist, is a freedom fighter and a hero, a martyr for the cause of freedom.[2]

Scholars like Francis Fukuyama were quick in forecasting a peaceful world after the dissolution of the Union of Soviet Socialist Republics (USSR) and the end of the almost-fifty-year-long Cold War.[3] The then US President George Bush famously proclaimed a new world order.[4] For some time, it appeared that the decade of 1990s would be a decade free of fear. This, however, proved to be an incorrect assessment as the 1990s turned out to be one of the bloodiest decades in recent history.

Ethnic conflicts in Bosnia–Herzegovina and Rwanda resulted in genocide, ethnic cleansing and mass displacement. Ethnic conflicts in Sri Lanka, Indonesia and elsewhere brought to fore the ugly reality that ethnic conflicts would continue, despite the current emphasis on terrorism and the war against terrorism, to be a major source of instability in the world. Cases like Bosnia–Herzegovina and Rwanda continue to pose a challenge to students of ethnic conflicts. A major question which continues to be discussed is what led to such violence. How those who

2   Introduction

are behind the most cruel and gruesome acts of violence justify it? What narrative they had which led to and justified such hatred? How and why these *new* rivalries, based on *older* differences and rivalries, emerged?

How the narrative based on the *collective memory* of past injustices came into play to instigate a new wave of violence? How significant was the role of the ethnic elite in the process of ethnic awakening, politicization and violence?

Over the years, a number of scholars have provided several explanations for the emergence of ethnic conflicts. These explanations range from ancient rivalries to political interests and sense of security dilemma. All such explanations have valid points, yet they fail to answer several questions, especially regarding the timing of the eruption of the ethnic conflict.

The *process* of an ethnic conflict involves *ethnic awakening, ethnic politicization* and *ethnic violence*, and the *role played by the ethnic elite* in this process and the *tools* these ethnic elite employ in this process.

Ethno-political conflicts occur due to the politicization of ethnicity. In the process of politicization of ethnicity, the elite or leadership of that ethnicity and ethnic group play the most important role. Once ethnicity is politicized, again it is the ethnic elite/leadership which decides whether the politically active ethnicity will turn violent or not. When it turns violent, government symbols and installations are targeted, as are other ethnic groups. This is done for two reasons: one, to signal resolve, and two, to achieve a stronger bargaining position vis-à-vis the central government. In the process of the politicization of ethnicity, the biggest tool used by the elite is a narrative based on the collective memory of an actual or perceived injustice to the ethnic group. However, the presence of a memory of a past injustice could only be used to politicize an ethnic group when an *actual* or *perceived* injustice is happening to the ethnic group at the time.

THE ROLE OF THE ETHNIC ELITE

A very important factor in ethno-political conflicts is the behaviour of the leadership/elite and how they politicize ethnicity.[5] The existence of ethnic differences and consciousness could not lead to violent conflict between two or more than two ethnic groups. It occurs when the ethnic elite of a particular ethnicity realize that they can achieve their objectives through politicizing the ethnic differences. The ethnic elite then use different methods such as a particular narrative based on the historical memory of an actual or perceived injustice committed against the ethnic group to politicize the ethnicity. They create fear of the *other* in the ethnic group by pointing out that what is or could be happening to the ethnic group is in fact the continuation of the past injustices. Gurr argued that this fear of other groups would then turn into aggression against what he called the *source* of that frustration.[6] Ivan Siber, also emphasizing the role of the ethnic elite, pointed to the choices and decisions made by the ethnic elite as a major factor in deciding what shape a particular ethnic conflict would take.[7] Siber argued that the ethnic elite have a choice of whether to deal with the problems or to create fear and hatred of the *other*.[8]

Introduction 3

Before surveying the role of the ethnic elite in ethnic conflicts, one needs to look at the term the ethnic elite.

Who are the ethnic elite? Are they the political and/or tribal leaders of an ethnic group who already hold a position of considerable influence and authority which they use during such situations *or* can an ethnic conflict create a situation which can provide an opportunity to someone who could identify and utilize the circumstances to emerge as a leader of a group? What strategies and techniques the ethnic elite use to achieve their objective and goals? More so, why the masses accept what the ethnic elite say and follow them? Why their, i.e. the ethnic elite's, position and plan resonate with the public?

David Laitin believes that the ethnic elite is someone who is in a position to provide incentives to people to join in the struggle. Traditionally, the ethnic elite is someone with a certain position of authority within the group. Barring a few exceptions, generally, he is not part of the masses and is in a position to provide a narrative of events linking it with the past and the collective memory of the group. He is aware of what to say and how to formulate his narrative within the group so that it resonates with the people. He presents the problem and conflict as a collective problem of the whole group. By doing this, he consolidates his position as the leader of the group and uses it to gain political legitimacy. He then uses this political legitimacy during negotiation with the centre/government. This point can be substantiated with several examples. Take for example the case of Kenya. Joseph Mboya,[9] a noted Kenyan politician, stated that in Kenya, a number of leaders used the memory of victimization and hostilities to achieve their own political objectives. According to Mboya (who was referring to his own country and the region, yet this principal has universal applicability), when a leader could not achieve his objective at the national level, he reverts to his tribal support base. He uses the political language that provides him the support of his tribe and strengthens his political standing.[10]

Gurr agrees. However, he argues that how the ethnic elite campaign to consolidate their position would have implications for how the situation would develop. According to Gurr, the danger of violence would increase if the ethnic elite accentuate the threats to the ethnic group and instigate fear and hatred of the rival or other groups.[11] Ivan Siber is of the view that most conflicts have political and economic causes, and how to deal with and contextualize the problems depend on the leader of the group. According to Siber, it depends on the ethnic elite whether he engages with the central government or the rival group to solve the problem or takes the route of confrontation and of utilizing people's feelings to create fear.[12] Nedegwa concurs and states that the choices made by the ethnic elite would decide the course of ethnic politics as well as conflict. He further states that as the ethnic elite's position depends on how much authority and following he commands within the ethnic group, he would ensure that he comes out as someone who is safeguarding the rights of and struggling for the needs of the masses.[13]

Rothschild also points to the role of the ethnic elite as the deciding factor in the politicization of ethnicity.[14] He argues that the ethnic elite, to achieve their objective, use certain myths and symbols as rallying points. They use the historical

4   *Introduction*

memory of the past glory and often the defeats that should not be repeated. By doing this, they embark on the path of using force and violence.[15] The existing literature on ethnic conflict points to the veracity of this view. Rene Lemarchand, while discussing the Hutu–Tutsi conflict, wrote:

> The crystallization of group identities is not a random occurrence; it is traceable to specific strategies pursued by ethnic entrepreneurs centrally concerned with the mobilization of group loyalties on behalf of collective interests defined in terms of kinship, region or ethnicity. ...clearly, one cannot overestimate the part played by individual actors in defining the nature of the threats posed to their respective communities, framing strategies designed to counter such threats, rallying support for their cause, bringing pressure to bear on key decision makers, and, in short, politicizing ethnoregional identities ...[16]

The role played by Milosevic in the Bosnian conflict is perhaps the best manifestation of how ethnic leaders can shape and decide the course of ethnic politics and conflict.[17] A number of scholars who have studied the ethnic conflict in Yugoslavia and the subsequent disintegration consider Milosevic as the main actor in the disintegration of Yugoslavia. According to Agneza Roberson, the disintegration of Yugoslavia was a logical outcome of Milosevic's politics.[18] Milosevic, quite early in the conflict, started referring to the power of the *people*. This was followed by his emphasis on the Serb grievances. Milosevic's speech to a large crowd of Serbs on 24 April 1987 could be considered the most important step in the politicization of the Serb politics. During this speech, Milosevic cautioned the police (mostly ethnic Albanian) not to be sturdy with the Serbs in attendance. During his speech, he stressed on the Serbian national pride and stated that the Serbs never stopped or backed off due to an obstacle in their way. In the same speech, he stereotyped the Albanians and warned them that "there will be no tyranny on this soil anymore."[19]

According to the literature, once the ethnic elite embark on the course of the politicization of ethnicity, among the first steps they take is to marginalize the moderate voices within their ethnic group. This could be done in a number of ways such as labelling the moderates the enemy's agent or motivated by personal gains and greed. Milosevic did exactly this once he started using the power of the people card. He made sure that all moderate voices and elements, especially those opposing his adopted course of action, are sidelined and eventually removed from party positions in the Serbian League of Communists. In the following months and years, Milosevic increasingly used the language grounded in ethnic terms and based on the selective historical memory of the Serbs. For instance, on the occasion of the 600th anniversary of the Battle of Kosovo, Milosevic stated that the defeat of the Serbs from the hands of the Turks was mainly due to the internal divisions and the lack of a united front and leadership of the Serbs. This internal division was the prime reason for the Serbs' suffering up till the communist era. He accused the Serb leadership of making compromises at the cost of the Serbian dignity and honour to enjoy their own petty benefits. He pledged that it would not

Introduction 5

happen again. Linking the past with what was happening at the time, Milosevic stated that after six centuries, the Serbs are once again facing similar battle fronts, though not armed battles yet, but this might not be the case for long.[20]

Over the course of time, Milosevic's political vocabulary got increasingly ethnic. At the same time, using selective historical narrative, he started stereotyping the *rival* ethnic groups. This narrative which was soon picked up by the Serbian media blamed the Albanians for the violence, accusing them of despoiling churches and graveyards. In this narrative, the rival ethnicities, especially the Albanians, were projected as terrorists and separatists, whereas the Serbs were the victim of massacres and were presented as endangered and as refugees or internally displaced due to the atrocities committed against them.

How the other side is perceived also plays an important role in the initiation of an ethnic conflict.[21] Brown is of the view that in a conflict situation, the other side is often demonized and *ethnic mythologies* are created.[22] Gurr and Harff argue that ethnic conflict is most likely to occur when there is a strong sense among a minority of imposed group disadvantages *and* where the ethnic group is characterized by strong group cohesion and represented by leaders with political agenda.[23]

The case study of Milosevic's use of a narrative based on the collective memory of a historical injustice (actual or perceived) during the Yugoslav crisis brings to our attention the most important tool which he and the ethnic elite in general use to manipulate the masses. This is important because this would provide an answer to the question why the ethnic elite often succeed in mobilizing the masses.

THE SIGNIFICANCE OF NARRATIVES

Milosevic's use of a narrative based on the Serbian collective memory of the historical events brings to our attention the significance of a clearly crafted, but based on what is generally perceived to have happened, narrative as a tool of the ethnic elite in the politicization of ethnicity. This is not unique to the ethnic conflict in Yugoslavia. A closer look at all the ethnic conflicts, especially those that emerged after the end of the Cold War and the break-up of the Union of Soviet Socialist Republics (USSR), points to the presence of a narrative based on the collective memory of the ethnic group which was used by the ethnic elite to mobilize the masses.

The significance of perceptions based on memory cannot be overemphasized. Memory plays an important role in our lives. A particular perspective of the past makes humans what they are today. The collective memory of a group, whether it is actual or perceived or a mix of both, serves two important purposes: one, it provides the group members an identity by providing an answer to who they (the group members) are; and second, who is the *other* and how the *other* has acted towards them (or us) in the past? Tilly argues that people often develop accounts about themselves. Tilly calls these accounts *boundary stories*. These boundary stories, according to Tilly, provide a sense of not only who these people are but also how they differ from and interact with other groups.

6   Introduction

A number of scholars have pointed the importance of the collective memory of the ethnic group in its relations with other groups. Van Evera, for instance, linking the past with the present, argued that whether the groups or nationalities will be peaceful or in a conflict would depend on how they have treated each other in the past. Conflict would be greater between groups where the history would be rife with mistrust and bad blood. The experiences of the past would result in conflict, and the chances of normalization would be minimal. Why the past would dictate a group's actions? Kaufman states that the answer lies in symbolic politics. According to Kaufman and other proponents of the symbolic politics theory, people, instead of making decisions rationally, follow their emotions. This, according to Kaufman, is the prime reason why the masses mobilize. The masses would react once the ethnic myths and symbols that they hold dear appear to be in danger. According to Kaufman, at the individual level, people respond to the emotionally laden ethnic symbols and collectively when other groups are blamed for their problems.

The idea of the *other* that is in most cases evil, inhuman, tyrannical, antagonistic and violent plays an important role in the formation and strengthening of the ethnic identity of a group. In ethnic histories, this *other* is often projected as a threat to the very existence of the group. This creates a fear of the other, which not only strengthens the identity of the group, but also consolidates and unites the members of the group. Such narratives, while blaming the other for whatever wrongs the group suffers, also create a sense of victimhood in the group. Once this happens, everything which the group does would be projected as self-defence. The other would be blamed for the hostilities and atrocities committed against the group. In such a situation, only one's sufferings would appear to be of any significance, whereas the other is portrayed as a total evil or whatever is happening to it would be justified under different pretexts. Renee Hirschon calls such behaviour victim complex. Almost all ethnic conflicts, especially in Bosnia and Rwanda, are prime examples of the fact that the groups involved were suffering from victim complex. Once this victimhood complex takes roots in a group, the members of the group could only anticipate the persistence of violence against them. Based on what he observed in Burundi, Jean-Pierre Chretien wrote:

> Fear … lies not in the décor of the drama, but becomes the principle actor. What does it mean to be Hutu or Tutsi? It doesn't mean being Bantu or Hamite, nor serf or lord. It means remembering who killed those closest to you fifteen years ago, and asking yourself who will kill your child ten years …[24]

Narratives

Bar-Tal, Oren and Zehngut define a narrative as "a story about an event or events that has a plot with a clear starting point and end point, providing sequential and casual coherence about the world and/or a group's experience."[25] According to Bruner, a narrative is a "community's collective experiences embodied in its belief system."[26]

Introduction 7

Bruner described narrative as:

> Social constructions that coherently interrelate a sequence of historical and current events: they are accounts of a community's collective experiences, embodied in its belief system and represent the collective's symbolically constructed shared identity.[27]

Beckerman and Zembylas argue that "historical collective narratives are embedded in particular emotional discourses about collective (national) belonging and otherness."[28] Beckerman and Zembylas further argued that such narratives create reality for the people and they identify with the narratives and believe in them passionately.[29]

Narratives do not exist or operate in isolation. It has been pointed that "rival groups in a conflict, motivated by contradictory goals and interests, adopt negating collective narratives, while viewing the other as a perpetrator with no legitimate claims, fostering a sense that acknowledging the other side's narrative undermines one's own narrative."[30]

Main elements of a narrative

Collective memory plays an important role in the creation of a narrative. Scholars such as Bukley-Zistel, Liu and Hilton who have worked on the subject are of the view that narratives are used to justify the case or cause of the group.[31]

It is normal to have more than one narrative in the group which might be dealing with and/or addressing the concerns of the subgroup within the main group. Take for instance the example of the Baloch. When we look at the Baloch narrative, we realize that it is a collection of a number of sub-narratives. There is a Kalat narrative, a Brahui narrative, a Bugti narrative, an Allah Nazar narrative, to name just a few. All these narratives focus on specific issues. Once all these narratives are combined, the Baloch narrative emerges. More of this would be discussed in subsequent chapters. This is exactly what Moscovici states in his study.[32] Moscovici states that in such a situation, a master narrative emerges that covers all sub-narratives and develops into a large, comprehensive master narrative.[33] According to Hammack, such master narratives incorporate "collective story lines that range from a group's history."[34]

Narratives do not exist in isolation. They are constructed and strengthened in the presence of competing and/or counter-narratives. Narratives are often used to justify a group's position and negate the opponent or rival group's position. Bar-On argued that "The negation of the other allows construction of a monolithic narrative, which excludes the other, including its narrative."[35]

Within such narratives, a group can focus on one or more than one issue. For instance, a number of groups emphasize the identity and purity of their race. In conflict narratives, one can see that groups focus on the atrocities committed against them by the rival or opposing group. This focus develops a sense of

8   *Introduction*

collective victimhood in the group. It is also used to justify any action taken by the group against the rival group(s).

Narrative and ethno-political conflict

Narratives play a significant role in ethno-political conflicts. Groups involved in ethno-political conflicts develop conflict-supportive narratives that "form a collective self-presentation and describe the causes of the conflict, its nature, the image of the rival, the conditions needed to win the conflict."[36]

Apart from the master conflict-supportive narrative, there could be event-specific narratives, but these narratives are also used in the master narrative.[37] If one looks at the Baloch narrative, one can see and identify a number of event-based and tribe- or personality-based narratives that are fed into the master Baloch narrative. These narratives, such as the narrative of Ahmad Yar Khan of how he was forced into joining with Pakistan, the narrative of Nauroz Khan's struggle against the Pakistan Army, the narrative of the battle of Chamalang, have been used by the relevant Baloch actors at various time periods in the history of the centre (Islamabad)–province (Balochistan) relations. When the Baloch master narrative is issued, all of these narratives are then fed into this master narrative. This would be discussed in the following chapters.

Scholars such as Paez, Liu, Bar-Tal and Oren point to the two main elements of a conflict-supportive narrative[38]: the eruption of the conflict and how it evolved play an important role in the development of the narrative. The second important element in this regard is the nature and orientation of the group or society involved in the conflict.[39]

Bar-Tal, analysing the Bosnian, Rwandan and other such conflicts,[40] argued that the master conflict-supportive narrative has eight key themes or points[41]:

> First, the master narrative justifies involvement in the conflict and the course of its development which at the same time, discrediting the goals of the other side as unjustified and unreasonable. Secondly, it delineates the dangers that the conflict constitutes to the security-threat to its cherished values, identity, and territory. Thirdly, it delegitimizes the opponent. In essence, delegitimization denies the adversary's humanity and serves as a psychological permit to harm the rival group. Fourth, in contrast to the opponent, the master narrative presents a glorified image of the in-group. Fifth, it presents the in-group as the sole victim of the conflict and the opponent. Sixth, it encourages patriotism, which is essential in order to mobilize people for achieving its group goals, especially for violent confrontations with the rival-including readiness to make the ultimate sacrifice life. Seventh, it emphasizes the importance of maintaining unity, by ignoring internal discords and disagreements, in the face of an external threat. The eighth and final theme consists of the desire to live in peace, as the conflict situation inflicts suffering and losses.[42]

The aim of a conflict-supportive narrative is not to provide an objective and accurate account of the development, but to unite the group for a struggle.[43]

Conflict-supportive narratives are constructed selectively and ignore facts and information that do not suit the story line. When the Baloch narrative is analysed in the light of these points, one can see that it suffers from the same shortcomings. The Baloch narrative ignores facts that do not support its claim that Kalat was an independent state (Chapter 1) and the British treatment of Kalat (Chapter 2), the failure of the NAP government and Marri–Mengal and Bugti rivalry (Chapter 4), the absence of violence (Chapter 5) and the lack of a unified position, structure or leadership (Chapter 6).

In conflict-supportive narratives, often the information that supports the case of the party is highlighted. At the same time, facts that do not fall in line with the overall theme are ignored. If that is not possible due to these facts being too well known, a justification/explanation is created. For instance, in the Baloch narrative, the decade of 1970s was a decade of bloodshed during which the centre committed grave atrocities against the Baloch. The narrative is totally silent on the role of the Baloch leaders, including Sardar Akbar Bugti, Ahmad Yar Khan and the Jam of Las Bela during this time period. When probed further, Baloch nationalists would argue that the centre always used the *divide and rule* policy in Balochistan and (without naming them) used its agents in Balochistan for this purpose. Regarding the *forcible* accession of Kalat to Pakistan, the Baloch narrative is totally silent on Ahmad Yar Khan's double speak. These and other issues related to the Baloch narrative would be discussed in the subsequent chapters.

The statement of Sardar Ataullah Mengal regarding the returning of the Punjabi civil servants to their parent departments is a clear manifestation of the point that in a narrative, actors often ignore information or fabricate it to support their position. After the dismissal from the chief ministership and the dissolution of the NAP government of Balochistan, Mengal claimed that it was Ghulam Mustafa Khar, the then Governor of Punjab, who called all the Punjabi civil servants to their home departments to create an administrative vacuum in Balochistan. By claiming this, he completely ignored the fact that returning the Punjabi and other non-Balochistani domiciled civil servants to their domiciled provinces and parent departments was the NAP's electoral promise that it repeatedly made during the election campaign (Chapter 4).

Nadir Tsur argues that in conflict-supportive narratives, a framing language is used "that triggers emotions, memory, cognition, and motivations related to past events, nurturing and shaping these in line with the current conflict-supporting narrative."[44]

In every narrative and especially conflict-supportive narrative, two factors play an important role in its construction: one, the cause the group is pursuing is just and worth dying for and, two, in the conflict, the group is the victim or the aggrieved party that must struggle to get justice. A closer look at all major ethno-political conflicts highlights that every group involved in the ethno-political conflict had a narrative justifying its position and actions in the conflict. These

10   *Introduction*

conflict-supportive narratives not only justify the group's action in the past but also provide motivation and justification for the current policy and action as well as the future course of action. It has been rightly argued that "each party's adherence to its own narrative fuels the conflict by further entrenching the differences at the root of the conflict and creating a new battle ground on the issue of historical fact."[45]

The ethnic elite and conflict-supportive narratives

The ethnic elite play the most important role in the construction and dissemination of a narrative. Brubaker and Laitin argue that the ethnic elite play this role by "engendering ethnic insecurity through highly selective and often distorted narratives and representations."[46]

Another aspect of the ethnic elite's role in narrative making is the framing of the *other*. How did the Sinhalese come to the conclusion that the Tamils are "superhumanly cruel and cunning"[47] or that the "Serbs really feared Croats as latter day Ustashas?"[48] This point can be further elaborated using the Baloch narrative. Who informs the common tribal and nomad Baloch, who may never have any direct contact with an outsider, that he is deprived of basic human needs because the Punjabis are looting and plundering the natural resources and wealth of Balochistan, his mother land? How Punjabis as an ethnic group emerged as a rival in the Baloch narrative because, before 1947, Punjabis were not present in the Baloch narrative and there is no evidence of any rivalry and resentment between the two before 1947.

An important point in this regard is that it is the elite that use this collective memory in a coordinated and well-crafted narrative emphasizing the grievances and injustices faced by the ethnic group. Such a narrative is not static, it evolves. New elements are incorporated in it to give a sense of enduring injustice. For instance, whatever Milosevic said in his various speeches and statements was not something new for the Serbs or that they were unaware of. Despite this, it was Milosevic who established a link between the past and the present.

It is the elite who decide what is to be included in the narrative. For instance, when US President William McKinley was assassinated on 11 September 1901, the New York Times declared that this event would be remembered and would have a number of effects on the coming generations of the USA. At present, nobody even remembers that event as it is not part of the overall US narrative. Perhaps, that is why, Richard Bulliet argued that "there are broad ideas that emerge from historical narratives. Perhaps most important is that the historical memory is fleeting and can be easily manipulated."[49] The elite use the historical memory to create a well-crafted narrative. Abdesselam Cheddadi is correct that "history is used to construct a version of events that is accepted as true and immutable...."[50]

The discussion so far about the narratives based on the collective memory of an actual or perceived past in which the other or the rival group (other, them) acted odiously against a group (us) raises three points: One, is the past experience or history a sufficient reason for the ethnic elite to politicize the ethnicity

Introduction 11

and mobilize the masses? Two, somewhat related to the first point, why *only* at a certain time and place the ethnic elite manage to politicize and mobilize the ethnic group? Three (perhaps a fundamental question in itself), why the elite opt for this course of action? Is this *the* only way certain leaders do their politics or is there some reason behind it?

To adequately answer the first two questions, we need to *first* seek an answer to the third question. Once it is established why the ethnic elite, instead of participating in the political activities at the national level, decide to revert to their ethnic group for support and making their presence felt, we would be in a better position to answer the first two questions. A closer look at various ethnic conflicts throughout the world and the actors involved in these conflicts indicates that most of these ethnic elite leading their groups during these conflicts were, at one point or the other, part of the political leadership of the country at the national level. Why these leaders decided to revert to their ethnic groups? Was it because they were not effective at the national level or were they no more in a position of authority or significance within the larger political set-up of the country?

The ethnic elite or, for that matter, all politicians seek political influence and power especially in the area in which they do their politics. Once they feel that their position is challenged and they might lose the power and authority, be it political, social and/or economic, they revert to their home base and use the ethnic card. Added to this could be another explanation: if the ethnic elite are operating in a state which is weak or dysfunctional, this could provide an altogether different set of incentives for the ethnic elite in using the ethnic card. However, the prime reason for the ethnic elite to use the ethnic card or the power of the people card is the fear of losing the political and economic influence.[51] According to Gagnon, if the ethnic elite fear that, apart from losing the power, they might be prosecuted for past crimes, the chances that he would use the ethnic card get maximized.[52] The most important tool the ethnic elite use to instigate the people's power is a narrative based on the collective memory of an actual or perceived injustice committed against them. The political career of Late Nawab Akbar Bugti is a case in point. He served as the Defence Minister of Pakistan and as the Governor and Chief Minister of Balochistan and was active in Pakistan's national politics during the 1990s. During this period, he projected his party, Jamhoori Wattan Party, as the third political force in the country. After the murder of Salal Bugti and developments that took place during General Musharraf's era, he restricted himself to Dera Bugti. After differences emerged and intensified between Nawab Bugti and the General Musharraf-led centre, he increasingly used ethnic language regarding the centre's policy towards him, his tribe and Balochistan. These points are discussed in Chapters 5 and 6.

This brings us back to the first two questions: Why the members of the ethnic group believe in this and why they follow the ethnic elite? And is the narrative of an historical injustice fed to them by the ethnic elite the only reason for mobilization? If so, it would be logical to ask why the masses or group members mobilize at certain times and not others.

12   *Introduction*

One of the common characteristics of different ethnic groups is the presence of people and leaders with extremist and uncompromising views. Despite the presence of such views and actors, ethnic group members go on with their lives. If the ethnic group is financially and politically secure and most of their political and economic as well as social rights are being met, the masses would ignore the extremist views. This would happen even if the past was ugly as only an ugly past is not a reason enough to lose all what they have today. Take for example the French–German and French–English experiences.

This would, however, change if the group members would feel that their political, economic and social rights are under threat. According to Joshua Smith, ethnic group members face four types of threats to their security: *physical, political, economic* and *social and cultural*.[53] They would be inclined to heed to the ethnic elite who would link what is currently happening with the historical experience of the group and the injustice committed against them by the ruling elite. In other words, in the process of the politicization of ethnicity, the biggest tool which the ethnic elite use is a narrative based on the collective memory of an actual or perceived injustice to the ethnic group. However, the presence of the memory of a past injustice could only be used to politicize an ethnic group when an actual or perceived injustice is happening to the ethnic group at the time. This is then linked by the ethnic elite with the memory. The current insurgency in Balochistan is a case in point. After the Baloch insurgency during the 1970s, the province was peaceful for more than two decades. This is discussed in detail in Chapter 5. However, the situation changed when differences emerged between Akbar Bugti and the centre on gas royalty payments. This was then linked by the Baloch leaders with the past grievances of the Baloch towards the centre (Chapter 6).

Once the ethnicity and the ethnic group are politicized, whether the group would remain peaceful or get violent would depend on the ethnic elite. A number of factors such as *geography, demography, state structure, regional environment, availability of weapons* and *external support* would play important roles in the ethnic elite's decision to use violence as a strategy.[54]

If an ethnic group is scattered in different parts of the country, it would be extremely difficult for it to start a violent movement against the rival group or the state. However, if an ethnic group is concentrated in one geographical area, it would be easier for it to launch an armed struggle. For an effective armed movement, a suitable terrain is an advantage.[55] A number of experts of guerrilla warfare have pointed to the advantages of the so-called rough terrain such as mountain or forest. Such a terrain provides the armed militants an advantage, and they can achieve successes despite being numerically inferior to the security forces.

How strong and effective a state and its institutions are would also be a very important factor. A state with a stable system and effective institutions would be in a far better position to rule and administer the area under its sovereignty. In most of the cases where violent ethnic mobilization took place, the state was either defunct or swiftly losing its sovereignty and its institutions were in disarray. Regional environment also plays an important role in the decision to use violence. If the region in general is unstable or if there is increasing instability, a war or a

Introduction 13

war-like situation in the neighbourhood, the chances of violence increase as it would provide a much more favourable environment to the ethnic elite to operate in.

The two most important factors which almost play a decisive role in the ethnic elite's decision to turn the mobilization violent are the external or regional support and the availability of arms. If there is a state in the immediate neighbourhood, be it a kinstate or a state that has its own objectives or score to settle, the chances of the ethnic elite deciding to turn the movement into a violent movement would increase as they can use the support of the neighbouring state. This support could be of different types such as direct military support, providing safe havens or moral and diplomatic support. Above all, however, is the availability of arms as, without weapons, there could be no armed struggle. A steady supply of arms would make the ethnic group bold and effective. The arms could be provided by the supporting state, sympathetic diaspora and arm traders through black market or through a crime syndicate. A number of studies point to the nexus between drug smuggling and weapon supply where a number of tribal elite facilitated drug smuggling through their area in return for arms and ammunition. If the ongoing Baloch insurgency is analysed, one will find all the above-mentioned elements in it (Chapter 6).

Pakistan, located at the junction of South, Central and West Asia, bordering Afghanistan, China, India, and Iran, is the world's sixth most populous country. It is the only nuclear state in the world with a predominantly Muslim population. At the same time, Pakistan is faced with a myriad of challenges stemming from economic mismanagement, competing political institutionsand multiple socio-economic problems. Pakistan's inability to forge a national identity has led to an intensification of ethnic, linguistic and regional nationalism, which has splintered and fragmented the country. The most dramatic example of this splintering occurred in 1971 when the government's failure to address the needs of the ethnic Bengali community led to East Pakistan becoming the independent nation of Bangladesh.[56]

Pakistan has been a frontline state in the ongoing global war against terror. It has made considerable contributions to combating global terrorism,[57] yet it has also been described as a nursery of global terrorism.[58] It is considered a part of the problem as it is alleged that at least some elements in Pakistan continue to support the Taliban in Afghanistan and have preserved their links with the Jehadi groups as an option.[59] Due to the global focus on the war against terror, whatever attention Pakistan gets, it is mostly because of the war against terror and its lawless tribal areas which are the alleged sanctuary for the Al-Qaeda and the Taliban leadership.

What is mostly ignored by the world and the Pakistan-watchers is the ongoing insurgency in Balochistan. Balochistan accounts for 43.6% of the total territory of Pakistan. At the same time, it is the least populated province of Pakistan. According to official figures, the population is 6.51 million (5.1% of the national population).[60] It is the least developed province of Pakistan.

In all the previous insurgencies in Balochistan (1948, 1958 and 1973–77), the demand for secession that exists today did not exist, which makes the Baloch

14 *Introduction*

insurgency dangerous for the security of Pakistan.[61] Balochistan has energy and mineral resources which, if utilized properly, can provide a way out of Pakistan's current economic downturn. The Port of Gwadar in Balochistan and the recently inaugurated China–Pakistan Economic Corridor (CPEC) also provide Pakistan with strategic and economic significance in an area close to the entrance of the Persian Gulf. The secession of Balochistan – if it occurs – would deny Pakistan this access. Furthermore, if the Baloch are ever able to establish a unified front, a successful separatist movement among the Baloch could create serious security concerns for the state by starting what could be referred to as the Balkanization of Pakistan.[62]

Using the historical analysis method, this study aims to understand and analyse the ethno-political conflict in Balochistan by focusing on the Baloch nationalist narrative(s). As narratives do not exist or operate in a vacuum, the study also looks at Islamabad's counter-narrative.

Outline of the book

This book has six chapters, an introduction, a conclusion and an epilogue. This book, loosely following the chronological model, looks at the *important milestones* in the centre–province relationship and uses them as *cornerstones* of various chapters. Every chapter focuses on the developments in the area during the time period and how they contributed to the Baloch narrative. The aim is to see how the narrative evolved and how each development contributed to or added to the existing narrative of grievance. In this way, a clear picture emerges of the Baloch narrative since the arrival of the British in Balochistan.

The book is divided into two parts. Part I includes Chapters 1 and 2. These chapters cover the history of the Baloch and Balochistan from the earliest record to the departure of the British from the Indian subcontinent. These chapters cover different views about the origin of the Baloch and the epic battles they fought against invaders as per the Baloch legends. Chapter 1 challenges the Baloch nationalist claim that before the arrival of the British, Kalat was an independent state.

Chapter 2 looks at the policy confusions of the British officers dealing with the Baloch throughout their engagement with Balochistan, arguing that it was this confusion that was capitalized by the last Khan of Kalat. He claimed that Kalat's status is different from other princely states of India. This confusion further complicated the situation when Pakistan and Kalat negotiated accession.

Chapters 3–6 comprise Part II. This part covers developments in the relations between the province (Balochistan) and the centre (Islamabad) that have taken place since Balochistan became a part of Pakistan.

Chapter 3 covers developments that took place from 1947 to 1969. A number of important developments took place during this period. Khan of Kalat claimed that Kalat enjoyed a special status during the British Raj and, with the lapse of paramountcy, became independent. He formally declared the independence of Kalat as well. However, this chapter challenges this view. The chapter argues that Ahmad Yar Khan failed to take a firm and singular position on a number of issues. He

Introduction 15

kept promising one thing to the founder of Pakistan, Quaid-e-Azam Muhammad Ali Jinnah, and another to his sardars. The effects of the policy of One Unit on Balochistan (a policy which was actually aimed at East Pakistan) have also been discussed in this chapter. The chapter argues that in the 1960s, with the political decline of Ahmad Yar Khan, a new nationalist Baloch leadership emerged. Khair Bakhsh Marri, Ghaus Bakhsh Bizenjo, Ataullah Mengal and Akbar Bugti were the main pillars of this leadership.

Chapter 4 covers arguably the most important time period in the history of Balochistan–Islamabad relations, *especially* in terms of its significance in the Baloch narrative of the centre's injustice towards the Baloch and Balochistan. The chapter starts with General Yahya Khan, the then President and the Martial Law Administrator of Pakistan, granting Balochistan, for the first time in the history of Pakistan, the status of a full-fledged province of the state of Pakistan. The 1970 national elections were tragic for Pakistan as the post-election developments resulted in the dismemberment of the country. For Balochistan, the elections were a positive development. For the first time since 1947, the Baloch got the opportunity to elect their own representatives. Barring Akbar Bugti, who could not contest the elections due to a legal issue, all other nationalist leaders, Mengal, Marri and Bizenjo, managed to reach the provincial assembly and eventually established the first Baloch provincial government. Ataullah Mengal became the Chief Minister and Bizenjo was appointed the Governor of Balochistan. This proved to be a short-lived government. The political developments in the country and the Bhutto-led centre and Mengal-led province soon got to loggerheads, which resulted in the dissolution of the provincial government. This resulted in the most serious insurgency in Balochistan, which left long-lasting scars on the memory of the Baloch political activists as well as on the centre–province relationship. This chapter also highlights the various factors and reasons that contributed to the worsening of the situation.

Chapter 5 covers a long span of almost twenty-three years of the centre–province relationship. I have titled this chapter Balochistan and the peace interval. This chapter is important as the developments that took place during this time period support one of the main arguments of this research that, in the process of the politicization of ethnicity, the biggest tool used by the elite is a narrative based on the collective memory of an actual or perceived injustice to the ethnic group. However, the presence of a memory of a past injustice *could* only be used to politicize an ethnic group when an *actual* or *perceived* injustice is happening to the ethnic group at the time. As it was not the case during this time period in Balochistan, there was an absence of violence, hence a peace interval in Balochistan. This peace interval started with General Zia's martial law and ended with General Pervez Musharraf's coup of 1999. During this period, however, most of the concerns/grievances of the Baloch nationalists, at least according to them, remained unaddressed, yet Balochistan remained largely and mostly peaceful. Let me clearly state here that by peace interval I mean the absence of violence (as it was witnessed in the 1970s). General Zia, due to a number of regional and international compulsions, took several conciliatory steps towards the Baloch

16   *Introduction*

political leadership and Balochistan. During the latter part of this peace interval, when democratic practices were restored in the country, not only the Baloch leadership participated in the national politics, but Baloch leaders like Akbar Bugti and Ghaus Bakhsh Bizenjo emerged as national-level leaders with political clout, influence and respect throughout the country. This, however, changed after 1999.

Chapter 6, The return of insurgency in Balochistan, covers the developments from 1999 onwards. During this time period, just like at the beginning of the peace interval, Pakistan was ruled by a military government led by General Musharraf (General Zia during the peace interval) followed by democratic governments of People's Party and Muslim League Nawaz, just like it was during the peace interval. The main reason that this chapter has combined both the military and the civilian government is that it focuses on the Baloch insurgency which returned and continued since early 2000. This chapter details the events which led to the return of violence in Balochistan. The chapter argues that the main reason for the return of violence in Balochistan is the clash of interests between the Baloch elite and the Central elite. Musharraf–Bugti personal clash further complicated the situation. Islamabad's lack of clarity and long-term policy towards addressing the Baloch grievances is the major reason why the violence continues.

The conclusion sums up the main findings of the research, and the epilogue looks at CPEC and the future of Pakistan, particularly focusing on Balochistan.

Notes

1 Archduke Franz Ferdinand assassinated, www.history.com/this-day-in-history/archduke-franz-ferdinand-assassinated.
2 "Gavrilo Princip Is Arrested after Assassinating Archduke Ferdinand," *The Guardian*, June 28, 2013, www.theguardian.com/artanddesign/picture/2013/jun/28/gavrilo-princip-franz-ferdinand; Gavrilo Princip, http://en.wikipedia.org/wiki/Gavrilo_Princip; Assassination of Archduke Ferdinand, 1914, www.eyewitnesstohistory.com/duke.htm.
3 Francis Fukuyama, "The End of History," *The National Interest*, 1989; Francis Fukuyama, *The End of History and the Last Man* (New York: Avon Books, 1993).
4 President of the United States of America, George Bush's speech to the Congress on 6 March 1991. A Youtube clip can be viewed at www.youtube.com/watch?v=byxeOG_pZIo.
5 See for instance, Tom Mboya, *Freedom and After* (Boston: Little and Brown, 1963); Neil Devotta, "From Ethnic Outbidding to Ethnic Conflict: The Institutional Bases for Sri Lanka's Separatist War," *Nations and Nationalism*, no. 1 (2005): 141–59.
6 Gurr, *Why Men Rebel* (Princeton: Princeton University Press, ND), 9.
7 Ivan Siber, "Psychological Approaches to Ethnic Conflict," in *Ethnic Conflict Management: The Care of Yugoslavia*, ed. Dusan Janjic (Ravenna: Longo Editore, 1997), 125.
8 Ibid.
9 Thomas Joseph Odhiambo Mboya (1930–69) was a Kenyan politician during Jomo Kenyatta's government. He was the founder of the Nairobi People's Congress Party, a key figure in the formation of the Kenya African National Union (KANU), and the Minister of Economic Planning and Development. Mboya was assassinated on 5 July 1969.
10 Mboya, *Freedom and After*.

Introduction 17

11 Gurr, *Why Men Rebel*, 9.
12 Ivan Siber, "Psychological Approaches to Ethnic Conflict," 125.
13 Ndegwa, *Citizen and Ethnicity*, 601.
14 Rothschild, *Ethnopolitics*, 137–71.
15 Ibid.
16 Rene Lemarchand, *Burundi: Ethnic Conflict and Genocide* (Cambridge: Cambridge University Press, 1996).
17 Agneza Bozic-Roberson, "Words Before the War: Use of Mass Media and Rhetoric to Provoke Ethnopolitical Conflict in Former Yugoslavia," *East European Quarterly*, 38, no. 4 (Winter 2004). Available at http://connection.ebscohost.com/c/articles/15370942/words-before-war-milo-evics-use-mass-media-rhetoric-provoke-ethnopolitical-conflict-former-yugoslavia.
18 Ibid.
19 Ibid.
20 Ibid.
21 Stuart Kaufman, *Modern Hatreds: The Symbolic Politics of Ethnic War* (Ithaca: Cornell University Press, 2001), 20, 21.
22 Brown, *The Causes of Internal Conflict*, 13.
23 Ted R. Gurr and Barabara Harff, *Ethnic Conflict in World Politics* (Boulder, CO: Westview, 1994).
24 Jean-Pierre Chretien quoted in Victor T. Le Vine, "Conceptualizing 'Ethnicity' and 'Ethnic Conflict': A Controversy Revisited," *Studies in Comparative International Development* 32, no. 2 (Summer 1997): 56.
25 Daniel Bar-Tal, Neta Oren, and Rafi Nets-Zehngut, "Sociopsychological Analysis of Conflict-Supporting Narratives: A General Framework," *Journal of Peace Research* 51, no. 5 (2014): 663. Also see, Jerome Bruner, *Act of Meaning* (Cambridge, MA: Harvard University Press, 1990); Janos Laszlo, *The Science of Stories: An Introduction to Narrative Psychology* (New York: Routledge, 2008).
26 Bruner, *Act of Meaning*, 76 as quoted in Meytal Nasie, Daniel Bar-Tal, Ruthie Pliskin, Eman Nahhas, and Eran Halperin, "Overcoming the Barrier of Narrative Adherence in Conflicts through Awareness of the Psychological Bias of Naïve Realism," *Personality and Social Psychology Bulletin* 40, no. 11 (2014): 1553.
27 Bruner, *Act of Meaning*, 76 as quoted in Bar-Tal et al., "Sociopsychological Analysis of Conflict-Supporting Narratives," 663.
28 Zvi Beckerman and Michalinos Zembylas, "Fearful Symmetry: Palestinian and Jewish Teachers Confront Contested Narratives in Integrated Bilingual Education," *Teaching and Teacher Education* 26, no. 3 (2010): 507–15; Zvi Bekerman and Michalinos Zembylas, "The Emotional Complexities of Teaching Conflictual Historical Narratives; The Case of Integrated Palestinian-Jewish Schools in Israel," *Teachers College Record* 113, no. 5 (2011): 1004–30 as quoted in Bar-Tal et al., "Sociopsychological Analysis of Conflict-Supporting Narratives," 663.
29 Beckerman and Zembylas, "Fearful Symmetry," 507–15; Bekerman and Zembylas, "The Emotional Complexities of Teaching Conflictual Historical Narratives," 1004–30 as quoted in Bar-Tal et al., "Sociopsychological Analysis of Conflict-Supporting Narratives," 663.
30 Nasie et al., "Overcoming the Barrier of Narrative Adherence," 1554. Also see Biton and Salmon, "Peace in the Eyes of Israeli and Palestinian Youths: Effects of Collective Narratives and Peace Education Program," *Journal of Peace Research* 43 (2006): 167–80.
31 Susanne Bukley-Zistel, "Nation, Narration, Unification? The Politics of History Teaching After the Rwandan Genocide," *Journal of Genocide Research* 11, no. 1 (2009): 31–53; James Liu and Dennis Hilton, "How the Past Weighs on the Present: Social Representations of History and Their Role in Identity Politics," *British Journal of Social Psychology* 44, no. 4 (2005): 537–56 as quoted in Bar-Tal et al., 664.

18   *Introduction*

32   Serge Moscovici, "Notes Towards a Description of Social Representation," *European Journal of Social Psychology* 18, no. 3 (1988): 211–50 as quoted by Bar-Tal et al., 644.

33   Moscovici, "Notes Towards a Description of Social Representation," 211–50 as quoted by Bar-Tal et al., 644.

34   Philip Hammack, "Identity as Burden or Benefit? Youth, Historical Narrative, and the Legacy of Political Conflict," *Human Development* 53, no. 4 (2010), 173–201 as quoted in Bar-Tal et al., 644. Further relevant information on the subject could be found in Philip Hammack, "Narrative and the Cultural Psychology of Identity," *Personality and Social Psychology Review* 12, no. 3 (2008): 222–47; Philip Hammack, *Narrative and the Politics of Identity: The Cultural Psychology of Israeli and Palestinian Youth* (New York: Oxford University Press, 2011).

35   Dan Bar-On, "Ethical Issues in Biographical Interviews and Analysis," in *Ethics and Process in the Narrative study of Lives*, ed. Ruthellen Josselson (Thousand Oaks, CA: Sage, 1996), 9–21; Dan Bar-On, *The Other Within Us: Constructing Jewish Identity* (Cambridge: Cambridge University Press, 2008) as quoted in Bar-Tal et al., 664.

36   Bar-Tal et al., 665 quoting Yeudit Auerbach, "National Narratives in a Conflict of Identity," in *Barriers to Peace in the Israeli-Palestinian Conflict*, ed. Ya'aacov Bar-Simon-Tov (Jerusalem: Jerusalem Institute for Israeli Studies, 2010), 292–318.

37   Bar-Tal, 665 quoting Auerbach, "National Narratives in a Conflict of Identity," 292–318.

38   Dario Paez and James Liu, "Collective Memory of Conflicts." In *Intergroup Conflicts and Their Resolution: A Social Psychological Perspective*, ed. Daniel Bar-Tal (New York: Psychology Press, 2011), 105–24; Neta Oren, *The Israeli Ethos of Conflict 1967–2005*, Working Paper 27, http://scar.gmu.edu/publication/isreali-ethos-of-conflict-1967-2006.

39   Bar-Tal, 665.

40   There is vast literature available on these conflicts. For details, see David MacDonald, *Holocausts? Serbian and Croatian Victim-centered Propaganda and the War in Yugoslavia* (Manchester: Manchester University Press, 2002); Nikki Slocum-Bradley, "Discursive Production of Conflict in Rwanda," in *Global Conflict Resolution through Positioning Analysis*, eds. Fathali Moghaddam, Rom Harre, and Naomi Lee (New York: Springer, 2008), 207–26 as quoted in Bar-Tal et al., 665.

41   Bar-Tal et al., 665.

42   For details see Daniel Bar-Tal, Dan Jacobson, and Aaron Klieman, eds. *Security Concerns: Insight from the Israeli Experience* (Stamford, CT: JAI, 1998); Roy Baumeisten and Stephen Hastings, "Distortions of Collective Memory: How Groups Flatter and Deceive Themselves," in *Collective Memory of Political Events*, eds. James Pennebaker, Dario Paez, and Bernard Rime (Mahwah, NJ: Erlbaum, 1997), 277–93; Susan Optow, "Moral Eclusion and Injustice: An Introduction," *Journal of Social Issues* 46, no. 1 (1990): 1–20 as quoted in Bar-Tal et al., 665.

43   Bar-Tal et al., 666.

44   Nadir Tsur, "Vocabulary and the Discourse on the 1967 Territories," in *Effects of Lasting Occupation: Lessons from the Israeli Society*, eds. Daniel Bar-Tal and Yitshak Schnell (New York: Oxford University Press, 2013), 471–506 as quoted in Bar-Tal et al., 667.

45   Nasie et al., "Overcoming the Barrier of Narrative Adherence," 1553.

46   Roger Brubaker and David D. Laitin, "Ethnic and Nationalist Violence," *Annual Review of Sociology* 24 (1998): 442.

47   Ibid., 443.

48   Ibid.

49   See for details, *Clash of Civilizations or Clash of Perceptions? In Search of Common Ground for Understanding* (New York: World Policy Institute, ND), 19.

Introduction 19

50 Ibid.
51 Joshua G. Smith, "Fighting Fear: Exploring the Dynamic between Security Concerns and Elite Manipulation in Internal Conflict," *Peace Conflict and Development* no. 8 (February 2006), available at www.peacestudiesjournal.org.uk.
52 Gagnon, "Ethnic Nationalism and International Conflict: The Case of Serbia," *International Security* 19, no. 3 (Winter 1994–95): 130–66 as quoted in Joshua G. Smith, ibid.
53 Smith, "Fighting Fear," available at www.peacestudiesjournal.org.uk.
54 Svante Cornell, *Autonomy and Conflict Ethnoterritoriality and Separatism in the South Caucasus-Cases in Georgia,* available at www.silkroadstudies.org/new/inside/publications/0419dissertation.pdf.
55 For details on this see; Walter Laqueur, *Guerrilla Warfare* (New Brunswick: Transaction, 1997).
56 For various challenges faced by Pakistan, see Anatol Lieven, *Pakistan A Hard Country* (London: Allen Lane, 2011); Husain Haqqani, *Pakistan between Mosque and Military* (Washington, DC: Carnegie Endowment, 2005); Ahmed Rashid, *Descent into Chaos* (New York: Penguin, 2008).
57 Islamabad's contribution to the WoT is well documented, and the allies have praised its role in it. According to a report published at the time of the American President's visit to South Asia: "Pakistan has to date arrested more than 700 members of Al-Qaeda and killed a further 850 of them. Pakistan's security forces, meanwhile, have suffered a loss of 350–400 personnel, with injuries to another 760 in this war. Some of the high-profile terrorists arrested include Abu Zubayda (March 2002), Ramzi bin Alshibh (September 2002), Khalid Sheikh Mohammad (March 2003), Mustafa Ahmed Al-Hawsawi (March 2003), Mohammad Omar Abdel-Rahman (March 2003) and Abu Faraj al-Libbi (May 2005). Pakistan has also helped in freezing bank accounts of Al-Qaeda and its affiliated welfare organisations, such as the Al-Rasheed Trust and the Rabeta Trust." For a detailed and comprehensive account of Pakistani contribution to the WoT, see Ghani Jafar and Rizwan Zeb, *Pakistan: Countering Global Terrorism* (Islamabad: Institute of Regional Studies, 2006); also see "General Musharraf Is Still Riding High," (editorial), *Daily Times*, available at www.dailytimes.com.pk/default.asp?page=2006\10\12\story_12-10-2006_pg3_1, "Al Qaeda Caught and Killed: Tally Highest in Pakistan: Cheney," *Daily Times*, Thursday, October 19, 2006, available at www.dailytimes.com.pk/print.asp?page=2006\10\19\story_19-10-2006_pg1_2.
58 For details, see "India Accuses Pakistan of Being Nursery of Global Terrorism," *Daily Times*, available at www.dailytimes.com.pk/default.asp?page=2006\09\27\story_27-9-2006_pg7_40.
59 "ISI on Agenda of Nato Official's Talks," *Dawn*, October 10, 2006, available at www.dawn.com/2006/10/10/top4.htm, Cyrus Hodes and Mark, "The Search for Security in Post-Taliban Afghanistan," *Adelphi Paper 391* (London: International Institute for Strategic Studies); Moren and Michael Hirsh, "Where the Jihad Lives Now," *Newsweek*, October 29, 2007.
60 www.balochistan.gov.pk/index.php?option=com_content&task=view&id=37&Itemid=741.
61 Jan Singfield, "Ascending from Chaos?," *Majalla*, Jeddah, April 16, 2010, www.thebaluch.com/041610_ahmedRashid.php.
62 Waheed Khan, "Pakistan's Other Problem Area: Baluchistan," *Time Magazine*, November 1, 2009; and Nicholas Schmidle, *To Live or To Perish Forever: Two Tumultuous Years in Pakistan* (New York: Henry Holt and Company, LLC, 2009), 74.

Part I

Baloch and Balochistan through history

1 Baloch and Balochistan through history

INTRODUCTION

Historically, Balochistan has been isolated from the great power struggle going on around it. The Baloch were left on their own most of the time, and there was hardly any outside interference in Balochistan. Baloch tribes were the masters of their own destiny and territories. A Baloch ballad often quoted by the nationalist and other readers of Baloch history described this sense of isolation in these words: *The lofty heights are our comrades, the pathless gorges our friends.*[1] Balochistan's only significance was that it was used as a route or a place to seek refuge by kings and princes on the run. The present significance that Balochistan enjoys is solely based on its strategic location and mineral wealth. As Selig Harrison once wrote, "were it not for its strategic location, long coastline at the mouth of the Persian Gulf, and potential for discoveries of oil and gas and other minerals, Balochistan may not have assumed the importance it currently enjoys."[2]

Balochistan is among the earliest human settlements in the world. The site discovered by French archaeologists in Mehrgarh or Mehregan arguably makes Balochistan the earliest civilization in the world, with a few claiming that it predates both the Egyptian and the Mesopotamian civilizations. The evidence collected at Mehrgarh indicates that it was inhabited from 7000 to 2000 B.C. Mehrgarh's inhabitants were cave-dwellers and fishermen. Mehrgarh is among the earliest Neolithic sites where evidence of domestication of animals and cereal cultivation such as wheat and barley was found. According to the available evidence, Mehrgarh was a centre for craftsmanship as early as 7000 B.C. Due to the lack of any available evidence or record, it is impossible to ascertain who these inhabitants were and how and whether they were are linked with the Baloch.[3]

Most historians contend that the origin of the Baloch cannot be precisely established. For them, it is an insolvable riddle of history. G.P. Tate, summing up this view, stated that due to the lack of historical evidence, the question cannot be finally disposed of. Among the many views on the origin of the Baloch, the most popular explanation and the widely held view, especially among the Baloch, is that they are a Semitic race lived in Syria and migrated from Aleppo to Kirman in the present-day Iran and from there finally to what is today called Balochistan.

24   *Baloch and Balochistan through history*

Another view is that they are Aryans from Asia Minor. Third explanation is that they are Arabs and migrated to Makran and Turan around the seventh century.

Who called it Balochistan first is also not clear. One view is that it was the British who called it Balochistan when they took control of it. What is not clear is why the British called it Balochistan and not Brahuistan after the Brahuis of Kalat. A noted Baloch historian, Gul Khan Naseer states that it was Nadir Shah who called it Balochistan.[4]

This chapter aims at providing an overview of the history of the Baloch and the land of the Baloch from the beginning up till the time when it was taken over by the British. As no verifiable historical sources are available, the reliance is on Baloch sources. An important point in this regard is that the British colonial officers, spies and administrators have published vast literature on Balochistan; however, even this literature relies too heavily on the Baloch oral tradition when discussing the history of the Baloch. The chapter begins with providing basic facts about Balochistan's geographical locations, and tribes, their types and their locations. The next section looks at the history of the Baloch. In this section, an attempt has been made to separate the information about the people and the land which appears in "outsider sources," although it is too limited, from what the Baloch sources provide us. Also, an attempt has been made to make sense of the relationship between the Khanate of Kalat and the tribal sardars and the relationship between the Khanate and the Afghan rulers, followed by a section on the Baloch tribal system, its core features, principles and players. The last section sums up the chapter.

BALOCHISTAN: BASIC FACTS

In terms of geography, Balochistan is the largest province of Pakistan, covering 134,000 square miles of the territory; at the same time, it is the least populated province of Pakistan.

Geographically, Balochistan is divided into three parts: north, central and south Balochistan. The Baloch are divided into seventy main groups and more than four hundred subgroups. However, the most prominent and significant of the Baloch groups include the Suleman Baloch or the Eastern Baloch and Makran Baloch or the Western Baloch.

The Suleman Baloch or the Eastern Baloch comprise tribes of Bugti, Buzdars, Dombkis, Kaheris, Khetrans, Magasis, Marris, Mugheris, Rind, and Umranis. The Makran Baloch or the Western Baloch comprise tribes of Dashti, Gichki, Kandai, Rais, Rakhshani, Rind, Sangu, and Sangrani.[5] The Rind tribe, the direct descendant of the eldest son of Mir Jalal Khan, the father of all Baloch and named after him, is considered to be the most prominent of the Baloch tribes. Other notable tribes are the Bugtis and the Marris.[6] The Brahuis constitute another significant group. Within the Brahuis, there are three main groups: the core Brahui group includes the tribes of Ahmadzai, Gurguari, Iltazai, Kalandari, Kambrani, Mirwari, Rodeni and Sumalari. The other two are Jhalawan Brahui and Sarawan Brahui. Among the Brahuis, the Ahmadzais hold the highest prestige, perhaps due to the fact that it was the Ahmadzai

Brahuis who established the Khanate of Kalat in 1666.[7] When exactly these tribes were formed is not clear. Take for instance major Baloch tribes such as Marri, Bugti, Mengal, Buzdar, and, Leghari. One finds no mention of these in Baloch poetry, indicating that at the time of writing of the classical poetry, these did not exist.

Among these tribes, there are serious differences, rivalries and feuds. Some of these feuds have a long history. Widely known tribal feuds in Balochistan include Bugti vs Kalpars and Ahmadan Bugti sub-tribes, Bugtis' feuds with Mazaris and Raisanis, Gazinis vs Bejranis, Marris vs Loonis, Hameedzais vs Ghaibezais, Rind vs Raisani and Suleman Khels vs Lawoons. Due to the tribal nature of the Baloch society and these feuds, the emergence of the unified leadership of the Baloch is not possible. Every tribe and the tribal sardar primarily works for his tribe.

The Baloch: Origin and development of the Baloch tribes

Who is a Baloch? What is the origin of the Baloch? What exactly is the meaning of the word Baloch?[8] These questions could not be satisfactorily answered, at least not any more. One explanation which has wide validity among the Baloch, especially the nationalist Baloch, is that the word Baloch was derived from Belus. According to the Baloch tradition, Belus was the title for the Babylonian kings. Nimrod, one of the most famous Babylonian kings, was called Nimrod the Belus. Muhammad Sardar Khan, a Baloch historian, claimed that Nimrod's followers were called Belusis.[9] The generally held view among the Baloch historians is that Belusis became Balos in Arabic. Balos further changed to Baloch.[10]

Late Akbar Bugti, apart from being one of the strongest Baloch sardars, was also credited to be an authority on Baloch history. He was reportedly in possession of the largest and perhaps the oldest collection of Baloch poetry, including the *Daptar Shaar* (Chronicle of Genealogies). He once opined that there is no need to glorify the Baloch past or link it to one great personality from history or another. He criticized those Baloch nationalist historians (Gul Khan Naseer, Inayatuallah, Taj Mohammad Breseeg, Malik Muhammad Saeed Dehwar, etc.) who link the Baloch to Babylon or claim that the Baloch are the descendants of the god, Baal and/or Nimrod. He wrote:

> I cannot understand why they shy away from the fact that the Baloch as a national group do not find mention in any history prior to the advent of the Christian era, and they never set up any empire nor made conquests of any consequence. At the most, they must have been simple nomads and pastoral people who led an uncomplicated life roaming the vast steppes of central Asia in search of sustenance.[11]

However, Late Nawab Akbar Bugti was in minority, perhaps singular in presenting this simple and uncomplicated account of Baloch history. Most Baloch believed otherwise. Baloch poetry including the daptar Shaar that dates back to the time of Chakar the Great, a legendary Baloch ruler (1479–1524 A.D.), described the Baloch as:

26 *Baloch and Balochistan through history*

We (the Baloch) are followers of Ali, firm in faith and honor through the grace of the Holy Prophet Lord of the earth. We are the offspring of Amir Hamza, victory rests with God's shrine. We arise from Halab and engage in battle with Yazid in Karbala and Bampur, and we march to the town of Seistan.[12]

One can infer from this passage that the Baloch, or at least some of the Baloch, were originally Shia. This fact is acknowledged by Rai Bahadur Hatu Ram. In his book on the history of the Baloch, Hatu Ram claimed that that was the case in the past, but since the 1800s, almost all of the Baloch are Sunni Muslims.[13] He, however, is silent on how exactly and when this conversion took place.

Firdosi, in his epic Shahnama, described the Baloch as[14]

An army of the Baloch & Kouch (Brahui).
bred and ready like Ewes.
They never turned their back to the battlefield.
They were armed to teeth – not even a finger uncovered.
Their brave heads could reach the glaring Sun.

Mir Khuda Bux Bijrani Baloch claimed that the Baloch, just like the Kurds, originated in Aleppo (Haleb) in Syria. The Kurds settled in the present-day Turkey, Iran, and Iraq, whereas the Baloch moved south and eventually settled in the present-day Pakistani and Iranian Balochistan.[15]

Baloch historians[16] emphasize the bravery of these Baloch and the epic wars they fought to defend their freedom and territory against the forces of the mighty empires of the time. For instance, the Baloch not only defended themselves against the advancing Sasanian forces during the reign of King Ardeshir but also raided deep into the Sasanian territory. One of the greatest battles of all time was fought between the Baloch and the mighty Persian Empire's army during the rule of one of the greatest and mightiest Persian Kings: Anosheervan. According to the Baloch sources, Anosheervan, fed up with the continuous Baloch defiance against him, personally led a Persian army against the Baloch. However, Baloch historians[17] do not shed much light on the actual fighting of this battle, and there is almost no authentic and/or independent historical record of this event to ascertain the outcome of this "one of the greatest battles of all times."

Vara Pishin-anha (valley of Pishin) is the first ever mention one can find of Balochistan or its parts in Avesta.[18] Throughout history, the present-day Balochistan or its parts, especially Makran, have been identified as Macka or Mecka, Mackiya and Mackiyan, Gedrosia, Gedroshia or Gedrozia.[19] Makoran or Makran was also used for Balochistan. Holdrich opined that the actual word was Mahi Khoran (fish eaters) which changed to Makoran.[20] Marco Polo referred to Balochistan as Kasmakoran or Kasehkoran.

Moreover, not much is known about the earlier inhabitants of Balochistan. Very little, if any, information regarding Balochistan is given by Herodotus.[21] A detailed and mostly authentic account is provided by Strabo.[22] Shahnama details how Kai Khusru (Cyrus the Great) occupied Makran and that during Darius

Baloch and Balochistan through history   27

Hystaspes reign, the whole of Balochistan was under the Achaemenian Empire.[23] Greek historian Arian claimed that when Alexander the Great passed through the present-day Balochistan, two different groups of people, *Ichthyophagi* and *Oreitai*, lived there. We don't know much about these people, especially whether there is any link between these people and the Baloch. One thing that stands out is that these people fought courageously to ensure their freedom, something acknowledged by the generals in the Alexander's army. The aspiration to retain their freedom at all cost was something which these people definitely shared with the Baloch.

After Alexander, Balochistan was ruled by Seleucus before being taken over by Sakas from Central Asia sometime between 140 and 130 B.C. During the time of Nausherwan (529–577 A.D.), Balochistan became a part of the Sasanian dynasty. Next, it came under the Rai dynasty when, around the 630s, Rai Chach occupied Makran.

The presence of Arabs in Makran is recorded around 643. After the conquest of Iran, the second Muslim caliph, Omer ibn-ul-Khatab sent two scouting missions to Balochistan. Both of these scouting missions provided negative reports and stated that the area is of little strategic value and would be a logistical nightmare as a smaller force would not be able to conquer it mainly due to a strong resistance it would face from the locals and that a larger army would require much greater logistical support than the strategic value of the area.[24] However, in the seventh century, Hajaj bin Yusaf's geostrategic and geoeconomic concerns resulted in the Arab conquest of parts of Balochistan and Sindh. The Arab conquest of Balochistan introduced Islam in Balochistan. The people of Balochistan converted from Zoroastrianism to Islam.

Balochistan suffered from the Mongol wrath as Chagatai invaded Makran. According to the local tradition, Timurlane passed through the Marri territory to attack India.[25]

In the fifteenth century, Mir Chakar of the Rind tribe, arguably the greatest Baloch in Baloch history, asserted and consolidated his position around the area of Kalat. In the 1530s, Mir Umer Qambarani took over Kalat from Zanoon Beg. However, Mir Umer was challenged by two rival tribal sardars: Mir Chakar Rind and Mir Gohram Lashari. For them, it was an insult to their tribal honour that a sardar from a minor tribe managed to occupy Kalat. They ganged up against Mir Umer and amassed a joint army against him. In the ensuing battle, Mir Umer got assassinated and Chakar and Gohram occupied Kalat.[26] They had no experience of ruling and targeted Kalat only due to tribal jealousy. They were free souls who earned their fortunes by raids. Soon after, major differences emerged between the two. Both decided to target Kacchi. It was decided that Mir Chakar will advance towards Kacchi via Bolan Pass and Mir Gohram will attack via Mulla. They agreed that, in this pincer movement, the point when they come face to face will be considered borderline between their tribes.[27] This was the last time Mir Chakar left Kalat and could never return to it. Before leaving Kalat, he appointed his father-in-law Mir Mundo incharge of Kalat.[28]

28 *Baloch and Balochistan through history*

According to Baloch historians,[29] Chakar the Great founded first independent Baloch kingdom. According to them, Chakar's kingdom included a vast territory and spanned from southern Afghanistan, the present-day Balochistan, to parts of Sindh and Multan in Punjab. Chakar the Great, according to the Baloch sources, ruled his kingdom from his capital in Sibi from 1487 till 1511. He died and was buried in Satygraha, the present-day Okara, in Punjab, Pakistan. Chakar's era is highly romanticized by the Baloch nationalists, but as a matter of fact, Chakar spent most of his time in fighting a civil war with Mir Gohram of the Lashari tribe.[30] An important aspect of the Chakar–Gohram bloody feud is how far a Baloch would go for his honour and to avenge an insult to his tribe.

According to the Imperial Gazetteer,

> The succeeding century is one of the great historical interest. The Baloch extended their power to Kalat, Kacchi, and the Punjab, and the wars took place between Mir Chakar the Rind and Gohram Lashari which are so celebrated in Baloch verse. In these wars a prominent part was played by Mir Zunnun Beg Arghun, who was the governor of north-eastern Baluchistan under Sultan Husain Mirza of Herat about 1470. At the same time the Brahuis had been gradually gaining strength, and their little principality at this time extended through Jhalwan country to Wad. [31]

From 1559 to 1595 and then again from 1638 to 1708, Balochistan was under the Safavids. Between these time periods, Balochistan remained under the Mughals (1595–1638) and eventually under the Pashtun Ghilazis.[32]

Establishment of the Khanate of Kalat

The rise of the Ahmadzais[33] and the establishment of the Khanate of Kalat is a historical riddle.[34] Dehawars played an important role in the rise of the Ahmadzai from the very beginning.[35] This alliance not only resulted in the rise of Ahmed Khan to a coveted position, but also provided him with the agricultural and economic resources and surplus, which played a significant role in his rise as he used these resources to win allies.[36] In return of this support provided by the Dehawars, Ahmed Khan appointed a Dehawar as his chief minister.[37] This practice continued for a long time.

The Khan utilized these agricultural resources to expand his influence and alliance with other Baloch sardars. In exchange for a pledge of providing military support to the Khan in case of a war, the Baloch sardars were provided cultivatable land.

The British records indicate:

> The Khan ... gradually engaged the assistance of the chiefs of their kindred tribes in the neighborhood by giving them fiefs in Kalat. In return for these fiefs they were bound to furnish troops, in certain specified cases and numbers, for the aid of the Khan. This is highly significant, as although primarily entirely independent in their own territories, these chiefs became, doubtless, as regards these fiefs,

Baloch and Balochistan through history 29

quasi-feudal vassals of the Khan. By means of the troops so raised, the territories of the Khan were extended by conquest, such conquest being on behalf of the khan only, and for the affiliated tribes ... thus bound together, and finding mutual cohesion essential against their powerful neighbors, Persia, Afghanistan, and Sind, the petty state of Kalat, the independent Baloch and Brahui tribes, and their joint conquests gradually became amalgamated into one feudal state under the authority of the Khan. The condition of this agreement, however, secured to the confederate chiefs practical self-government in their previously independent territory.[38]

With the passage of time, the Khan of Kalat managed to convert Kalat into a centre of elite interaction by maintaining a lavish court.[39] The Baloch–Brahui coalition resulted in later khans despite being Ahmadzai Brahui able claiming to be Khan-e-Baloch. Nina Swidler claimed that with the advent of the Khanate of Kalat, this area upgraded from a borderland refugee area to chiefdom.[40]

In 1740, Kalat formally accepted the sovereignty of Nadir Shah of Persia. Nadir Shah rewarded Kalat with the Kacchi Plain.[41] This further expanded Kalat's agricultural resources. Nasir Khan I further refined Kalat's administration. Under Nasir Khan, Kalat comprised two different types of areas. One belonged to Kalat, and the Khan of Kalat directly ruled it through his Naibs (deputies). He also established a proper administrative set-up and appointed a prime minister and a council of sardars. Second area comprised two provinces of Sarawan and Jhalawan.[42]

Akbar Bugti, commenting on Nasir Khan and Kalat, stated:

Mir Nasir Khan (Nuri) set up a loose tribal confederacy on some parts of Balochistan. Most Balochi speaking people were never a part of this confederacy, for example: The Marri, Bugti, Buledi, Khosa, Bijrani, Sundrani, Mazari, Lund, Drishak, Leghari, Gishkori, Dashti, Ghulam-Bolak, Gophang, Dodai, Chanday, Taalbur, and a number of other smaller clans never vowed allegiance to the Khans of Kalat.[43]

Nasir Khan established an army of 25,000 men and 1,000 camels. He paid tribute to Nadir Shah. However, Nadir Shah's assassination in 1747 freed him. But this turned out to be just a change of masters for Nasir Khan. Ahmed Shah Abadali, who provided Nasir Khan refuge for almost nine years when as a young boy he was exiled from Kalat by the then Khan of Kalat and his step brother, established a new kingdom of Afghanistan. Nasir Khan accepted his suzerainty. He agreed to ensure the safe passage and security of the Afghan trade caravans, to pay Rs. 2,000 annually to Abdali and to station and maintain 1,000-strong military contingent at Kandahar. This had a number of favourable outcomes for Kalat: Kalat received a vast area including Quetta and Mastung. In 1758, after a brief clash, both Nasir Khan I and Ahmed Shah Abdali negotiated a new treaty. Under the new treaty, Kalat would provide military contingent to Afghanistan in case of a war. Nasir Khan also agreed that Kalat would not support or provide shelter to any anti-Abdali element. Ahmed Shah Abdali, on his part, agreed not to interfere in Kalat's internal affairs, to provide financial support and to return all captured areas of Kalat

30   *Baloch and Balochistan through history*

on these favourable terms. Nasir Khan I readily accepted Abdali's suzerainty and Afghanistan as the dominant power. As per the tribal tradition, to further strengthen the relationship, Nasir Khan's niece was married to Ahmed Shah Abdali's son.[44]

Baloch nationalists[45] claimed that this was a treaty signed by two equals, a claim Nina Swidler, a leading historian of Kalat, disputes.[46]

After securing his position with Afghanistan, Nasir Khan turned his focus to his southern neighbours and one by one captured and incorporated Makran, Les Bela and Kharan into Kalat.

In 1766, after the death of his father, Jam Ghulam became the sardar of the Jamotes. He got married to Nasir Khan's daughter Sultana Bibi. As part of her dowry, Nasir Khan gave her 50 percent of the annual income from Gwadar.[47] After Jam Ghulam Shah's death in 1776, Nasir Khan got informal control of Gwadar. In 1783, Saeed Sultan, the ruler of Oman, after a successful coup against him, fled to Balochistan. He requested Nasir Khan to provide him military support. Instead, Nasir Khan offered him refuge and the remaining percentage of Gwadar's income as stipend. The understanding they reached was that when the time is ripe and Saeed Sultan manages to return to Muscat, he would return Gwadar to the Khan. Unfortunately, when he managed to return to Muscat, he chose not to honour this and held on to Gwadar.[48] He maintained his control of Gwadar through an Arab governor or Wali.[49]

Nasir Khan died in 1795. Unfortunately for Kalat, his successors could not match Nasir Khan's charisma or his achievements. Kalat plunged into a civil war between several claimants to Kalat's throne. Different claimants were supported by various tribal sardars. A number of sardars, who previously pledged allegiance to Kalat, defected. A number of areas of the Khanate of Kalat were captured or reclaimed by Sindh and Afghanistan. Kalat's financial and trade domination was severely diminished as much of the trade activity shifted to Karachi. Trade caravans, due to increased threat and multiple taxing, were rerouted.[50]

Akbar Bugti wrote:

> Nasir Khan started his career in the service of Nadir Shah of Persia as a "Yasawal." Later, after Nadir Shah had been assassinated, he shifted to Ahmad Shah Abdali, who had also been in service of Nadir Shah before his death. Ahmed Shah appointed Nasir Khan to the gadi of Kalat in place of his elder brother, and Ahmed Shah remained as a loose suzerain to whom Nasir Khan ever remained loyal. Soon after Nasir Khan's death, his confederacy almost immediately fell back into anarchy, and the powers of his successors as rulers diminished even more rapidly than Nasir Khan had augmented it.[51]

According to the British record,

> The rulers of Kalat were never fully independent. There was always, as there is still, a paramount power to whom they were subjects. In the earliest times they were merely petty chiefs; later they bowed to the orders of the Mughal emperors of Delhi and to the rulers of Kandahar, and supplied men-at-arms

Baloch and Balochistan through history   31

on demand. Most peremptory orders from the Afghan rulers to their vassals of Kalat are still extant, and the predominance of the Sadozais and Barakzais was acknowledged so late as 1838. It was not until the time of Nasir Khan I that the title of Beglar Begi (Chief of Chiefs) and Wali-i-Kalat (Governor of Kalat) were conferred in the Kalat ruler by the Afghan kings.[52]

Khanate of Kalat's chequered relationship with the tribal sardars

The Khan of Kalat always had a chequered relationship with the Baloch sardars. In the court of the Khan of Kalat, a sardar of Sarawan sat to the Khan of Kalat's right and a sardar of Jhalawan to his left. The hierarchy of the sardars was clearly indicated by the presents given to them by the Khan of Kalat. A Zarakzai sardar would receive a Kashmiri shawl, one length of brocade, a horse with silver harness and a dagger with a golden hilt. A Mengal sardar would also receive all these items except the dagger, whereas a Bizenjo sardar would only get a shawl and brocade. When an influential sardar would die, the Khan would personally visit the grieving family for condolences, whereas, on the death of a minor sardar, the Khan would send his son or a representative for condolences.

The Khan of Kalat's army comprised of a Dasta Khas (special regiment), Dasta Sarawan (regiment of Sarawan) and Dasta Jhalawan (regiment of Jhalawan). Dasta Khas comprised soldiers of the Khan's own Brahui tribesmen numbering 1,750, whereas the Dasta Sarawan and Dasta Jhalawan were provided by sardars of Sarawan and Jhalawan. Dasta Sarawan had 1,750 tribesmen, and Dasta Jhalawan had 4,800 tribesmen. These two dastas were part of the ghami lashkar. Each dasta was further subdivided into sections Palu Sherik (partners).

One twelfth of these ghami lashkar was permanently stationed at Kalat and was maintained by the Khan of Kalat. This group was known as the *Saan*. These troops were loyal to their sardars and not to the Khan of Kalat. Charles Masson, a British soldier and spy, who visited Kalat, witnessed a clash between a group of Saan soldiers and soldiers loyal to the Khan of Kalat. Masson's assessment was that Saan soldiers were ill-trained, under-disciplined and of questionable loyalty.[53]

The Khan of Kalat might have had a lavish court attended by most of the sardars, yet he and his court had little relevance to and had no direct connection with the Baloch tribesmen. For these tribesmen, the tribal sardar was the authority, and they were dependent on their tribal sardar. Hence, joining the Khan of Kalat's court offered a number of benefits to the sardars, but on the ground, it further reinforced their hold on their tribes and tribal affairs.

Baloch tribal system and the centrality of the sardars

The true origin of the Baloch is shrouded in mystery. Even the Baloch sources are divided on the question of the origin of the Baloch. One can find varied information about their migration to Iran and from there to the present location. They arrived in bolaks (groups) under the overall leadership of Amir Jalal Khan, the

32 *Baloch and Balochistan through history*

father of all Baloch. These groups or *bolaks* comprised blood relatives. These bolaks roamed the land and earned their living from robbery, assault, looting and plundering the land and enslaving people. How effective and bold these bolaks were in their escapades mostly depended on the leadership of the bolaks. A charismatic leader drew larger numbers and, at times, other bolaks under his leadership. The gathering of various bolaks under a common leadership gave birth to the *tuman*. Unlike a bolak, a tuman was not homogeneous and consisted of a dominant bolak which constituted its main and several other bolaks.

According to Dame, the Baloch comprised forty to forty-four bolaks. These bolaks then evolved into five tumans: Rind, Lashari, Hot, Korai and Jatoi. These tumans derive their names from the direct descendants of Amir Jalal Khan, the father of all Baloch. These five tumans are considered to be the *cream de la cream* of the Baloch tribes.[54]

Scarcity of natural resources such as water and pastoral lands resulted in these tumans to claim certain areas as their territories. Each and every member of the tuman contributed to whatever little economic activity that occurred, and every member had unlimited access to whatever pasture-land and water resources the tuman held in its possession.

Fred Scholz in his book described the structure of a Baloch tribe:

> The amalgamation of several clans (takkar, paro), each in their turn consisting of subtribes (shalwar, phalli) which, yet again, were composed of families (pira, para, firqah) marked the organizational structure of the tribe (tuman, qom). Amongst the individual organizational units and their leaders there existed at the respective levels, a hierarchy determined by genealogy. A group that genealogically was not connected with the ruling class and unrelated to it, the lower class, the class of the dependents (hamsayahs), had associated itself with the thus organized and socially structured actual tribe, upper or ruling class (raj-o-kabila). This lower class was divided into three groups in accordance with its members occupations, and the social esteem the ruling class accorded those occupations: slave (Maratha, gadra, ghulam), traders, artisans, musicians (hindus, lohars, doms), and peasants, farmhands, shepherds (gosbi, khafi).[55]

The Brahui, just like the Baloch, were divided into several smaller bolaks. Ahmadzai is considered the most prominent of the Brahui tribes. Mir Ahmad Khan I is often credited for bringing the Brahui tribes under some form of a joint organizational set-up of Kalat. Nasir Khan I is credited to have converted this gathering into some sort of a loose/preliminary confederation.[56] He divided the Brahui tribes into Jhalawani (lowlanders) and Sarawani (highlanders).[57] These Brahui tribes, following the rule of shadi-ghum, were obligated to provide military force to the Khan of Kalat Nasir Khan I, in case of a war. Nasir Khan I, like all following Khans of Kalat, paid homage to the ruler of Kandahar.

While discussing the Baloch, Bath emphasizes the role of patrilineality and honour in the Baloch tribal structure,[58] and Huges-Buller claims that the main pillars of the Baloch tribal structure are the shadi-ghum (common good/joy and

Baloch and Balochistan through history   33

sorrow/grievance) and Khun Bha (blood feuds), shared history, place and identity.[59] Looking at various works on the Baloch tribal structure, one could sum up the main features of the Baloch tribal structure as the sense of a common identity, belonging, shared history and place and the need to maintain and retain the honour of the tribe. In the Baloch tribal set-up, the tribe, not an individual, is the core. This is why an insult to an individual would be taken as an insult to the whole tribe. As per the concept of shadi-ghum, the whole tribe would share the agony and the joy of its individual members. The Baloch tribal principle of honour emphasizes that a Baloch must fulfil its commitment, whatever might be the cost. This principle of honour should be kept in mind when looking at the battles the Baloch have fought throughout history. [60]

The whole tribe collectively shared the responsibility for the behaviour of its individual members. Nina Swidler, in her seminal and widely quoted research on Kalat, quoted how a tribesman described this collective responsibility in the Baloch tribal society:

> In our tribal law the whole family is responsible for a man's actions, even the tribe is responsible, A man who absconded, his relatives were responsible, along with his chief, his tribe, his village. If anything took place in the old days ... if there were tracks going to a village, the people of the village were accountable for them, to explain them or show that they had gone on to another area. If the tracks went on to the Rind's (another tribal unit) village ... we handed the tracks over to him. He either gave us the thieves or he showed us the tracks (leading out of the village) ... Ultimately when the tracks got lost, those people had to produce the thieves or they had to pay the compensation.[61]

The Baloch tribal culture, like most other tribal cultures in the world, considers loyalty and hospitality as a vital part of its value system. The Baloch are fiercely independent and follow a traditional code of honour, the *Rivaj*.[62] The Rivaj has certain commonalities with the Pashtunwali (the traditional law of the Pashtun tribes). According to this code of honour, a Baloch could go to any length to maintain its independence and would be extremely suspicious of an outsider who, for a Baloch, is a potential threat to his independence, would provide unconditional sanctuary to any one requesting it, would provide the best possible hospitality and could go to any length to ensure security of his guest. However, when targeted, he would not settle down till he has achieved his revenge.[63] Henry Pottinger, a British spy, who was sent to Balochistan in the nineteenth century to scout the area, wrote: "When they once offer, or promise to afford protection to a person who may require or solicit it, they will die before they fail in their trust."[64]

The main unit in the Baloch tribal culture is the tribe and the tribe's loyalty to its sardar (chief of the tribe). Baloch tribes are governed by a tribal system, the Rivaj. This tribal system, which is often mistakenly referred to as the sardari system, follows a multi-tier leadership system: *motebars, takkaris* and the *sardar*. Motebars and takkaris work under the sardar, who is the overall chief of the tribe. The position of the *sardar* of the tribe is *hereditary*. Traditionally,

34   *Baloch and Balochistan through history*

the eldest son of a sardar becomes the sardar. If, for some reason, the eldest son could not be considered fit for the position, a council comprising motebars and takkaris would elect another sardar, mostly from other sons or close relatives of the deceased sardar.

The traditional justice system of the Baloch is the sardar and the jirga. Within a Baloch tribe, the sardar is the final authority. The jirga system in Balochistan has three tiers: *local, joint and shahi*. Local jirgas address local issues, joint jirgas handle inter-tribal disputes. In such jirgas, sardars of different tribes would sit together and reach a collective decision binding to all parties. In principle, such jirga decisions would be respected as an overall ruling related to a certain situation even by those Baloch sardars who were not part of this jirga. Shahi Jirga is the highest level in which tribal sardars would take a decision which would be extremely important for the Baloch qom (tribe). It was a Shahi Jirga in which the majority voted in favour of joining British Balochistan to Pakistan in 1947.

The sardar plays the most important and authoritative role in the Baloch tribal system. Within a Baloch tribe, the sardar is the centre of the Baloch tribal universe. However, a sardar is very much part of the tribe, and both the sardar and the tribe are interdependent in a number of ways. The sardar's income comes from various sources. One major source is the sardar land. The sardar also collected a tax called maliya on all types of items such as land produce and/or animal husbandry in the tribe. Maliya, however, is not a standard or permanent source of income for the sardar because in certain parts of Balochistan it is collected regularly, whereas in other areas, the collection of maliya is sporadic. For instance, in Jhalawan (lowlands), maliya is an important and regular source of income for the sardar, whereas in Sarawan (highland), it is collected intermittently. Before the advent of the modern mode of transportation, especially trains, the sardars also charged a fee for the caravans crossing through their territory. Other sources of income for sardars are shishak, an agricultural tax, and bajar, a tax collected at marriages and other festivities.

In the past, sardars had to be static as well as mobile. The sardar's camp included not only the sardar but also his staff and servants.[65] Traditionally, a sardar's public court is held daily. Tribesmen would bring in their cases, disputes and problems to the sardar. The sardar is bound by the tribal code to give all of them a proper hearing and provide some solution to their problems. According to the tribal code, the sardar could not close the business of the day unless he has heard each and every one.

These issues and cases could range from property disputes, marriage settlement to theft. The sardar plays the role of a counsellor, a mediator and a magistrate. The sardar uses the traditional Baloch code, the Rivaj, and the Islamic law, the Shariah, to work out the solution of these problems. Baloch tribesmen want their sardar to be authoritative, decisive and autocratic. Yet the sardar is mostly a fatherly figure, a strict, no-nonsense disciplinarian father but a father nonetheless. Professor Akbar S. Ahmed, who aptly pointed to the centrality of the sardar in the Baloch tribal system, stated,

Baloch and Balochistan through history   35

The tribe is a self-contained world. At its centre is the Sardar or chief of the tribe. Tall, full-bearded, in flowing clothes and heavy turban, the Sardar is not unlike Sean Connery playing a tribe chief. He symbolizes Baloch custom and tribal tradition. Honor, hospitality, and bravery are displayed in his behavior. The tribe revels in his glory. The word of the Sardar is law, his authority total. In an area threatened by nature, and often, invading tribes, unity under the Sardar became the key to survival. The Baloch have a saying the Baloch will swear on the Holy Quran but never on the head of the Sardar.[66]

CONCLUSION

Very little authentic and historically verifiable information about the Baloch and Balochistan is available. Most of the scholars of Baloch history agree that Balochistan, for a very long time, served as a corridor for invaders going to India or Afghanistan and returning from Afghanistan and India. Scholars like Axmann and Swidler suggest that prior to the establishment of the Khanate of Kalat in 1666, the country served primarily as a refuge area for kings and princes who needed refuge or sanctuary after being uprooted from their thrones by their rivals.

Little is known of Balochistan before the fifteenth century. Therefore, one has to rely on the Baloch sources when discussing the history of the people and the area. The British have left considerable historical works on the various tribes of Balochistan. However, they have relied on the Baloch oral tradition and mostly translated the Baloch historical narrative. Henry Pottinger and other such British spies, who have written the earliest books and monographs on Baloch history, have nothing in their writings except what they heard from the people of Balochistan.

Like most of the tribal groups, the Baloch too regard themselves as the descendants of a single eponymous and mythical ancestor, to whom they turn when they wish to extol the valour and dignity of their own tribal group and lineage.[67] One thing which clearly stands out by this overview is that the Baloch strongly believe that they once were part of a mighty empire and have fought and defeated other empires. During this period, the establishment of the confederacy of Kalat was indeed a significant development. Kalat operated at a level ahead of a tribe, but it was still far away from attaining the status of a state.[68] Despite the infighting and the internal fissure and instability after the death of Nasir Khan Nuri, had the British not intervened, there was a fair chance that, under a more assertive Khan, Kalat might have been able to inch towards statehood.[69] However, Kalat's internal conflicts, combined with the movement of Russia into Central Asia, led the British to intervene and initiate policies which froze the chiefdom.

It also brings to our attention the Baloch belief that Kalat was an independent state representing the sovereignty of the Baloch and was equal to Afghanistan. It is claimed that the then Khan of Kalat and the ruler of Afghanistan Ahmed Shah Abdali negotiated as equal sovereigns. This constitutes the first major point of the Baloch nationalist narrative that before the arrival of the British, Kalat (Balochistan) was an independent state. As it is demonstrated in this chapter, this

36 *Baloch and Balochistan through history*

is incorrect, and the narrative that Kalat was an independent and sovereign state before the arrival of the British is a later construct.

Notes

1 Selig Harrison, *In Afghanistan's Shadow* (Washington, DC: CEIP, 1981), 7.
2 Ibid.
3 "Baluchistan: Conflicts and Players," *PIPS Report* (Islamabad: PIPS, 2009).
4 Gul Khan Naseer, *Tareekh-e-Balochistan* (Quetta: Kalat Publishers, 2010), 5.
5 For details, see Muhammad Sardar Khan Baluch, *History of Baluch Race and Baluchistan* (Quetta: Gosha-e-Adab, 1977); Ricardo Redaelli, *The Father's Bow The khnatate of Kalat and British India* (Ilmastrale, 1997); Gul Khan Naseer, *Tarikeh Balochistan* (History of Balochistan. In Urdu) (Quetta: Kalat Publishers, 2005); Rai Bahadur Hatu Ram, *Tarikeh Balochistan* (in Urdu) (Lahore: Sang-e-Meel, 2001); Mir Ahmed Yar Khan, *Inside Balochistan* (Karachi: Royal Book Company, 1975); Mir Khudabux Bijarani Marri Baloch, *The Baloch through Centuries History versus Legend* (Quetta: Islamic Electric Press, ND).
6 Ibid., also see, Deny Bray, *The Life-History of a Brahui* (Karachi: Royal Book Company, 1977).
7 Bray, Ibid.
8 Rizwan Zeb, "Khans and Fractious Chieftains," *The Friday Times*, July 22, 2016, www.thefridaytimes.com/tft/khans-and-fractious-chieftains/.
9 Muhammad Sardar Khan Baloch, *History of Baloch Race and Balochistan*, 16–26.
10 Ibid.
11 For details, see Akbar Bugti's Foreword in Aziz Bugti, *Balochistan* (in Urdu) (Lahore: Fiction House, 1996).
12 Mir Khud Bakhsh Bijrani Marri Baloch, *The Baloches through Centuries: History verses Legend* (Quetta: Mir Baloch, 1965).
13 Hatu Ram, 34.
14 *Shah Nama* (Lahore: Sang-e-Meel Publications, 2002).
15 Baloch, *History of the Baluch Race and Baluchistan*, 5.
16 Gul Khan Nasir, Inayatuallah, Taj Mohammad Breseeg, and Malik Muhammad Saeed Dehwar to name a few.
17 Ibid.
18 *Imperial Gazetteer Provincial Series Baluchistan* (Lahore: Sange-e-mee, 2002), 11.
19 Taj Muhammad Breseeg, *Baloch Nationalism: Its Origin and Development* (Karachi: Royal Book Company, 2004), 55–56.
20 T. H. Holdich, "The Perso-Baloch Boundary," *The Geographical Journal* 9, no. 4 (April 1897): 418.
21 *Imperial Gazetteer Provincial Series Baluchistan*, 11.
22 Ibid.
23 Ibid.
24 Breseeg, *Baloch Nationalism*.
25 *Imperial Gazetteer Provincial Series Baluchistan*, 13.
26 Naseer, 7–8.
27 Ibid., 8–9.
28 Ibid., 9.
29 Gul Khan Naseer, Inayatuallah, Taj Mohammad Breseeg, and Malik Muhammad Saeed Dehwar had made significant contributions to Baloch history.
30 For details, see Aziz Bugti, *Balochistan, Saksiyat key ayney mian* (in Urdu) (Lahore: Fiction House, 1996), 29–41.
31 *Imperial Gazetteer Provincial Series Baluchistan*, 13.

Baloch and Balochistan through history 37

32 For details, see Malik Hatu Ram, *Tarikeh e Balochistan* (in Urdu) (Lahore: Sang-e-Meel, 2001).

33 The Mirwaris, from whom the Ahmadzais are descended, claim Arab origin. "Baluchistan," *Imperial Gazetteer Provincial Series* (Lahore: Sang-e-Meel, 2002), 14.

34 Nina Swidler, "The Development of the Kalat khanate," in William Irons and Hudson, 115–21, Nina Swidler, "The Development of the Kalat Khanate," in Rao and Casimi, 73–80.

35 Axman, *Back to Future*, 20.

36 Swidler, *Kalat.*

37 Ibid.

38 Government of India, *Frontier and Overseas Expeditions from India*, 5 vols. (Quetta: Nisa Traders, 1982), 33–34 as quoted in Martin Axmann, *Back to the Future* (Karachi: OUP, 2009), 21.

39 Axamann, *Back to Future*, 21.

40 Ibid.

41 Zeb, Khans and Fractious Chieftains, *The Friday Times*, July 22, 2016, www.thefriday-times.com/tft/khans-and-fractious-chieftains/.

42 Nina, *Kalat.*

43 Akbar Bugti's Foreword in Bugti, *Balochistan, Saksiyat key ayney mian*, 6.

44 Gul Khan Nasir, *Tarikh-i-Balochistan* (Quetta: Kalat Publishers, 2005), 110–14.

45 See the works of Gul Khan Nasir, Inayatuallah, Taj Mohammad Breseeg, and Malik Muhammad Saeed Dehwar for this.

46 For details, see Nina, *Kalat.*

47 In 1651, the Portuguese attacked and burned Gwadar.

48 Gul Khan Nasir, *Tareekh-e-Balochistan* (Quetta: Kalat Publishers), 91, 94–95.

49 "Baluchistan" *Imperial Gazetteer Provincial Series* (Lahore: Sang-e-Meel, 2002), 186.

50 Nina, *Kalat.*

51 Akbar Bugti, Foreword, 7.

52 *Imperial Gazetteer Provincial Series Baluchistan*, 14.

53 Charles Masson, *Narratilat* (London: Richard Bentley, 1843), 144–67.

54 M. L. Dames, *The Baloch Race*, 5, 39 as quoted in Fred Scholz, *Nomadism and Colonialism* (Karachi: OUP, 2002), 50.

55 Muhammad sardar Khan Baloch, op.cit, Aziz M. Bugti, *Balochistan, Adab, Saqafaat aur Samaj* (in Urdu) (Quetta: Spensors, 1995), Aziz Bugti, *Baloch Qabayal* (in Urdu) (Quetta: Kalat Publishers, 2004), Henry Pottinger, *Travels in Beloochistan and Sinde* (Karachi: OUP, 2002), Shah M. Marri, *Baloch Qom* (in Urdu) (Lahore: Takhleqat, 2007).

56 Mir Ahmed Khan, op.cit.; Brey, op.cit.; Nina Swidler, op.cit.

57 Ibid.

58 Barth, "Ethnic Processes on the Pathan-Baluch-Boundary," in *Indo-Iranica melanges presente a Georg Morenstierne al'soccassion de son soixante-dixieme anniversarie*, 16 as quoted in Scholz, 56.

59 Hughes-Buller, "Balochistan," in introduction in C.J. 1901, Vols. V, VA, pp 117, 119, 128, as quoted in Scholz, 56.

60 Ibid.

61 Nina Swidler, *The Political Structure of a Tribal Federation: The Brahui of Balochistan* (PhD., Columbia University, 1969).

62 Aziz Bugti, *Tahrik-e-Balochistan* (in Urdu) (Quetta: Spensors, 1995).

63 Ibid.

64 Henry Pottinger, *Travels in Balochistan and Sinde* (Karachi: Oxford University Press, 2003).

65 Hatu Ram, Bugti, *Tahrik-e-Balochistan.*

38   Baloch and Balochistan through history

66 Akbar S. Ahmed, *Pakistan Society: Islam, Ethnicity and Leadership in South Asia* (Karachi: Oxford University Press, 1986), 188, also see, Akbar S. Ahmed, *The Thistle and the Drone*, 139.
67 Masson, *Narratilat*, 38.
68 Nina, *Kalat.*
69 Ibid.

2 Balochistan during the British rule in India

INTRODUCTION

In the previous chapter, we saw how, for the first time, various Brahui and Baloch tribes came under the leadership of the Ahmadzais and established a tribal confederacy at Kalat. Although it was not a state per se, the emergence of a tribal confederacy in Kalat was an important step in the direction of statehood. During the reign of Mir Nasir Khan Nuri, a significant number of Baloch were united under his leadership. His tenure can rightly be called the golden era in the Baloch as well as Kalat's history, but the unity faded after his death and a civil war-like situation emerged in the land of the Baloch, where the Khan of Kalat and the Baloch sardars were competing for influence and territory.

The warring Baloch tribes were not aware of a bigger threat looming on the horizon: the so-called rivalry or the great game between Russia, France and England. Afghanistan, which was to be the centre of this great power competition, eventually dragged the land of the Baloch into the British area of influence. For the first time in history, the Baloch had to deal with an invader who was not just crossing their land but wanted to stay and establish military posts and camps.

The initial British interest in Balochistan was purely geostrategic. The initial British policy towards Kalat was to strengthen the Khan of Kalat and provide full support to him so that he can control the sardars. However, soon the British realized that this policy is not working, and under Sandeman, the British decided to actively engage the sardars. This policy resulted in strengthening the sardars immensely.

This period of Baloch history is very important in understanding the Baloch narrative. Nationalist Baloch historians[1] claim that the British treated Kalat as an independent and non-Indian state. They claim that the British treatment of Kalat was similar to its treatment of Nepal.

British policy and position, however, are different as it is demonstrated in this chapter. British policy makers in India considered Kalat as an Indian state at least from the 1920s onwards but could not incorporate it into the British India due to administrative and political reasons. A number of British documents and statements point to this inconsistency in British policy. This failure in bringing clarity to its position on Balochistan created problems for Pakistan after 1947. Another

40   *Baloch and Balochistan through history*

important factor of the period under discussion is the role of Ahmad Yar Khan, the last Khan of Kalat. He was a man of contradictions. Above all, he was a British loyalist to the core, yet he was highly ambitious and aspired to be a king and had a self-constructed illusion of greatness and grandeur of Kalat and the Khans of Kalat.

This chapter covers the British involvement in Balochistan and analyses how the British policy evolved in Balochistan. The chapter is divided into six sections: the first section looks at the initial geostrategic concerns of the British and the place of Balochistan; the second section looks at the various approaches adopted by the British to engage the Baloch leadership and the change in the British perception and policy towards Kalat; the third section looks at the Sandeman system and how it changed the British–Balochistan relations; the fourth section looks at the appointment of Ahmad Yar Khan as the Khan of Kalat and how he started projecting himself as the king of the independent state of Kalat; the final section before concluding the chapter analyses the British position and debates about the status of Kalat, leased areas and the British Balochistan.

BRITISH COLONIZATION OF INDIA AND THE GEOSTRATEGIC COMPETITION BETWEEN ENGLAND, FRANCE AND TSARIST RUSSIA

Steam engine, arguably one of the greatest inventions of all time, made it possible for the European powers to voyage deeper into the sea and compete for naval supremacy. India, the so-called land of the spices, was one of the destinations which at the time held almost mythical charm for the European admirals. By the time the Portuguese and the Dutch reached India, who were the first to arrive in India, the golden era of the Mughals was inching towards oblivion. The English and the French followed the Portuguese and the Dutch and soon overshadowed them. The Europeans who arrived as traders established their East India companies and started trading. As the Mughal Empire lost its prime and started to fizzle into a number of smaller fiefdoms, these states or fiefdoms locked in disputes and rivalries. As these states were weak, almost all of these states aspired to win the Europeans as their allies so that they can share with them their much needed financial support and superior military might. The European companies were eager to oblige as they saw it as an opportunity to increase their influence in the Indian subcontinent.

This expanded the traditional rivalry between France and England into the Indian subcontinent as the French and the English East India companies struggled to win allies and compete for influence. Due to a shortage of European manpower, the French initiated a programme of military training for local recruits. The sepoys (soldiers) turned out to be an effective force and soon caught the eye of the local princes, who were willing to exchange land and capital to acquire French-trained sepoys to guard their interests. This resulted in French gaining influence in most parts of the southern India. The prime example of this is Tipu Sultan, the most respected and feared British rival who was in alliance with the French. The British followed the French model and started training their own sepoys.

A number of factors such as the seven-year war (1756–63), British overall naval supremacy and effective leadership of Robert Clive almost eliminated the French threat to the British interest and presence in the Indian subcontinent. Clive effectively used his superiorly trained sepoy force in the Battle of Plassey (1757) and made England a dominant player in the Indian subcontinent.

However, the British also had to worry about another more serious rival to their interest in the region: tsarist Russia. Lacking an all-weather port of its own, Russia, since the days of Peter the Great (1672–1725), was desperately looking for an access to warm waters. After the Russian forces managed to conquer the khanates of Central Asia, it started sending diplomatic missions to Persia (the present-day Iran), Afghanistan, Sindh and Punjab (at that time under the rule of Maharaja Ranjit Singh). The British forces in India viewed these developments as a threat to the British interest in the Indian subcontinent. When the Russians defeated the Persian force at Arpatch and signed the Treaty of Fars with Iran, to counter the ever-increasing Russian threat, the British approached the Shah of Iran and offered him all types of aid and support against their common enemy, Russia. At the same time, the British officials in India reached out to Afghanistan. The Governor General of India commissioned the Governor of Bombay to approach Shah Shuja, the ruler of Afghanistan. The mission was successful, and a treaty was signed in 1809. However, Shah Shuja was forced out as the ruler of Afghanistan and, after struggling for some time to recapture his lost throne, fled to Lahore in 1813. The British continued to court Shah Shuja and sanctioned a monthly stipend for him.

In 1838, a trilateral agreement was signed between the British government in India, Maharaja Ranjit Singh and Shah Shuja. According to this agreement, the British and Ranjit Singh agreed to help Shah Shuja regain the throne of Afghanistan in exchange of him accepting Ranjit Singh's control over Peshawar and the areas currently part of the Pakistani province of Khyber Pakhtunkhwa and Kashmir. According to this agreement, the British raised an army known as the Army of Indus in support of Shah Shuja. According to the plan, the Army of Indus would attack Kabul and install Shah Shuja on the throne in Kabul. However, both Ranjit Singh and Shah Shuja had their differences, and Ranjit Singh withdrew his support from the plan and denied the Army of Indus the passage from his territory.

Desperate to find an alternative route for the Army of Indus to reach Afghanistan, General Keane decided to explore alternative routes via Sindh and Balochistan. By that time, the British had almost no official contact with Balochistan and their knowledge of Balochistan was limited and, at best, sketchy. Earlier, as part of their strategy to contain the emerging French and Russian threat, the British sent expeditions to neighbouring areas as it wanted to identify the areas which can be used as buffer states between the British India and Russia. Two such expeditions were sent to Balochistan. In 1809, Captain Grant was sent with the task of identifying the possible route of an invading army from Persia.[2] He scouted Makran and the surrounding area. In 1810, one year after the Grant mission, Colonel Henry Pottinger was sent to Kalat. Pottinger failed to understand the complex dynamics of the tribal Balochistan and was fascinated with the Khan of Kalat. His account

42 *Baloch and Balochistan through history*

of Kalat emphasized the centrality and sovereignty of the Khan of Kalat, without any clear indication of the position of sardars. With this limited and almost inaccurate understanding of the Baloch affairs, General Keane approached the Khan of Kalat for a passageway for the Army of Indus to reach Afghanistan through Balochistan.[3]

At the time, the Khan of Kalat Mir Mehrab Khan was engaged in a bitter and intense competition with Baloch sardars to consolidate his position as the Khan of Kalat. An agreement was reached between the Khan of Kalat and the British on 28 March 1839. As per the agreement, Mir Mehrab Khan acknowledged the sovereignty of Shah Shuja over him. Although he was not happy about it, he had to accept this as a condition because he was under tremendous pressure in his constant struggle with the tribal Baloch sardars. The Khan of Kalat agreed to facilitate the movement of the Army of Indus to Kandahar through Khangarh (later renamed Jacobabad), Dhadar, Bolan Pass, Quetta, and Khojak Pass and to provide supplies and protection to the Army of Indus while it is on the move. In return, the British agreed to pay Mir Mehrab Khan an amount of 150,000 rupees. It was a much need sum which would provide the Khan of Kalat, Mir Mehrab Khan, a desperately needed support in his struggle against the sardars.[4]

However, what the British were not aware of was that the Khan of Kalat was not in total control and that there were Baloch tribes that operated independently and outside his control. When the British forces were passing through the Bolan Pass, they were attacked by the tribes of Kacchi and Bolan area. The British accused the Khan of Kalat of double-crossing them and violating the treaty agreement. General Willshire besieged Kalat. The great Khan of Kalat, Mir Mehrab Khan, refused to surrender and stood against the British might and fought till his last breath in a heroic battle against the British forces which deserves a glaring mention in the annals of military history.[5] After his death, the British occupied Kalat and installed a new and more amiable Khan.

On 6 October 1841, the British signed a new treaty with the new Khan of Kalat. According to the newly reached understanding, the British government in India would station British troops in Kalat and control its foreign relations, and a British resident would oversee and conduct the business of the state of Kalat. Although the Khan of Kalat was a mere figurehead, even if he wanted to shed away with the British shackles, it would have been almost impossible as the British occupied neighbouring Sindh in 1843 and Punjab in 1849. After further strengthening their hold by occupying Sindh and especially Punjab, the British decided to make further inroads into Balochistan as well as to minimize their too visible involvement in the area. Despite being involved in Balochistan and especially Kalat affairs, the British were still operating under the assumption that the Khan of Kalat was an independent and sovereign ruler.[6]

Under this assumption, in 1854, the British signed a new treaty with the Khan of Kalat on May 14 at Mastung. Under this treaty, the British authorities in India recognized the Khan of Kalat as an independent ruler and also recognized the Khan's authority from south of Kalat to the Arabian Sea and Las Bela. The British also promised to pay 50,000 rupees annually and to provide military training

Balochistan during British rule in India 43

and assistance in case of an invasion or attack on Kalat. In return, the British demanded that the Khan of Kalat ensured that the Bugti and Marri tribes were reined in by the Khan of Kalat. In exchange of this recognition, the Khan of Kalat pledged not to get into an alliance with any British rival/adversary and to facilitate the British and its allies. The agreed subvention was doubled in 1862 by the British. The treaty was revisited by both sides in 1863. According to the revised treaty, the Khan pledged to ensure the safety and security of the British personnel and installations stationed in the area. The British agreed to pay the Khan of Kalat Rs. 20,500 annually.

As the British got involved in the affairs of Balochistan, they continued to treat the Khan of Kalat as the sole authority in the area, a policy which was ignorant of the basic structure of the tribal federation and the role of sardars in it. Throughout this period, the British supported and on occasions encouraged the Khans of Kalat (Nasir Khan II and Khudadad Khan) to centralize the power. The Baloch sardars viewed the British policy and its support to the Khan of Kalat as an attempt to contain and minimize their position and hold. As a consequence, the sardars started revolting against the Khan. Soon, one group of sardars was fighting against the Khan of Kalat and the sardars supporting him. In this power struggle, the Khanate of Kalat and larger Baloch territory got increasingly anarchic. The Khan of Kalat, Mir Khudadad Khan, in his effort to assert his position and maintain the balance of power, got more and more dependent on the British in his struggle against the sardars. A closer look at the Treaty of 1854 clearly illustrates the fact that under this treaty, the Khan of Kalat was answerable and accountable much more to the British thanto his fellow sardars. As the British officials dealt with the Khan of Kalat and with the political realities of the Baloch tribal politics, the romanticized account of Pottinger started to appear hollow. This led a few officers in the British government in India to start questioning the wisdom of following the policy of supporting the Khan of Kalat. The particular puzzle for the British was the relationship between the Khan of Kalat and the sardars. Were the sardars mere rebels or part of a confederation and a disgruntled part at that, who wanted their share of the pie? Colonel Graham, the Commissioner of the Derajat, and Colonel Phayre, the political superintendent of the Upper Sindh Frontier, were not even sure whether Balochistan was a confederacy or a state with a sovereign ruler. Henry Green wrote:

> The Khan is absolutely powerless to exert unaided by any physical force over his unruly Chiefs and their followers: he can but rule by setting Chief against Chief and the tribe against tribe, and he can only do this with the assistance of money and by its use maintaining on his side the most powerful of his Chiefs. By depriving him of his subsidy we have reduced him to equality with the weakest of his Sardars. We have deprived the country of any semblance of a head.[7]

Robert Sandeman, who later became one of the most effective and prominent British officer to serve in Balochistan, was of the view that the British authorities

44 *Baloch and Balochistan through history*

in India have almost given up on the idea that even with their full support, the Khan of Kalat cannot actually assert his authority and establish a stable and functioning government in his state. The British tried everything, provided military aid and financial support, and did everything else to raise the stature of the Khan of Kalat as a ruler, yet nothing worked. Sandeman proposed that the British policy should be reworked and the British officials should take charge to ensure the safety and security of the British interests, personnel and installations.

Another reason for the increasing anxiety among the British officials in India about the instability in Balochistan was the traditional fear of a possible Russian encroachment into the area. The British authorities in India feared that once the Russians were successful in establishing themselves in these areas, it would be much easier for them to further spread into the settled areas directly under the British sovereignty and suzerainty.[8] Due to this uncertainty of how to deal with their Balochistan problem,[9] the British soon found themselves playing the role of a power broker and mediator between the Khan and the sardars. To address this uncertainty, the British officials in India involved in dealings with the Baloch and met at Mithankot in February 1871. This event was later recorded in the history as the Mithankot conference.

The officials in attendance were clearly divided into two groups. The group spearheaded by Sir W. Merewether, Chief Commissioner of Sindh, and Captain Harrison (Political Agent at Kalat) strongly voiced their view in favour of the Khan of Kalat and urged that the Khan of Kalat should be treated by the British as the sovereign ruler of Kalat and the sardars as his subjects. Merewether was totally against negotiating with the Baloch tribes and sardars directly and interfering in the internal affairs of Kalat and strongly advocated strengthening the Khan.[10] The other group which included Colonel Graham, Colonel Phayre and Robert Sandeman mostly represented the British government in Punjab with a noted exception of Col. Phayre, who was of the view that the Khan of Kalat was just a head of a confederacy and that the British needed to actively and directly support the tribal leaders/sardars.[11] The Mithankot conference remained inconclusive as both sides failed to reach an agreement on what would be the correct course of action. Despite the fact that the Mithankot conference was inconclusive, as later events proved, the group that advocated reaching out to the tribes and working with them as well as the Khan of Kalat decided to approach the tribes. This difference in approach towards the Baloch resulted in a serious clash between Merewether and Phayre, who eventually lost his job when Merewether dismissed him for disobeying his orders.

Regardless of these developments, it became obvious that London was inclined towards exploring various options to address this policy dilemma. Robert Sandeman, who had experience of dealing with the Baloch tribes during his posting in Punjab, was tasked to go to Balochistan and prepare the ground for a further interaction between the sardars and the British government in India. Sandeman's expedition to Balochistan failed to achieve desired results, and he had to return to Punjab due to a fresh wave of tribal violence in Balochistan. Despite this, Sandeman managed to make contact with several tumandars. Merewether strongly

Balochistan during British rule in India   45

objected Sandeman's mission and accused him of operating beyond his orders or knowledge of the authorities concerned. This was only partially correct. Sandeman went to Balochistan with full knowledge and approval of the British government in India. However, he transgressed his orders and established or at least attempted to establish contacts with the tribal sardars.

The Viceroy of India Lord Northbrook provided Sandeman one more opportunity to establish contact with the Baloch tribes. Armed with a letter from the Viceroy of India Lord Northbrook, Sandeman reached Kalat in May 1876. He presided a meeting in which the Khan of Kalat and the sardars voiced their grievances against each other. The Khan of Kalat's and the Baloch sardars' willingness to make Sandeman their arbitrator spoke volumes about who they thought was the true sovereign holding the authority in the area. In July 1876, Sandeman worked out the Mastung Settlement which, on the one hand, authenticated the Khan of Kalat's status as the ruler of Kalat and increased his stipend and, on the other, pressed the Khan to acknowledge the position of the sardars and address their grievances. Sandeman's arbitration was accepted by both the Khan of Kalat and the Baloch sardars. The acknowledgement of British ascendancy and its role as the arbitrator in disputes between the Khan and the sardars was perhaps the most important outcome of this agreement. This agreement reinforced the 1854 Treaty between the then Khan of Kalat and the British. The success of Sandeman's mission won him a number of accolades.

By the time of Sandeman's mission to Balochistan, London was once again caught in its fear of Russian expansion into British areas of influence. British strategic planners in London envisaged the creation or identification of buffer states and/or areas to counter the perceived Russian thrust towards British India via Afghanistan. The British decision to follow the forward policy in Afghanistan and the idea of developing buffer zones was one of the tasks given to the new Viceroy of India, Lord Lytton. The significance of Kalat as one of the buffer states could be gauged from what Lytton once said, "if, at length, we succeed in binding more closely to us the people of Khelat... We shall have added an additional bulwark to our Empire." As a consequence, the British forward policy and Sandeman's effective penetration into Balochistan's political and tribal affairs, as demonstrated by his arbitration between the Khan of Kalat and the Baloch sardars, minimized the status of the Khan to a mere ceremonial head of the state by reducing his status as nothing more than a tribal sardar with sanguine ego[12] and also indirectly sabotaged any chances of integration of the tribes into the state of Kalat and the Khan of Kalat's status as an independent ruler of Kalat.[13]

In January 1877, Lord Lytton, the Viceroy of India, invited the then Khan of Kalat Mir Khudadad Khan to attend the royal *darbar*. This event is highlighted by Baloch nationalist historians as a proof that the British had a special relationship with Kalat and did not treat it as an Indian state. They argue that the fact that the British did not give the Khan of Kalat a banner like other Indian princes implies that he was not treated like the rulers of the Indian states. They further argue that due to their sovereign status, the Viceroy not only received the Khan of Kalat and the Sultan of Oman but also paid them return visits.[14]

46 *Baloch and Balochistan through history*

What is ignored in this narrative is that the Khan objected to this treatment. When he was informed that he was treated as such because he was not one of Her Majesty's feudatories, he responded "I am feudatory quite as loyal and obedient as any other. I don't want to be an independent prince and I do want to have my banner like all the rest. Pray let me have it." And so it happened. At the end of the *darbar*, Mir Khudadad Khan was bestowed with the rank of Knight Grand Commander of the Most Exalted Order of the Star of India. So, even if he was not considered an Indian prince when he came to the *darbar*, by the time he left, he was transformed into one by his own will. In an official communication, the British authorities stated:

> The extraordinary reception given to the Khan of Kalat at the Darbar of 1877 is to be explained by the fact that it was the first occasion in which a Khan had attended an Imperial Indian gathering... on the other hand, when the Khan of Kalat attended the Darbars of 1903 and 1911 he was received in exactly the same footing and was accorded identically the same treatment as other Indian princes of equal rank.[15]

In 1877, the British administration in India transferred the administration of the Derajat to the Punjab government. This change brought a number of Baloch tribes, Buzdar, Khetran, Khosa, Leghari and Mazari, under the administration of the Punjab government. In 1877, Robert Sandeman was appointed as the Agent to the Governor General at the newly established Balochistan Agency, headquartered at Quetta.

Sandeman's policy towards Balochistan

Sandeman, a Scot highlander himself, realized quite early in his career that to secure British interests in Balochistan, the British authorities must cultivate strong and effective relationship with the tribal sardars. This section points to the policy and its main points devised by Robert Sandeman to deal with the Baloch tribes, especially the Baloch sardars. It also looks at the effectiveness of this policy in achieving the British interest in Balochistan and its effects on the Baloch tribe and how it brought Baloch sardars to the fore and made them in the process the most effective and decisive factor in the Baloch tribal society.

Sandeman's initial contact with the Baloch took place when he was working for the Punjab government. He was able to deal with them successfully. He then started making inroads and established contacts with the Baloch tribes in Balochistan. He convinced the Khetrans and Hasni tribes, who had age-long feud with the Kakars and Lunis, Pashtun tribes of Balochistan, to come under British protection. However, the high time of Sandeman's interaction with the Baloch came when in 1879 he established contact with Marri and Bugti tribes and convinced them to tone down their activities and accept British officials as advisors.

As it was stated in the previous section, Sandeman belonged to the so-called Punjab group versus Sindh group in the policy debate about Balochistan. His sole

Balochistan during British rule in India   47

concern was to uphold the British supremacy in the region. His primary concern in dealing with the Baloch tribes was to ensure the security of British imperial interests in Afghanistan and against the tsarist Russia. Sandeman argued that having a strong British presence in Balochistan would provide the British forces a strategic advantage in case they have to move into Afghanistan. He believed that Balochistan corridor would play an immensely important role in case of a war in Afghanistan. To ensure that Balochistan stayed peaceful and secure for such a movement, Sandeman advocated the creation of a community of interest with the Baloch tribes. According to him, as long as the British would address the interest of the Baloch tribes, these tribes would uphold British interest as their own.

Sandeman, from his experience of dealing with the Baloch tribes while serving in the British government in Punjab, understood the centrality of the sardar in the Baloch tribal system. He argued that once the British authorities established an understanding with the sardars and ensure them of its full support, these sardars would turn out to be excellent guardians of the British interest in Balochistan. To achieve this objective, Sandeman took several steps that clearly compromised the Khan of Kalat's suzerainty and clipped his wings of already very limited power. The 1876 Treaty, as mentioned in the previous section, was one such instrument using which Sandeman not only ensured that the British are recognized as the arbitrator in any dispute between the Khan of Kalat and the sardars but also by default lowered the status of the Khan to a level where the Khan and the sardars were to be treated at the same level. He also managed to ensure that the British have a permanent military presence in Balochistan and the expansion of railway and telegraph into Balochistan.

Sandeman was successful in achieving most of the above because of an intelligent manipulation of the Baloch tribal culture. Quite early in his interaction with the Baloch tribes, he realized the pivotal role of sardars in the Baloch tribal culture. The most important point of his policy was that he provided the Baloch sardars with the financial support, administrative functions, glamorous titles and the assurance of continued British support. These steps strengthened the position of a sardar within his tribe as well as in the Baloch tribal culture as he was no more accountable to his tribe and had other sources than his tribe to derive power, authority and support. Sandeman also introduced jirga (council of elders) to address and solve inter-tribal disputes. Over the years, it became an effective forum for the British to interact with the Baloch wherever and whenever there was a problem. The Baloch sardars also found it useful, and this system of negotiation and mediation achieved wider acceptability. Sandeman also setup a levy system in Balochistan as a local law and order body. According to Thornton, this system was primarily aimed at inculcating judicial responsibility among the tribesmen.[16] The main purpose of the levy force which was recruited from the Baloch tribes was to be the eyes and ears of the British authorities.[17] The levy force served a dual purpose; they were recruited from and served in their own tribal area and were paid a stipend by the sardar who was provided a special levy fund by the British. This enhanced not only the stature of the sardar but also that of the personnel of the levy force. At the same time, this provided the British Political Agent in

48   Baloch and Balochistan through history

Balochistan a financial leverage over the sardars as, whenever the sardars failed to achieve the desired results or tried to act independently, their levy fund was suspended.[18]

The Baloch sardars prospered under the British administration. With the British support, they were politically empowered in their tribe and were no longer dependent on their tribe and tribal loyalty as they used to be in the past. They also used the levy system to strengthen their position by appointing their family members and loyalists in the force and, according to Redaelli, integrated the levy system with the traditional tribal society.[19]

These policy steps enhanced the role and status of the sardars in the Baloch tribal system. The levy system and the introduction of the jirga also had long-term effects on the Baloch tribal society and structure. This policy which later came to be known as the Sandeman system also redefined the nature of the relationship between the Khan of Kalat and the Baloch sardars. Unlike the earlier policy of the British authorities, especially the Sindh group, spearheaded by Merewether that relied on the Khan of Kalat to achieve British interest in Balochistan, Sandeman's policy reduced the status of the Khan of Kalat to a mere ceremonial head of a state that was administratively under tight control of the British. According to the administrative report of the Balochistan Agency, 1886:

> The Agent to the Governor-General has practically taken the place of the Khan as head of the Baluch confederation. His Highness is still the nominal head; the Sarawan and Jhalawan chiefs still sit on his right hand and his left in the durbar as of old, and till he is invested by the Khan with the khilat or mantle of succession, a sirdar is not to be legitimized as the representative of his tribe. But in the essential questions of the nomination of sardars, the summoning of jirgahs for the settlement of inter-tribal disputes, and the general preservation of peace in the country, the Agent of the Governor-General is recognized all over Baluchistan as having taken the place of the Khan, and his mandate naturally commands a great deal more respect and obedience than ever did that of His Highness.[20]

On 29 January 1892 in Las Bela, Sandeman passed away after a short illness. By the time of his death, he was successful in securing the British interests in Balochistan. The effects of his policy towards the Baloch and Balochistan were interminable. It transformed the Baloch tribal system, and almost after 110 years of his death, his model of dealing with the tribesmen of Balochistan, the so-called Sandeman system, was considered perhaps the most effective case of dealing with a tribe. In the post-9/11 world, there was a renewed interest in understanding the Sandeman system and perhaps implement it.

However, by the time Sandeman died, despite the fact that he achieved British interests in Balochistan, views were divided about him and his methods. This division of opinion indicated the existence of personal and professional rivalries among the British authorities in India and also of a persistence of policy confusion on how to deal with Balochistan. Sandeman system's effectiveness might

Balochistan during British rule in India 49

have been able to silence the likes of Merewether, but they were not completely sidelined. A number of British officers had not so favourable view on Sandeman and his way of dealing with Balochistan. Henry Mortimer Durand, the Foreign Secretary, for instance, stated "it seems impossible to make him ever understand that Balochistan is not his private property. His attitude always seems to me to be rather that of a suspicious native chief than that of a British officer." Later, Durand accused Sandeman of being the real danger to the British interest and working beyond the British foreign office's control.

An important development which took place in 1895 was the demarcation of the border between Balochistan and Afghanistan. In 1895, a Baloch–Afghan commission was established to finalize the demarcation of the international border between Balochistan and Afghanistan. This commission, under the chairmanship of Colonel McMahan, worked on extending the international border, part of which covered Afghanistan and NWFP was demarcated by Durand and was named after him. The part of the border between Afghanistan and Balochistan was named after McMahan and was called the McMahan line.

At the turn of the twentieth century, Balochistan was divided into four parts:

1   British Balochistan
2   Agencies
3   Tribal Areas
4   Khanate of Kalat, Kharan, Las Bela and Makran

As the name indicated, British Balochistan comprised the area that was directly administrated by a chief commissioner representing the British government in India. It included the areas it acquired under the Treaty of Gandermak of 1879.

Agencies included Quetta, Bolan and Chagahi. These were the areas which the British acquired on lease from the Khan of Kalat due to the strategic significance of these areas. Bolan was strategically a very important passage route which the British had to keep under their control as it would be the key to any military expedition to Afghanistan. The areas acquired through the Treaty of Gandamak, Zhob and Loralai, also constituted agency areas. The Agent to the Governor General of India was the administrative head of agency territories.

The Marri and Bugti areas comprised the tribal area. This was the most difficult and delicate area for the British to handle as the Marri and Bugti tribes were fiercely independent. Here, the British control was exercised indirectly without any provocation to the Marris and Bugtis.

The states comprised Kalat, Kharan, Las Bela and Makran. Out of these, Kalat was the most important state with territorial claims on the remaining three states. Here, the British retained some kind of ceremonial political set-up in the sense that these states had their rulers and government despite the fact that the real power and decision-making authority was held by the British.

Soon after the beginning of the Great War (World War I), the Khan of Kalat and the Baloch sardars assured the British authorities in India of full support to

50   *Baloch and Balochistan through history*

the British forces and the British war effort. The Khan of Kalat contributed handsomely to the war relief fund. The Khan of Kalat also, as a gesture of support, offered the British his Kalat and Las Bela camel crop and also fully supported and encouraged the British policy of recruitment from Balochistan, a fact fully appreciated and acknowledged by the British authorities in India. The administrative report of Balochistan (1917–18) noted the efforts of the Khan and the sardars in this regard. The report stated that most of the sardars responded positively to the British authority's call for recruitment.[21]

During this period, there were a number of uprisings in Zhob, Killa Saifullah and Loralai areas. However, the views were divided on the reasons and causes for the emergence of these uprisings as a number of British sources linked these uprisings with the situation in Afghanistan, especially the third Afghan war (1919).

The Marri and Bugti tribes were of particular concern for the British authorities in India. The British were worried that the Bugtis and Marris would create trouble and revolt against them. Serious troubles occurred in Jhalawan (1915–16) and in Marri and Bugti areas (1918). There were British intelligence reports about the presence of German spies in Afghanistan and Balochistan. The death of two British officers in Makran in Balochistan was attributed to these German agents.

To counter the ever-increasing German threat who the British authorities in India believed were considering invading India via Balochistan, Brigadier Dyer[22] was sent to Balochistan to assess the nature and scope of the threat and possible counter-measures.[23] However, as it turned out, most of the British intelligence reports were incorrect. Yet Brigadier Dyer's mission to Balochistan was successful, as he managed to make useful contacts and inroads into Balochistan with the help of Baloch tribesmen.[24] However, the biggest satisfaction for the British authorities in Balochistan and India came at the end of the war and during the post-war period: when the whole of India was going through a frantic Khilafat Movement, Balochistan remained totally aloof and completely unaffected by this movement.

KALAT'S GROWING ADMINISTRATIVE QUANDARY

In Balochistan, the increasing instability and administrative mismanagement in the Khanate of Kalat presented a challenge for the British. On 29 March 1893, the nominal Khan of Kalat, Mir Khudadad Khan was arrested by the British authorities and was kept captive along with most of his family members at Pishin. He remained under captivity till his death almost fifteen years later on 21 May 1907. The British appointed Mir Mahmud Khan II as the new Khan. This Khan of Kalat had no interest in the affairs of the state and remained confined into Miri, the traditional/official residence of the Khans of Kalat. He had a weird personality and suffered from a mania of collecting stuff and then destroying it. During this reign, the administration of Kalat was completely run by the Agent to the Governor General of the British India. Nawab Sir Mir Shams Shah was appointed Wazir-e-Azam (Prime Minister) by the Khan of Kalat Mahmud Khan in later years of his so-called rule but was later sacked by Mir Azam Khan, who succeeded Mahmud

Balochistan during British rule in India   51

Khan as the Khan of Kalat. Mir Mahmud Khan died on 2 November 1931. His reign as the Khan of Kalat was equally erratic and inefficient. As it turned out, the Khanate of Kalat was increasingly becoming ungovernable.[25]

It became clear to the British that their objective of having a politically stable and secure Kalat that is capable of providing a stable base for the British forces in British India's western borderlands could not be achieved unless some drastic measures were taken to improve the situation. The policy confusion of the British authorities on Kalat and Balochistan persisted. With the political developments in the Indian subcontinent and the emergence of political activities in Balochistan, a group of British officers were of the view that the British government in India had to revise its treaties with Kalat and introduce administrative reforms.

Edward Wakefield was appointed as Kalat's first British Wazir-e-Azam (Prime Minister). His appointment was an indication that the British authorities in India were not happy about the way the state was run. This was rather ironic, in keeping with the fact that since the sacking and imprisonment of the then Khan of Kalat, Mir Khudadad Khan in 1883, the Political Agent to the Governor General of India was running the state as almost a de facto ruler of Kalat.[26] Another important point that emerged from Wakefield's appointment was that the so-called Sandeman system could no longer resolve all the issues faced by the British in Balochistan. Even Wakefield expressed this view when he wrote:

> Sir Robert Sandeman, in the last quarter of the nineteenth century, had temporarily reconciled ancient enmities and established a modus vivendi for the Khan and the sardars. But the maladministration of recent years had placed too great strain on the Sandeman compromise. The old system had broken down, and some new relationship between the Khan and the sirdars had to be established.[27]

Political awakening in Balochistan

Although Balochistan was mostly quiet and peaceful during the Great War and the Khilafat Movement, a group of educated Baloch was privy to and was influenced by the All India Congress and its struggle against British colonialism. An underground group Anjuman Itahaad-e-Balochan was operating in Kalat under the leadership of Mir Abdul Aziz Kurd.

Mir Yusuf Ali Magsi, though not part of the Anjuman at that time, also played a significant role in the political awakening in Balochistan. He wrote an article that was published in the 17 November 1929 issue of weekly Humdard published from Lahore. In his article, addressing the Balochistani people, Mir Yusuf Ali wrote that the Baloch should rise above tribal differences and rivalries and struggle for freedom.[28] This article caused a major commotion among the administration in Kalat and Balochistan. Mir Yusuf was charged with attempting to instigate rebellion in Kalat and was arrested and sent to the Mastung Jail.

A jirga comprising Sardar Muhammad Khan Shahwani, Sardar Muhmmad Khan, Sardar Behram Khan Leghari, Sardar Rasul Bakhsh Zarakzai, and Sardar

52   *Baloch and Balochistan through history*

Rasul Bakhsh Mengal in their ruling declared Yusuf guilty of instigating unlawful activities in the state in general even before the publication of this article. The publication of this article, according to them was just another attempt by Yusuf to stir trouble in Kalat state. The jirga fined Yusuf with Rs. 12,900 plus Rs. 10,000 bond money as insurance for good behaviour. He was also given 1-year imprisonment under strict supervision of his uncle Sardar Rasul Bakhsh Zarakzai.

While he was in Mastung Jail, he was approached by the Anjuman. After he was released, Yusuf decided to start political activities in Kalat. Among the first campaigns Yusuf and his political comrades Mir Abdul Rehman Bugti, Mir Abdul Aziz Kurd, Malik Faiz Muhammad Yusafzai and Muhammad Hussain Unqa took part was to struggle in favour of appointing Mir Azam Jan as the next Khan of Kalat. This pitched them directly against the all-powerful Sir Shams Shah, the Prime Minister of Kalat, who was campaigning in favour of Mir Anwar Khan (the elder son of terminally ill Khan of Kalat Mir Mahmud Khan). A delegation was sent to the Viceroy of India to complaint against Sir Shams Shah. A booklet published as part of this campaign in November 1931 highlighted the crimes of Shams Shah against the Baloch and the Balochistani people. They also approached Baloch sardars to campaign in favour of Mir Azam Jan's appointment as the Khan of Kalat. They achieved their goal when, despite Sir Shams Shah's efforts, Mir Azam Jan was appointed as the Khan of Kalat. Sir Shams Shah was sent packing, and Bahadur Gul Muhammad Khan was appointed the new Prime Minister of Kalat.[29] However, once appointed the Khan of Kalat, Mir Azam Jan failed to appoint a more consultative political set-up and warned against any political activity in Kalat.

When Mir Ahmad Yar Khan became the Khan of Kalat, he had a puzzling relationship with the progressive and politically active Baloch.[30] While Mir Abdul Aziz Kurd was arrested and sentenced to three years of imprisonment, Mir Yusuf Ali was sent to England as an emissary of the Khan of Kalat. As this trip was part of a secret understanding between Yusuf Ali and Ahmad Yar Khan, it was taken as a betrayal of his political comrades by many. After spending almost ten months in England, Yusuf Ali returned to Karachi on 31 January 1935. The talks with the British authorities went inconclusive and Yusuf charted out a road map to continue political struggle. Unfortunately, he died along with thousands of others during the tragic earthquake on 31 May 1935 in Quetta.

The next milestone in this regard was the creation of Kalat State National Party (KSNP) on 5 February 1937. KSNP played an important role in Kalat politics, especially at the time of Kalat's accession with Pakistan.

The appointment of Ahmad Yar Khan as the Khan of Kalat

After the death of the Khan of Kalat Azam Jan, his second-born Ahmad Yar Khan was appointed as the new Khan of Kalat on 10 September 1933. He remained the Khan of Kalat till 1948 when the Khanate of Kalat acceded with Pakistan. Unlike the previous Khans of Kalat, the British authorities had closely followed Ahmad Yar's upbringing and played a role in training him for his future duties. He, at one

Balochistan during British rule in India 53

point of time, served as an intelligence officer in the levy forces of Balochistan.[31] His loyalty to the British throughout this period remained unquestionable, yet a number of British officers considered him to be fickle, vacillating and easily influenced. Wakefield, who was the Wazir (Prime Minister) at the time of Ahmad Yar's appointment as the Khan, described him as fickle and vacillating to a degree and that due to this reason, he would never become a good and strong ruler.[32] According to Wakefield, Ahmad Yar Khan could be easily dominated and influenced and swiftly change his opinion. His loyalty to the British, according to Wakefield, was the only constant factor.[33] The Agent to the Governor General Carter agreed with Wakefield's assessment. He wrote:

> (He) has yet little experience of government and it would be wrong to disguise the present fact that he is of a somewhat vacillating character and liable to be swayed by the last opinion or advice offered to him.[34]

Regardless of these views, Ahmad Yar Khan was educated and intelligent enough to soon realize, notwithstanding the realities on the ground, the loopholes in the British legal position on Kalat. He understood that the treaties which the British authorities in India have signed with his predecessors provide him enough space to manoeuvre and assert his position as the Khan of Kalat. This was exactly what a group of British officers in India assumed would happen and suggested that the British should revise and sign a new treaty with Kalat. Axmann in his book argued that Ahmad Yar Khan's dissatisfaction regarding his entitlement as the Khan of Kalat soon became obvious. One year after Ahmad Yar's appointment as the Khan of Kalat, Frederick Squire, Political Agent of Kalat, wrote in November 1934, "the present Khan after waiting a year to find his feet discovers that he does not know where to put them."[35] Ahmad Yar Khan in his autobiography wrote:

> The Agent to the Governor-General in Balochistan ... the administrative head of Kalat. The Khan-e-Baluch functioned merely as a figure head with no powers at all. He was, as it were, a mechanical contraption which could function as an instrument by putting his signature on the dotted line on orders issued by the political agent, who also functioned as the prime minister (i.e vezir of Kalat) ... The Khan-e-Kalat was the head of state merely on paper.[36]

Ahmad Yar Khan was aware that if he wanted to assert his position as the Khan of Kalat, he needed the support of the Baloch sardars. Historically, the Khan of Kalat provided the Baloch sardars with financial subsidies in return of their support when required. Since the Second Anglo-Afghan War (1878–80), the British continued this practice which resulted in the shift of the Baloch sardars' loyalty from the Khan of Kalat to the British authorities. Ahmad Yar Khan knew that if he had to assert his position as the Khan of Kalat, he should be in a position to provide subsidies to the sardars.

In keeping with these two factors, in February 1935, Ahmad Yar Khan, to reclaim his status of the Khan of Kalat and to assert his position, wrote a letter

54   *Baloch and Balochistan through history*

to the Agent to the Governor General requesting that the power of the Political Agent to be transferred to him. In his letter, he thanked the British for taking care of the affairs of Kalat up till now. Ahmad Yar Khan reproduced this letter in his autobiography. He wrote:

> I do not for a moment deny that during this period circumstances have in fact required that certain functions of government, which might ordinarily have remained with the Khan, should be exercised by the political agent; and I personally am conscious of the debt which the Kalat state owes to those officers who have done so much for it. But I would ask you now to consider whether such circumstances still exist. I am myself willing, and I believe myself to be capable, of assuming the full responsibility of my position as Khan of Kalat and head of the Brahui confederacy; and I feel confident that it will be to the advantage alike of the British government and of the Kalat state that I should do so. I am well aware of the special position which the sardars hold in my state, and I have therefore been careful to consult my state council before sending this murasila to you, and they are in accord with my views.[37]

What was surprising for the British authorities in India was not that Ahmad Yar Khan wanted more powers but his claim that the sardars of Sarawan and Jhalawan fully supported him in this request. Ahmad Yar Khan in his autobiography quoted from the memorandum of support the sardars presented to him on 27 January 1935:

> We the sardars, the dignitaries and citizens assure you on behalf of our followers, dependents and we, of our full faith and confidence in your leadership. We would remain faithful to you in the same manner and degrees as our forefathers were in the past to the Khan-e-Azam of the blessed memory and his ancestors.[38]

A closer look at this memorandum points to an interesting element. The sardars promised to support Ahmad Yar Khan exactly how their forefathers supported previous Khans of Kalat. This clearly meant that this pledge of allegiance was based on a give and take. There was a mixed response from the British authorities on the letter by Ahmad Yar Khan. Riccardo Redaelli in his book *The Father's Bow* maintained that the British were willing to transfer certain powers to the Khan *provided* he accepted the Political Agent and the Wazir as his advisors in all decisions.[39] At the same time in an official communication,[40] it was made clear to Ahmad Yar Khan that the British authorities in India would not accept the demand that Ahmad Yar Khan should be the one paying financial subsidies to the Baloch sardars.[41]

However, by this time, Ahmad Yar Khan had a change of heart. He realized that it would be almost impossible for him to achieve this demand and decided not to pursue it further.[42] Three years later, in 1938, Ahmad Yar Khan once again raised the issue of transfer of power. This time, the British response was straightforward. Ahmad Yar Khan was informed that he neither had the authority nor the resources

Balochistan during British rule in India   55

to run the state and that even if the British transfer the power to Ahmad Yar Khan, the sardars would reject such a transfer of power.[43]

Ignoring this rebuttal, Ahmad Yar Khan's next move was even more daring. He announced and implemented a number of political and administrative reforms in the Khanate of Kalat. He created a cabinet and a council of state. He contained the powers of the Wazir and made him answerable to the cabinet.[44] The British, although clearly not happy with this, adopted a cautious approach and asked Ahmad Yar Khan to appraise them of what exactly he intended. Ahmad Yar Khan's response, according to Redaelli, surprised the British even further. It became clear that Ahmad Yar Khan wanted to establish himself as the king of the Khanate of Kalat which would incorporate Kharan and Las Bela into Kalat.[45]

After exhaustive discussions, the British agreed to transfer the powers of the Political Agent to Ahmad Yar Khan as the Khan of Kalat.[46] At the same time, the British authorities also expressed their willingness to allow the Khan of Kalat to pay allowances to the Baloch sardars.[47] However, in a separate communication, the British authorities made it quite clear to Ahmad Yar Khan that it was the British who were calling the shots and would continue to do so. It was made clear to him that he could not make any decision without consulting the British authorities first and, whatever directive comes from the British authorities in India, the Khan of Kalat would have to follow it in letter and spirit.

Persistent policy confusion of the British about Kalat/ Balochistan

The introduction of the Sandeman system in Balochistan resolved the dilemma of the British authorities on how to deal with the Baloch leadership (both the Khan of Kalat and the Baloch sardars) so that the British geostrategic interests could be ensured. However, by the 1920s, a debate started to resurface among the British officers in India and Balochistan about the states and the future course of the British interaction with states, especially Kalat. Although, by that time, British authorities faced no problem in Kalat and Balochistan due to the loyalty of the Baloch sardars and British-backed but administratively and politically toothless Khans of Kalat, an emerging view among the British authorities in India was to revise its treaties with Kalat and legally declare it an Indian state.[48] Under this line of thinking that Kalat would eventually be included into the British India federation, two seats in the council of the states and one seat in the federal legislative assembly was allocated to Kalat.[49] That the British were planning to include Kalat into the Indian federation could be substantiated from a communication between London and Delhi (British government of India) of January 1935: "the ultimate sanction for relations with these frontier states will be paramountcy of the crown, exercise through the viceroy, to the same extent as in the case of other Indian states which are units in the federation."[50]

Axmann, quoting British official communication, argued that by 1939, Ahmad Yar Khan, realizing that the British would rebuke his attempts to assert his position

56 *Baloch and Balochistan through history*

as an independent and authoritative Khan of Kalat, demonstrated an interest in the affairs of the Indian federation. The AGG in Quetta, according to Axmann, also stated that Ahmad Yar Khan wanted to be informed whether Kalat would be incorporated in the Indian federation so that he could start participating in the Indian affairs. However, the British authorities continued to debate the issue and failed to come up with a clear stance on whether Kalat was an Indian state or not. Interestingly, another caveat was included in the debate: whether Kalat was as a state administratively and politically ready to be incorporated into the Indian federation. The answer was an overwhelming no. Regardless of the fact that it was the failure of the British authorities in India who were virtually in control of Kalat since 1842 but used it only to secure its geostrategic interests, it was now stated that administratively Kalat could not meet the requirements to join the Indian federation.

On the issue of Kalat joining Indian federation under the Government of India Act 1935 that required all heads of states to sign instruments of accession to join the Indian federation, Foreign Secretary Olaf Caroe, addressing the issue of Kalat's joining of Indian federation, commented that the Khan of Kalat was not in a position to ensure that he was the sole authority in Kalat and that the rulers of Las Bela and Kharan would never accept the Khan's sovereignty over them.[51] Equally problematic was the issue of the Baloch sardars. Caroe was of the view that at that point of time, moving forward with making Kalat a part of the Indian federation would result in an interstate and tribal war.[52]

By 1940, it emerged that the British viewed Kalat as an Indian state. The British authorities claimed that Ahmad Yar Khan demonstrated willingness to participate in Indian affairs as a ruler of an Indian state yet Kalat could not be incorporated into the Indian federation because it lacked proper administrative and political institutions. The advent of the decade of 1940s witnessed the intensification of the Second World War, and the geostrategic significance of Balochistan for the British strategists was reinforced, which obscured the British policy and position about when to legally incorporate Kalat into the Indian federation.

In the light of Ahmad Yar Khan's communication of 1941 stating that Kalat is not an Indian state, the Joint Secretary for External Affairs, on 31 December 1941, stated as follows:

> It would appear that His Highness bases his estimate of his constitutional position on a misperception of Article 3 of the Treaty of 1876…reinforced by family recollections of the special position accorded to his grandfather, Khan Khudadad Khan, at the Darbar of 1877. Article 3 of the treaty of 1876, however, expressly saves the provisions of Article 3 of the Treaty of 1854, by which the Khan of Kalat bound himself, his heirs and successors, in all cases to act in subordinate cooperation with the British Government. Thus the engagement of the British Government to respect the independence of Kalat must be read subject to the Khan's undertaking to act in subordinate cooperation with them, and the position this arrived at does not differ materially from that reached in the treaties with various other Indian states …[53]

Balochistan during British rule in India 57

Furthermore, in a communication by the Secretary of State, it was stated: "The treaties of 1854 and 1876 do not lead to the inference that Kalat is an Independent and sovereign state and it has, in fact, always been regarded as an Indian state."[54]

Effects of British involvement in Balochistan

The lack of knowledge of the British about the Baloch and Balochistan was the prime reason why the British authorities in India could not formulate a policy to deal with Kalat and Balochistan. It was the perceived threat from tsarist Russia to the British interests in the southern Asian region, including Afghanistan, that the British authorities decided to scout the area. In retrospect, Pottinger, who was tasked for this job, gave a faulty and inadequate assessment about the Khan of Kalat, his powers and his authority over the Baloch sardars. British initial policy was heavily reliant on Pottinger's account and suggested that to ensure the security of the British India, the British government of India should adopt a policy of non-interference in the internal affairs, strengthen the rulers of the buffer states and cultivate strong economic and trade relations with them and eventually expand the trade into Central Asia to develop an economic incentive against any war effort against the British India. The proponents of this policy were called the closed border policy school. Another view, the forward policy school, was that the British authorities in India should establish a network of states that would be dependent on British protection. This view gained prominence with the British authorities in India dealing with Balochistan, especially once the initial policy of strengthening the Khan of Kalat failed. The Forward policy school argued for cultivating strong relations with the Baloch sardars. The British managed to firm their grip on Balochistan when Robert Sandeman successfully penetrated the Baloch tribes and brought the Baloch sardars in his hold. However, as the primary interest of the British in Balochistan was geostrategic, they hardly paid any attention to uplifting the standard of living of the Baloch and provide them with basic human needs. They constructed roads, built railway lines and established cantonment cities such as Quetta, which had affected the Baloch, but that was an unintended outcome. That is why, Balochistan had the Command and Staff College in Quetta but no medical facility like the Lady Reading Hospital in Peshawar or educational institution like Government College, Lahore.

This lack of interest in economically and socially improving Balochistan became the prime reason why, despite their repeated assertion that Kalat is a normal Indian state, the British authorities in India could not incorporate Kalat into the Indian federation, as the widespread poverty, the lack of administrative structure and minimal population would have put a huge financial and administrative burden on the British India. Despite a lack of direction and a clear-cut policy towards Balochistan, the British involvement affected the Baloch and Balochistan in a number of ways. According to Nina Swidler, there was a rise in sedentarization, and as a result, new villages were founded and urban population increased manyfold.[55] Kalat as the centre of financial activity had to back-step as Quetta emerged as the new power centre and the financial capital of Balochistan. Traders moved

58 *Baloch and Balochistan through history*

their businesses from Kalat to Quetta. A number of sardars built houses in Quetta so that they could stay closer to the corridor of power. The British introduced the modern taxation system and the ownership of private property in Balochistan, something that was alien to the Baloch tribes up till that time. The advent of railway in Balochistan affected the Baloch tribes in a number of ways. It eventually disrupted and almost minimized the caravan trading. This had an effect on camel breeding in Balochistan and affected particularly those tribes that economically relied on this. This affected the trade patterns of the Baloch tribes. As a result of the advent of railway, Karachi Port became a major trade hub.

However, the biggest effect of the British involvement in Balochistan was that the evolutionary process of Kalat from a tribal confederacy to a state was halted. With the British takeover, the subsequent Khans of Kalat increasingly became irrelevant as all powers resided with the Agent to the Governor General, and for all practical purposes, he was the ruler of Kalat. The Baloch sardars, who understood this transformation of power, soon shifted their loyalties to the AGG. Ahmad Yar Khan, the last Khan of Kalat, understood that unless the British signed a new treaty with Kalat or officially incorporated Kalat into the Indian federation as an Indian state, he was arguably in his legal rights to demand more authority, but what he forgot was that he was in no position to demand anything from the British. Another impediment for him was that he was ignoring the ground realities and envisaged a great Baloch state with himself as the ruler of it. His mythical independent state of Kalat never existed. Even if it did, Ahmad Yar Khan lacked the leadership quality and political perspicacity to acquire it. His attempts to become a king of Balochistan and at the same time remain a loyal subject of the British crown were irreconcilable. He failed to acknowledge this dichotomy.

It is a fact that the British authorities used Balochistan as a military outpost and failed to bring it at par to other parts of British India. A Baloch historian, M.S.K. Baluch stated that the British rule of eighty years centred round the policy of how to divide and create a wider gulf of enmity and hatred between the same tribes of the same country. The country stands politically, economically and socially in the backwaters of civilization.

This chapter overviewed the second element of the Baloch nationalist narrative: the British treatment of Balochistan, especially Kalat. The Baloch nationalist narrative claims that the British, throughout their engagement and involvement in Kalat and Balochistan, always treated Kalat as an independent state. This chapter aimed at analysing this part of the Baloch narrative and has demonstrated that Baloch nationalists' position regarding Kalat's status is incorrect.

Notes

1 Gul Khan Naseer and Inayatullah prime among them.
2 Martin Axmann, *Back to the Future, The Khanate of Kalat and the Genesis of Baloch Nationalism 1915–1955* (Karachi: OUP, 2009).
3 Ibid.
4 Rizwan Zeb, "Khans and Fractious Chieftains," *The Friday Times*, July 22, 2016, www.thefridaytimes.com/tft/khans-and-fractious-chieftains/.

Balochistan during British rule in India   59

5 Ibid.
6 Ann Kalayil, *British Relations with the Khanate of Kalat, Baluchistan, 1838–1882* (PhD., University of Wisconsin-Madison, 1997).
7 Ibid.
8 Axmann, op.cit.
9 Government of India, *Kalat Affairs: Selection from Government Records* (Quetta: Nisa Traders, 1977).
10 Ibid.
11 Ibid.
12 Swidler, *Kalat*, 53–54.
13 Kalayil, op.cit.
14 Rizwan Zeb, "The Raj and the Khan," *The Friday Times*, November 25, 2016, www.thefridaytimes.com/tft/the-raj-and-the-khan/.
15 Ibid.
16 Thornton, *Colonel Sir Robert Sandeman*, op.cit.
17 Government of India, *Administration Report of the Baluchistan Agency for the Year 1920–21* (Quetta: Qasim Printers, 1989), 7.
18 Swidler, *Kalat*, 52–53.
19 Redaelli, *Father's Bow*, 62–74.
20 Government of India, *First Administrative Report of the Baluchistan Agency for 1886* (Lahore: Combine Printers, 1988).
21 Government of India, *Administration Report of the Baluchistan Agency 1917–18* (Quetta: Quetta Printing Press, 1989), 133.
22 General Dyer, *Balochistan key sarhadi chapa maar*, trans. Mir Gul Khan Naseer (in Urdu) (Quetta: Nisa, 1990).
23 Ibid.
24 Ibid.
25 Wakefield, *Past Imperative*, 109–12, 134.
26 Ibid., 109–12.
27 Ibid.
28 Gul Khan Naseer, *Tareekh-e-Balochistan* (Quetta: Kalat Publishers, 2010), 448.
29 Ibid., 468.
30 For details on this point of view, Naseer, *Tareekh-e-Balochistan*, 481–84.
31 For details, see Zahid Chaudhray, *Pakistan ki Siayasi Tareekh*, volume 4 (in Urdu) (Lahore: Idera Mutaleya –e-Tarekh, 1994).
32 Redaelli, *Father's Bow*, 118; and Axmann, *Back to the Future.*
33 Axmann, *Back to the Future*, 82.
34 Ibid.
35 Ibid.
36 Mir Ahmad Yar Khan, *Inside Baluchistan: A Political Autobiography of His Highness Baiglar Baigi Khan-e-Azam XIII* (Karachi: Royal Book Company, 1975), 123–24.
37 Khan, *Inside Baluchistan*, 121–22.
38 Ibid., XIX.
39 Redaelli, *Father's Bow*, 22–23.
40 Ibid.
41 Ibid., 123.
42 Ibid., 125.
43 Ibid., 127.
44 Khan, *Inside Baluchistan*, 121, 125–29.
45 Redaelli, *Father's Bow*, 130.
46 Ibid., 132.
47 Ibid.
48 For details, see Axmann, *Back to the Future.*
49 Ibid.

60 *Baloch and Balochistan through history*

50 Ibid.
51 Ibid.
52 Ibid.
53 Zeb, "The Raj and the Khan," *The Friday Times*, November 25, 2016, www.thefridaytimes.com/tft/the-raj-and-the-khan/.
54 Ibid.
55 Swidler, "The Political Context of Brahui Sedentarization," *Ethnology* 12 (1973): 299–314.

Part II

Centre–Province (Islamabad–Balochistan) relations post-independence

3 Independence of Pakistan, accession of Kalat and centre–Balochistan relations (1947–69)

INTRODUCTION

The last chapter demonstrated how Khan of Kalat Mir Ahmad Yar Khan, after becoming the Khan, tried hard to convince the British to accept the independent status of the Kalat state and him as the undisputed ruler of Balochistan. Now, with the British decision to leave the Indian subcontinent in 1947 and grant India and Pakistan independence, the Khan of Kalat made one last attempt to achieve his goal.

He got partial success when Quaid-e-Azam Muhammad Ali Jinnah, as a starter to further negotiation, agreed to accept Kalat's status as different from the rest of the princely states of the subcontinent. Quaid-e-Azam Muhammad Ali Jinnah, as his policy and statements regarding princely states that would join Pakistan indicate, was more than willing to provide Kalat maximum autonomy, with Pakistan only taking responsibility of the defence, foreign and economic affairs. In keeping with his personal relations with Ahmad Yar Khan, Quaid-e-Azam Muhammad Ali Jinnah hoped that Ahmad Yar Khan would accede to Pakistan. Quaid-e-Azam Muhammad Ali Jinnah underestimated Ahmad Yar Khan's intentions, who dreamed of becoming the ruler of an independent country. However, Ahmad Yar Khan apparently played a double game as it is demonstrated in this chapter, not only with Pakistan and especially with Quaid-e-Azam Muhammad Ali Jinnah but also with the Baloch sardars and the people of Kalat and Balochistan.

On the one hand, he kept ensuring Quaid-e-Azam Muhammad Ali Jinnah and the Pakistani government that everything would be sorted out which would be mutually acceptable. On the other hand, to Baloch sardars and the so-called elected representatives of Kalat, he discussed Kalat's historical place and destiny. His decision to not take the decision to accede to Pakistan alone but to ask his rather hastily and dubiously *elected* House of Lords and Commons was nothing but delaying tactics as the details provided in the chapter demonstrate.

However, despite all this, Ahmad Yar Khan had to sign Kalat's accession agreement with Pakistan, although the seeds of discontent and misperception between Pakistan and the Baloch were sown deep by then.

Once Pakistan managed to get the accession of Kalat and British Balochistan voting in its favour, it started working on administrated reforms in the province.

64 *Centre–Province relations post-independence*

A number of steps and measures were taken with mixed results. The One Unit policy, the ill-conceived arrest of Ahmad Yar Khan in 1958 on dubious charges and the mishandling and disrespectful treatment of Nauroz Khan added to the Baloch grievances towards the centre, which, according to Baloch nationalist narrative, was strongly anti-Baloch and consisted of the Punjabi ruling elites.

This chapter covers the first 23 years of Pakistan and Balochistan history. It is divided into two parts. The first part briefly looks at the process of partition of the Indian subcontinent and the creation of Pakistan and the challenges of state and nation building faced by the Pakistani leadership. The second part, which is the main body of this chapter, looks at the whole process of accession of Kalat with Pakistan, challenging a number of established myths in Baloch as well as in Pakistan's history. Looking at the whole process of negotiations between the Khan of Kalat and Quaid-e-Azam Muhammad Ali Jinnah and between Mir Ahmad Yar Khan and his team (the Prime Minister of Kalat Muhammad Aslam Khan and the Foreign Minister Douglas Fell) and his speeches to the two houses of Baloch sardars and notables, this chapter argues that it was the Khan of Kalat who made the whole process difficult and complicated, which could have been straightforward. The use of different narratives and tone by him in his communication with Quaid-e-Azam Muhammad Ali Jinnah and with Baloch sardars not only resulted in confusion between the Baloch opinion makers and the centre but also developed the perception that Pakistan wanted to occupy Kalat. It was this role played by Mir Ahmad Yar Khan that resulted in Prince Karim's localized armed struggle against Pakistan. The letter which Prince Karim wrote to Ahmad Yar Khan is a clear indication of the fact that Baloch perception about Quaid-e-Azam Muhammad Ali Jinnah and Pakistan became extremely negative as early as 1948. The chapter also demonstrates the failure of Pakistani policy makers in moving beyond the British model and policy of ruling Balochistan. With increased political instability in the country and differences between the East and the West Pakistan, the leadership of Pakistan could not do much about backward areas like Balochistan. The proceeding sections cover the developments of the decades of 1950s and 1960s and the implications of these developments on perceptions and policies of both the centre and Balochistan towards each other. The chapter concludes with the end of the Ayub's regime in 1969.

This chapter covers a number of important points of the Baloch nationalist narrative. The Baloch narrative argues that Pakistan forced the Khan of Kalat to sign the agreement of accession. After occupying Kalat, the centre treated the Baloch as second-class citizens and used the resources and wealth of Balochistan for its own needs, completely ignoring the Baloch and depriving them of the basic human needs.

Partition of the Indian subcontinent and the creation of Pakistan

Soon after winning the 1945 elections, the British Prime Minister Clement Attlee sent a three-member Cabinet Mission to the Indian subcontinent to work out the best way of transferring of power to the Indian political leadership.[1] It soon became

Independence of Pakistan 65

clear to the Cabinet Mission that the differences between All India Congress and All India Muslim League are irreconcilable as both parties remained firm on their stated positions: Congress for a united India, Muslim League for a Muslim Pakistan.[2] On 16 May 1946, the Cabinet Mission announced its own plan. According to this plan, the federal government of the Indian subcontinent would only be responsible for foreign affairs, defence and communications. The provinces would be divided into three groups. Group A would include Madras, Bombay, United Provinces, Bihar, Central Provinces and Orissa. Group B would comprise Punjab, North-West Frontier Province and Sindh. Group C would comprise Bengal and Assam. A closer look at these groups indicates that the Cabinet Mission plan separated the Hindu-majority provinces from the Muslim-majority provinces by placing them in separate groups. According to the Cabinet Mission plan:

> The constitution of the union and of the Groups should contain a provision whereby any province could, by a majority vote of its Legislative Assembly, call for reconsideration of the terms of the constitution after an initial period of 10 years and at 10 years intervals thereafter.[3]

This plan was unacceptable to All India Congress which stood for a united India. In a resolution passed on 24 May 1946, All India Congress rejected the plan on the grounds that it supported a weaker centre.[4] All India Muslim League accepted the plan as it was quite close to what it had been demanding.[5] The differences between the leadership of All India Congress and All India Muslim League, in the subsequent months, reached a point of no return.

On 20 February 1947, Atlee announced that the British government would transfer power to the Indian leadership by June 1948. Lord Louis Mountbatten was appointed the last viceroy of India and incharge of the process of the transfer of power. On 3 June 1947, a partition plan was announced by the British, according to which the transfer of power would take place in August 1947. As the name suggested, the partition plan envisaged the division of the Indian subcontinent into two states: India and Pakistan. Sir Cyril Radcliffe was appointed the Chairman of the Boundary Commission which divided the Indian subcontinent into India and Pakistan.

Views are extremely divided on the performance of Sir Radcliffe and the Boundary Commission. The partition award, though ready by 13 August 1947, was only announced four days later on 17 August 1947, when India and Pakistan had already attained the status of dominion states. Both India and Pakistan expressed dissatisfaction on the award. All India Muslim League leadership, which was already suspicious of the trio of Nehru, Edwina Mountbatten, and Lord Mountbatten, declared the award a conspiracy against Pakistan.[6]

Pakistan's state- and nation-building challenges

Pakistan, as Emerson aptly described it, was a state that "almost no one had fore-seen and few could credit in advance as even a possibility."[7] In Clifford Geertz's

66 Centre–Province relations post-independence

terminology, Pakistan belonged to the category of old societies and new states.[8] Perhaps the biggest challenge for the leadership of Pakistan was to build a Pakistani nation, as there was no such thing as a Pakistani nation prior to 1947. Ironically, the area that comprised Pakistan (West Pakistan in 1947) was not in the forefront of the struggle for a separate homeland for the Muslims of India. The biggest reason for this was that these were Muslim-majority areas and had no fear of Hindu domination and discrimination against Muslims. Punjab, which became the most important province of Pakistan, was under the rule of the Unionist Party till 1946. The political leadership of Punjab sided with the Muslim League only when it became obvious that Pakistan would be created and that Punjab would be a part of it.

NWFP (now Khyber Pakhtunkhwa) had a significant pro-Congress/united India sentiment under the leadership of charismatic Khan Abdul Ghaffar Khan, the frontier Gandhi. Using Joseph Strayer's view on successful nation building, those states

> correspond closely to old political units; those where the experience of living together for many generations within a continuing political framework has given the people some sense of identity; those where the political units coincide roughly with a distinct cultural area; and those where there are indigenous institutions and habits of political thinking can be connected to forms borrowed from outside.[9]

One cannot disagree with Emerson's claim that "by the accepted criteria of nationhood there was in fact no such thing as a Pakistani nation."[10] Moreover, the problems that emerged and multiplied such as the flow of migrants from India, the problem of Kashmir, Nehru's decision to block the supply of Pakistan's share from the assets to Pakistan created an atmosphere of distrust between the two states, and despite Gandhi and Quaid-e-Azam Muhammad Ali Jinnah's intention of good relations,[11] both countries went on a path of adversity. Pakistan being a weaker state became a national security state. As early as 8 October 1948, the Prime Minister of Pakistan Liaquat Ali Khan in an address to the nation declared "the defence of the state is our foremost consideration ... we will not grudge any amount on the defence of our country."[12]

The lack of democratic values and in Ian Talbot's words, the overarching tradition of bureaucratic authoritarianism or viceregalism[13] in West Pakistan, especially in Punjab, differences between the East and West Pakistan and the threat it faced from India made the task of nation building and state building for the leadership of Pakistan, most of which were migrants themselves, including Quaid-e-Azam Muhammad Ali Jinnah (Quaid-e-Azam, great leader), extremely difficult, if not impossible.

Balochistan and the separation of India

It was decided by the British authorities in India that a referendum would be held in the British Balochistan to decide its future. For Kalat (and also Kharan and Las

Independence of Pakistan 67

Bela), it was decided that according to the partition plan, Ahmad Yar Khan had a choice to decide his future course in negotiation with Pakistan.

Referendum in British Balochistan

The referendum took place on 29 June 1947. The Electoral College included the members of the Baloch Shahi Jirga, excluding the members from the states and the non-officially elected members of the Quetta Municipal Committee. The last Khan of Kalat, Ahmad Yar Khan tried to get members from the leased areas excluded from participating in the referendum on the grounds that these leased areas should be returned to Kalat. He was not successful in this. The referendum in British Balochistan would decide not only which way the British Balochistan would go, but also the very fate of Pakistan. According to a number of historians of the Pakistan movement, the result of the referendum would have impacted the outcome of a similar referendum to be held in NWFP in July 1947.[14] If the British Balochistan voted against joining Pakistan, these historians implied that NWFP would follow suit and there would be practically no Pakistan.[15] Nawab Muhammad Khan Jogezai and Mir Jafar Khan Jamali aided by M. Masud[16] were spearheading the campaign for Pakistan, whereas Abdul Samad Achakzai, a leading Pashtun nationalist leader popularly known as the Balochistani Gandhi, and Ghaus Bakhsh Bizenjo were leading the pro-united India camp in the British Balochistan. There are a number of conflicting accounts of this referendum, varying from that the British conspired to hold the referendum a day earlier so that the British Balochistan become a part of Pakistan to that there was no referendum held at all. The Pakistani camp believed that the British and pro-Congress elements joined hands and conspired against Balochistan becoming part of Pakistan. However, voting did take place and the majority voted in favour of joining Pakistan.

According to the partition plan, the princely states of the Indian subcontinent had a choice between staying independent and joining India or Pakistan. However, the British communicated to the princely states that the British would like them to join with India or Pakistan. Quaid-e-Azam Muhammad Ali Jinnah, on 30 July 1947, declared that Pakistan would follow a policy of non-interference towards the states and that they would be free to decide their own future.[17]

Kalat and Pakistan: The issue of accession

As it was located on the periphery of the Indian subcontinent, Kalat was never a key issue between India and Pakistan. Certainly, Kalat did not hold the same importance as Kashmir and Hyderabad. On 19 July 1947, Kalat was discussed in a meeting. In the meeting, Lord Mountbatten as the Crown representative made two important points. One, the status of Las Bela and Kharan was disputed as the rulers of Las Bela and Kharan have declared that they were not under the suzerainty of the Khan of Kalat.[18] Second, referring to the partition plan, Mountbatten stated that although Kalat had the option of independence, it would be appropriate for Kalat to work out a working relationship with Pakistan. Mr. Aslam Khan, the Prime

68   *Centre–Province relations post-independence*

Minister of Kalat, responded that the Khan of Kalat Ahmad Yar Khan wanted to reach a mutually acceptable understanding and agreement with Pakistan.

After ensuing discussions between Kalat and Pakistan, a joint communique was issued. This communique is an important document. It was a huge achievement for Ahmad Yar Khan as he achieved, though short-lived and on adhoc basis, his biggest objective. Pakistan accepted that Kalat was an independent sovereign state in treaty relations with the British government in India. This was a huge mistake on part of the Pakistani negotiating team. It also demonstrated their lack of understanding of the dynamics of Kalat–British relations as well as their inadequate homework on the subject. It was agreed between both parties that expert legal opinion would be sought about the leased areas and whether there would be any legal problem in Pakistan inheriting them. What was most important was that both Pakistan and Kalat agreed to a *standstill* till a final agreement was reached between them especially on defence, external affairs and communications.[19] According to the Baloch historian Dr. Abdul Rehman Brahui, there was another point of agreement: that if Pakistan and Kalat failed to establish a solid working relationship, Kalat, if it so desired, could join Afghanistan.[20]

The standstill agreement between Pakistan and Kalat

Following is the text of the standstill agreement agreed to by Pakistan and Kalat.

1   The Government of Pakistan agrees that Kalat is an independent state, being quite different in status from other states of India and commits to its relations with the British government as manifested in several agreements.
2   Legal opinion will be obtained to find out whether the Pakistan government is legally bound by the agreements and the treaties that already exist between Kalat and the British government.
3   Further talks will be held between the nominees of Pakistan and the Khan-e-Azam of Kalat after obtaining the legal opinion of the above points.
4   In the meantime, a standstill agreement will be made between Pakistan and Kalat by which Pakistan shall stand committed to all its responsibilities and agreement signed by Kalat and the British government from 1839 to 1947, and by this, Pakistan shall be the legal, constitutional and political successor of the British.
5   In order to discuss finally the relations between Kalat and Pakistan on matters of defence, foreign relations and communications, deliberations will be held in the near future in Karachi.

A closer look at this document indicates the contradictions in different points/clauses. Apparently, in an attempt to satisfy each other, the authors of the document have incorporated points which both parties were sensitive about. First point was acknowledgment of what Ahmad Yar Khan had been struggling for from the day he became the Khan of Kalat. Through this agreement, Ahmad Yar Khan finally

Independence of Pakistan 69

achieved what British refused to acknowledge and accept. The fourth point, on the other hand, acknowledged Pakistan as the constitutional and legal heir of the British in its relations with Kalat. Ahmad Yar Khan himself alluded to this fact when, in a meeting with Quaid-e-Azam Muhammad Ali Jinnah, he informed Quaid-e-Azam Muhammad Ali Jinnah that because of the standstill agreement, Kalat–Pakistan relation would be administered exactly as between the British and Kalat since 1938.[21] More so, he suggested to Quaid-e-Azam Muhammad Ali Jinnah that Quaid-e-Azam Muhammad Ali Jinnah should order the Agent to Governor General (AGG) to Balochistan to use his position and influence to convince the sardars in favour of accession.[22]

Kalat's declaration of independence and reforms

Regardless of the standstill agreement with the government of Pakistan, Khan of Kalat Mir Ahmad Yar Khan declared independence and promulgated a constitution.[23] Speaking on the occasion, Ahmad Yar Khan stated that Kalat would take every step necessary to preserve, ensure and defend its independence.[24] Going one step further, he expressed his resolve to work for a single and unified Balochistan.[25] Outlining his foreign policy priorities, Ahmad Yar Khan stated that Kalat's foreign policy would be based on the principle of non-interference and would particularly sought friendly relations with neighbouring states, Pakistan, India, Afghanistan, Iran and the Muslim world.

Inayat Baloch, a noted Baloch historian, quoted from an official document issued by the government of Kalat which ensured the people of Balochistan that the Khan of Kalat had consulted Quaid-e-Azam Muhammad Ali Jinnah in everything and that both are in agreement and following the same policy.[26] It was also claimed in the document that Quaid-e-Azam Muhammad Ali Jinnah was in total agreement with the independence of Kalat, the return of the leased areas and the merger of Baloch areas with the state of Kalat and that Quaid-e-Azam Muhammad Ali Jinnah assured all kind of support.[27]

These claims were in total contradiction with the understanding reached between the negotiating teams of Pakistan and Kalat. According to the joint communique, legal opinion would be sought on leased areas, and Kalat and Pakistan would further negotiate on the issue of accession. The so-called other Baloch areas that comprised British Balochistan had already voted in favour of joining Pakistan.

Soon after declaring independence, the Khan of Kalat Ahmad Yar Khan also issued a number of political and administrative reforms. The Khan promulgated a bicameral legislature in the state comprising the Dar-ul-Umra (House of Lords) and Dar-ul-Awam (House of Commons). Dar-ul-Umra comprised the sardars. Dar-ul-Awam comprised elected representative of the Baloch.[28] The biggest puzzle was when and where the elections were held in which the people's representative were elected. In the absence of an administrative apparatus, resources and electoral machinery, how the elections were conducted? More so, were the elections conducted on adult franchise? Who exactly voted in these elections? Who were the candidates? How and for how long the candidates campaigned for the

70   *Centre–Province relations post-independence*

elections? The fact is that these elections were not conducted in the sense elections are conducted. Local jirgas acted as the local electoral college. There were no proper candidates. Khan of Kalat's representatives went to the local jirgas, and the jirga members nominated people from their area who *they* thought were most suitable for the job. In 2000, Agha Nasir Khan, who was the governor of Jhalawan at the time of these elections, in an interview with Martin Axmann, explained how these elections were conducted:

> The governors of the provinces were called (and told) that you should go to your areas and that every area has got some seats; now you should go there and according to the rules and regulations conduct the elections. At that time, I was the governor of the province of Jhalawan, so I went to Khuzdar and there I took a public leader – Ghous Bukhsh Bizenjo who became later on Governor of Balochistan – he was a political leader and I took him as public leader and went throughout the area of Jhalawan and we conducted the election. The principle was adopted that in every tehsil the Jirga members (i.e. members of the local Jirga of village elders) will be the electorate. ... so, all those Jirga people elected their members (to the House of common) according to the seat given to the different categories of society of Kalat ... we went to every tehsil and conducted the election through those people and all those that were elected by them became members of the House of Commons of Kalat state. We finished this work within a week...[29]

The selected members of the House of Commons were all active members of their areas. This was perhaps the only criterion which was considered when selecting the members to the House of Commons. This explains why a significant number of activists and members of the Kalat State National Party (KSNP) were elected.

Agha Nasir Khan further explained:

> Elections were held on a non-political basis when these elections were conducted the people who were very energetic were elected by the people. Generally, during the British period, there was a political party in Kalat state called Kalat State National Party. Though, when the Khan of Kalat declared the constitution of the House of Commons, generally, the people, because the Party had served the causes of the people so much that they generally, during that elections, elected their (i.e. KSNP's) members. Though, the party didn't work for the elections. The people themselves were so much in favor of that party. But the elections were conducted without any political parties. [30]

According to Inayatullah Baloch, the KSNP won thirty-nine seats out of the total fifty-one seats.[31] The remaining were independent candidates who toed the KSNP's line.[32] Members of the House of Commons belonging to the KSNP established a block in the House of Commons and spoke with a unified voice.

Independence of Pakistan 71

This suited Ahmad Yar Khan and his political agenda as KSNP members were nationalists and against accession with Pakistan.

Despite declaring independence and claiming that Quaid-e-Azam Muhammad Ali Jinnah fully supported his position, Ahmad Yar Khan was scheduled to meet Quaid-e-Azam Muhammad Ali Jinnah in October 1947 to discuss the future of Kalat. Ahmad Yar Khan had a detailed meeting with Kalat's Prime Minister and Foreign Minister to discuss the possible options available to Ahmad Yar Khan regarding the future of Kalat. Inayatullah Baloch in his book has provided details about this discussion.[33]

In this meeting, five options were discussed: *accede to Pakistan, accede to India, join Afghanistan, join Iran* and *apply to UK for a protectorate status.* Ahmad Yar Khan considered accession with Pakistan complicated as he claimed public and political opinion was against it. How exactly he gauged it or what exactly he meant by that is something we don't know. It was a unanimous view of the participants that accession to India would be impossible. Other than the fact that there is no direct geographical link between Kalat and India, this action would be considered extremely adversarial by Pakistan and even London might not approve it. Ahmad Yar Khan also claimed that Nehru hated him and All India Congress never trusted him.[34] Kalat's Foreign Minister Douglas Fill had a favourable opinion about joining Iran. Elaborating on the historical ties between Iran and Balochistan and the fact that a significant number of Baloch lived in Iran, Mr. Fell argued that joining Iran would be good for the Baloch and the unity of the Baloch. The Khan of Kalat and a number of family members were positively inclined towards the option of joining Afghanistan. Douglas Fell argued against it on the grounds that Afghanistan was already an instable state and a close ally of communist USSR. Ahmad Yar Khan, being a devout Muslim, rejected this option. The Khan of Kalat was personally quite keen on the last option and considered it most suitable for his personal ambitions and vision for Kalat. Fell, however, reminded him that the British consider Kalat an Indian state and would never accept this request.[35] This meeting ended without reaching an agreement on what should be the future course of action for Kalat.

Quaid-e-Azam Muhammad Ali Jinnah and Ahmad Yar Khan met in Karachi in October 1947. Quaid-e-Azam Muhammad Ali Jinnah asked Ahmad Yar Khan to accede and assured him that he (Quaid-e-Azam Muhammad Ali Jinnah) would personally make sure that his (Ahmad Yar Khan) concerns were addressed. Ahmad Yar Khan stated that this is a decision he cannot take on his own.[36] He claimed that he needed to consult his tribes and ascertain their view on the issue.[37] This claim had a little historical validity. Perhaps the only positive outcome of this meeting was that both sides agreed to meet again. Ahmad Yar Khan, during the meeting, presented a draft treaty to Quaid-e-Azam Muhammad Ali Jinnah. According to the draft, Ahmad Yar Khan wanted Pakistan to recognize Kalat as a sovereign and independent state and sign a friendship and mutual defence treaty against any aggressor.[38]

On his return to Kalat from Karachi, Ahmad Yar Khan summoned the inaugural session for both houses on 14 December 1947. During his address to the joint

72   Centre–Province relations post-independence

session, he highlighted his role and support to Pakistan's freedom struggle. He went on to say that recently, on certain issues between Pakistan and Kalat, the Baloch are getting concerned and want the Khan to resolve the matter. He urged the members to remain peaceful and give Pakistan some time as it was going through a very difficult time[39] and he did not want to create further problems for Pakistan.[40]

This address raised a number of questions. What exactly Ahmad Yar Khan wanted? The developments of the past five months (August–December 1947) and his varied stances would puzzle any student of this period. Why was he giving conflicting messages to Quaid-e-Azam Muhammad Ali Jinnah and his sardars? Was he trying to say that Pakistan was not thankful for his role during the freedom struggle? Or was he projecting himself as an ally of Pakistan?

Mr. Douglas Fell presented detailed report to the house about the status and stage of negotiation with Pakistan on the issue of accession.[41] He emphasized Ahmad Yar Khan's stated position that Kalat was not an Indian state and had a different status in British India.[42] The most important announcement was made by the Prime Minister Muhammad Aslam Khan. He informed the members of both houses that Ahmad Yar Khan had decided that the decision whether to accede with Pakistan would be taken by the house.[43]

This decision could be viewed through various angles. One way of looking at it is that Ahmad Yar Khan, through this decision, was introducing and empowering democratic values and practices in a tribal society. It could be argued that this was consistent to Ahmad Yar Khan's policies throughout his tenure as the Khan of Kalat as he tried several times in the past to introduce political, democratic and administrative reforms in Kalat. Another way of looking at it would be that this was an intelligent move and a safe bet on his part. He knew a handpicked parliament dominated by the KSNP which was politically closer to the Indian Congress would never vote for accession with Pakistan. In this way, Ahmad Yar Khan would be able to argue to his negotiating counterpart in Pakistan that it was a decision of the elected representatives of people which, as the Khan-e-Baloch, he had to respect.

What followed was hardly unexpected. When the issue of accession was debated in the Dar-ul-Awam (House of Commons), the leader of the KNSP in the house, Ghaus Bakhsh Bizenjo in his speech stated:

> Why should we be asked to join Pakistan, merely, because we are Muslims? For that matter, then Iran and Afghanistan, as they are Muslim countries, must also join Pakistan. Under no circumstances would we join Pakistan and sign the death warrant of 1.5 crore (ten and a half million) Baloch of Asia. We have unlimited resources and if we are forced, we will fight back to preserve our independence.[44]

A number of other members spoke on more or less same line. A resolution was passed against the accession of Kalat with Pakistan. Dar-ul-Umra (House of Lords) met on 4 January 1948. The house passed a resolution, which was

Independence of Pakistan 73

different in wording but similar in spirit to the one passed by Dar-ul-Awam on 14 December 1947.

In his meeting with Quaid-e-Azam Muhammad Ali Jinnah, who came to Sibi for this meeting and to attend the Royal Sibi Darbar, the Khan of Kalat Ahmad Yar Khan informed Quaid-e-Azam Muhammad Ali Jinnah that Kalat's accession with Pakistan is not possible as people's representatives disapproved it. However, instead of ending it at this point, during the two meeting sessions with Quaid-e-Azam Muhammad Ali Jinnah, Ahmad Yar Khan made a startling claim. He told Quaid-e-Azam Muhammad Ali Jinnah that "the sardars were totally against accession but I tried hard to convince them and shared with them the advantages of acceding to Pakistan."[45] He claimed that after his personal effort and reasoning in favour of acceding to Pakistan, the sardars have agreed to a conditional accession with Pakistan.[46] In Ahmad Yar Khan's book, there is no mention of the names of the sardars who he convinced or how and when he discussed these issues with them. There is no other information available to verify this claim of Ahmad Yar Khan. Ahmad Yar Khan claimed that the sardars had set the following conditions[47]:

1   Without the consent of the Baloch, no interference will be made in the Rivaj (traditional practices/customs) of the Baloch, and as an assurance and guarantee to this, Quaid-e-Azam Muhammad Ali Jinnah and Ahmad Yar Khan should sign a document.
2   When a formal accession agreement is signed by the Khan of Kalat and Quaid-e-Azam Muhammad Ali Quaid-e-Azam Muhammad Ali Jinnah, the sardars should be there to witness it.
3   Quaid-e-Azam and the government of Pakistan should officially acknowledge the contribution of the Khan of Kalat and the Baloch in the creation of Pakistan and should issue a declaration in this regard.
4   Quaid-e-Azam, in a traditional gathering of the Baloch, should recognize and acknowledge the participation and contribution of the sardars in the freedom struggle.

It seems that Pakistan, which was closely monitoring the political developments in and the statements coming from Kalat, in the meanwhile, revised the draft instrument of accession, which Quaid-e-Azam Muhammad Ali Jinnah shared with Ahmad Yar Khan during their meeting. According to Ahmad Yar Khan, the revised draft had references to the Government of India Act 1935 and the Independence Act 1947 which were not present in the earlier draft.[48] He claimed that this amounted to his month-long hard work going to waste. He was so shocked that he had a nervous breakdown.[49]

Quaid-e-Azam Muhammad Ali Jinnah, who up till now was personally negotiating with Ahmad Yar Khan, on his return from yet another meaningless round of discussion with Ahmad Yar Khan decided to hand over the issue of accession of Kalat to Pakistan and any further negotiation with Khan of Kalat Ahmad Yar

74 *Centre–Province relations post-independence*

Khan to the Ministry of Foreign Affairs (MFA). Colonel S.B. Shah, the Secretary General of the Ministry of Foreign affairs, was tasked with this job. Baloch historians accused the Prime Minister of Kalat Muhammad Aslam Khan to be working on Colonel Shah's pay role. Ahmad Yar Khan, though still living in his world of denial, claimed that this change (from Quaid-e-Azam Muhammad Ali Jinnah to Colonel Shah) happened due to Quaid-e-Azam Muhammad Ali Jinnah's illness. Ahmad Yar Khan continued to give conflicting signals and informed Islamabad[50] that he would sign the accession agreement in three months.

In the meanwhile, the rulers of Kharan and Las Bela indicated to Pakistan that they would accede to Pakistan regardless of Kalat's decision. Moreover, Makran, which was a district of Kalat, also wanted to part ways with Kalat and become a part of Pakistan. The ruler of Kharan and the Jam of Las Bela wrote a number of letters to Quaid-e-Azam Muhammad Ali Jinnah. The ruler of Kharan, Mir Mohammad Habibullah Khan had developed his argument more or less on similar lines as Ahmad Yar Khan. According to Mir Habibullah Khan, before coming under the British rule in 1883, Kharan was under the influence of Afghanistan. Under the British, Kharan was an independent state. Kalat never accepted this fact and attacked Kharan in 1939 to subjugate it. Habibullah Khan declared that after the departure of the British, Kharan became independent. He as the ruler had decided to accede to Pakistan. Pakistan's initial response to Kharan and Las Bela's offer was mute as Pakistan was optimistic that Kalat would also accede with Pakistan.

On this lack of enthusiasm on Pakistan's part, Habibullah declared that whether Kharan joined Pakistan or not, Kharan would under no circumstances accept Kalat's domination. In March 1948, the Jam of Las Bela and the ruler of Kharan met Quaid-e-Azam Muhammad Ali Jinnah in Karachi. During the meeting, they accused Ahmad Yar Khan of stirring trouble in Makran and spreading false propaganda about Quaid-e-Azam Muhammad Ali Jinnah and Pakistan. They also informed Quaid-e-Azam Muhammad Ali Jinnah that they might have to reconsider their options if Pakistan continued to show cold feet on Kharan and Las Bela's request of accession to Pakistan.[51]

The government of Pakistan was already fed up with the doublespeak of Ahmad Yar Khan. The new team handling the case of accession of Kalat with Pakistan saw this as an opportunity. After a detailed emergency meeting, Pakistan accepted Kharan and Las Bela's offer of accession.[52] At the same time, Pakistan also accepted Makran's request for acceding with Pakistan.[53] On 18 March 1948, a press note was issued by the government of Pakistan that announced this development.

Losing Kharan, Las Bela and Makran limited Ahmad Yar Khan's ambition to rule an independent state of Kalat. Now Kalat became a landlocked state without any direct access to the outside world. Ahmad Yar Khan threatened to appeal to the United Nations.[54] A declaration was made that if Kalat was to be forced into accession, this accession would not be a voluntary one.[55] The government of Pakistan, on its part, accused the Khan of plotting against them and seeking British protection, all the while approaching India through an agent.[56] These

Independence of Pakistan 75

allegations echoed the discussion which the Khan had earlier had with his Prime Minister and Foreign Minister. Ahmad Yar Khan, in his book, totally ignoring the timeline and historical facts stated that it was the *accession* of Kharan, Las Bela and Makran to Pakistan that adversely affected Pakistan's regional relations.[57] He listed four major adverse effects: *firstly*, relations with Afghanistan soured; *secondly*, the humiliation of the Baloch persuaded the Nizam of Hyderabad to accept accession with India; *thirdly*, Maharaja of Kashmir changed his decision of acceding to Pakistan and joined India; *fourthly*, the sheikhs of Gulf states who had initially favoured Pakistan aligned themselves with India.

The last straw on the camel's back: All India Radio's report about the Khan's contact with India

The Khan of Kalat Ahmad Yar Khan consistently denied considering accession with India as an option. Even during the meeting with his Prime Minister and Foreign Minister in which various options available to Kalat were discussed, Ahmad Yar Khan reportedly was not enthusiastic about the accession with India option. Yet the diplomatic circles in Pakistan were rife with reports that Ahmad Yar Khan has used the option of joining India as a bargaining chip in his negotiation with Pakistan. The UK High Commissioner to Pakistan wrote "there is good reason to believe that he (Ahmed Yar Khan) has been flirting with both India and Afghanistan."

On 27 March 1948, All India Radio in Delhi broadcasted a report that in January 1948, Ahmad Yar Khan, the Khan of Kalat, approached New Delhi to discuss Kalat's accession with India. New Delhi rejected the request/offer.

Denying that he ever made such a request, Ahmad Yar Khan sent a telegram to the Governor General of India to protest on this false report and asked New Delhi to release any communications they had, if he really did approach them.[58]

However, the damage was done. Pakistan, which was already annoyed with Ahmad Yar Khan's indecisiveness and doublespeak, took this as a dangerous development. In view of the minimal options left for Ahmad Yar Khan, Baloch nationalist historians have argued that the Khan of Kalat at this juncture had two choices: accede to Pakistan or refuse to accede and prepare for any eventuality, including armed resistance. Ahmad Yar Khan went for the first option. He announced that Kalat would accede to Pakistan and signed the instrument of Accession. Ironically, before acceding to Pakistan, he did not call an emergency session of his council or the parliament to debate/discuss the matter in the light of the latest development (All India Radio report). In his biography, Ahmad Yar Khan, denying that he ever intended to accede to India, claimed that the moment he heard the report on All India Radio he decided to accede with Pakistan.[59]

Commenting on Ahmad Yar Khan's decision, Inayatullah Baloch wrote:

> The ruler of the Khanate of Baluchistan, Mir Ahmed Yar Khan, was forced to sign the document of accession. The Khan was not an absolute monarch; he was required to act under the provisions of the Rawaj (the Baluch constitution)

76   *Centre–Province relations post-independence*

and had no authority to sign the merger document without the consent of the parliament. The Khan, in his biography, has admitted that he violated his mandate by singing the merger document. The Khan claimed that despite his unconstitutional step; the Baluch nation did not raise a single voice of any nature to protest.[60]

Another Baloch historian Sardar Khan Baluch, commenting on this decision, commented:

> Nasir I united all. Nasir II endeavored to maintain it. Khudadad Khan fought for the whole of his life to organize a government. Mahmud Khan II prepared the coffin for the state. And Ahmed Yar, the present Khan, buried all the glory and vanity of his line.[61]

The All India Radio broadcast has been projected as the final factor in pushing Ahmad Yar Khan into acceding to Pakistan. Ahmad Yar Khan himself gave the same impression; however, this might be stretching it too far. After the accession of Kharan and Las Bela to Pakistan, Ahmad Yar Khan's dream of becoming the ruler of an independent kingdom of Kalat had ended, and as it was stated, he had only two options, accede with Pakistan or lead a struggle against Pakistan. As he lacked the will and resolve to lead a guerrilla struggle, he was left with only one option: accede to Pakistan. The All India Radio broadcast just provided Ahmad Yar Khan an opportunity to claim that he was acceding to Pakistan to prove himself an honest and pro-Pakistan person.

The All India Radio report: What exactly happened?

Gul Khan Naseer in his magnum opus *Tahreekh-e-Balochistan* (History of Balochistan) wrote that on the 27 March 1948, All India Radio reported the press conference of Mr. V.P. Menon in which he claimed that two months earlier, the Khanate of Kalat approached New Delhi with a request for accession, but New Delhi rejected the offer. According to Gul Khan Naseer, who was quoting Ahmad Yar Khan, this was a white lie aimed at creating bad blood between Pakistan and Kalat. Another purpose of this false report was to agitate the Pakistani leadership so that they act rashly, giving India an opportunity to move ahead against Hyderabad Deccan. This is not the first time that Kalat and India were mentioned together.

Throughout the negotiation between the Khan of Kalat Ahmad Yar Khan and Pakistan, diplomatic circles in Pakistan were rife with reports that Ahmad Yar Khan was using the option of joining India as a bargaining chip in his negotiation with Pakistan. The British High Commissioner to Pakistan wrote, "There is good reason to believe that he (Ahmed Yar Khan) has been flirting with both India and Afghanistan."[62]

What exactly was the nature of the contact between New Delhi and the Khan of Kalat Ahmad Yar Khan? During his campaign aimed at the British to accept his

Independence of Pakistan 77

position about the independence and sovereignty of the state of Kalat, Ahmad Yar Khan tried to solicit the support of the All India Congress leadership for his case. In 1946, Samad Khan, a prominent pro-Congress Pashtun leader from Balochistan, discussed Kalat's situation with the top leadership of the Congress. It was reported that Jawaharlal Nehru was not very keen to support it. *Baba-e-Balochistan* Ghaus Bakhsh Bizenjo, then a leading member of the Kalat State National Party, met *Imam-ul-Hind* Maulana Abul Kalam Azad, who was the President of All India Congress in New Delhi. Maulana Azad was of the opinion that Kalat cannot survive as an independent state and would have to seek British protection. Such an action would leave a serious question mark on the sovereignty of the Indian Subcontinent.[63] The details of the proceeding of the meeting between Ahmad Yar Khan, his Prime Minister and Foreign Minister indicate that Ahmad Yar Khan was not inclined to – or even willing to consider – New Delhi for accession. It is also important to note that during his negotiation with Pakistan and even later, the Khan of Kalat Ahmad Yar Khan consistently denied considering accession with India as an option.

Denying the All India Radio's report of 27 March 1948 that in January 1948 he approached New Delhi to discuss accession with India who rejected it, he demanded evidence to support this claim.

Regardless of the effect this report might have had on Ahmad Yar Khan's decision on the future of Kalat, the report caused a stir in New Delhi where a number of questions were raised. What exactly had happened? When and how did the Khan of Kalat contact New Delhi, if at all? As it turned out, the issue was also discussed in the Indian parliament and during an Indian cabinet meeting. On the floor of the house, Balkrishna Sharma raised this issue and asked the government to provide details. The Indian Prime Minister Jawaharlal Nehru, responding to this question, stated:

> I am glad to have this opportunity to clear up a misapprehension that has unfortunately arisen. I greatly regret that owning to an error in reporting, the All India Radio announced on the night of the 27th March that His Highness, the Khan of Kalat, had approached the Government of India about two months ago through his agents to seek permission to accede to India, but the Government of India did not agree. This statement is incorrect. No mention had been made at any time either by the representative of the ruler of Kalat or by the Government of India to the accession of Kalat state to India. In view of the geographical position of Kalat state, the question did not arise at all. I might also add that certain reports, which have appeared in the foreign press about political negotiations between the government of India and Kalat state, are also completely without foundation. The statement that any sum of money has been paid to Kalat state on behalf of the government and that the government have sought airbases in Kalat are also wholly without foundation. The facts are as follows: In August last, soon after the declaration of independence in India, the government of Kalat drew the attention of the government of India to a press communique in which it was said that the government of Pakistan had recognized Kalat as an

78 *Centre–Province relations post-independence*

independent sovereign state, in treaty relations with the British Government, with a status different from that of the Indian states. They invited the government of India to make a similar declaration. Sometime later, a request was made on behalf of Kalat state for permission to establish a trade agency of the state in Delhi. No formal reply was sent to either of these requests. Informally, the representative of Kalat state was informed that these requests could not be considered then. No further communication of any kind has been passed between the government of India and the government of Kalat.[64]

When the issue was discussed in a meeting of the Indian cabinet on 29 March 1948, according to reports, it was claimed that the statement attributed to V. P. Menon was a distortion of what he said and that he made no such claim or statement.[65]

THE MYTH OF MILITARY INTERVENTION AND FORCIBLE ACCESSION OF KALAT

The developments detailed above clearly indicate that in this whole process of accession of Kalat with Pakistan, Pakistan Army was neither involved nor played any role in the actual accession of Kalat, yet it is one of the most tenacious myth propagated by the Baloch historians.[66] One of the most authoritative experts on Balochistan, Professor Akbar S. Ahmed in his book wrote that in March 1948, the Pakistan Army troops crossed into Balochistan and the Khan of Kalat agreed to join Pakistan.[67] What exactly happened? The answer to this lies in Makran and its decision to join Pakistan. Unlike Las Bela and Kharan, Makran was a part of the Khanate of Kalat. It was administrated by the nawabs and sardars of Kech, Panjgur, Tump and an official appointed by the Khan of Kalat. It seems that once the government of Pakistan got disappointed and frustrated by the behaviour and doublespeak of Ahmad Yar Khan, it decided to accept any application for accession.

When Nawab Bai Khan Gichki applied for accession with Pakistan, Pakistan readily accepted it. Makran along with Las Bela and Kharan joined Pakistan on 17 March 1948.

At the time, Prince Abdul Karim, the younger brother of the Khan of Kalat Ahmad Yar Khan, was representing Kalat in Makran. He publically refused to accept Makran's accession with Pakistan and continued to operate from his office. Tension rose between Prince Karim and Nawab Bai Khan, the newly appointed Wali (ruler) of Makran. Soon the situation reached an impasse. All the communication lines to Makran were abstracted. Heavy rainfall added to this. Furthermore, Ahmad Yar Khan stopped rations and other supplies to Makran levy corps. In such a situation, the only option left was to air-drop or supply them through Jiwani.

Under such circumstances, under the advice of AGG Sir Ambrose Dundas, a high-level meeting took place in which it was decided, to ensure that no unpleasant event takes place and to avoid any further disturbances, to send enforcements. It was

Independence of Pakistan 79

decided to send security forces for securing the key installations and communication lines and roads. It was also decided that the Khan of Kalat would be informed of this development beforehand so that no unpleasant event occurs. However, before any of this happened, the Khan of Kalat, Ahmad Yar Khan, after listening to the All India Radio report, announced an unconditional accession to Pakistan.

First Baloch insurgency

At the time of acceding Makran with Pakistan, Nawab Bai Khan demanded that Pakistan should make sure that Prince Agha Abdul Karim, the younger brother of the Khan of Kalat Ahmad Yar Khan and Kalat's governor in Makran, must leave Makran before his return to Makran. Prince Karim was asked to leave. Prince Karim felt disrespected. On his way back to Kalat, he met a number of Baloch notables including Ghaus Bakhsh Bizenjo. On Ahmad Yar Khan's suggestion, Prince Karim also acquired the support of the sardars of Sarawan. 16 May 1948 is often cited as the date when Prince Karim started his armed resistance against Pakistan. Inayatullah Baloch later claimed that prince Karim's armed resistance was a national liberation movement.[68] There is hardly any evidence to substantiate this claim. Prince Karim's armed resistance was a reaction to his sacking from the position of the governor of Makran and what he thought was an unwarranted accession of Kalat to Pakistan. He crossed over to Afghanistan and tried to win the support of Afghanistan against Pakistan. The Afghan government refused to support him.[69]

The Khan of Kalat Ahmad Yar Khan on 24 May 1948 issued a statement in which he claimed that Prince Karim rebelled against the state of Pakistan against his wishes and issued an order in which he prohibited the Baloch tribesmen from supporting Prince Karim.[70]

Baloch historian Dr. Marri contested this claim and pointed that Ahmad Yar Khan was again playing a double game. According to Dr. Marri, at the time of issuing this farman (order), he was in contact with Prince Karim and he sent his emissary to Prince Karim encouraging him to continue the armed resistance.

In June 1948, Prince Karim wrote a letter to Ahmad Yar Khan in which he outlined his reasons for taking up arms against the state of Pakistan. He claimed that forced and illegal accession of Kalat, Kharan, Las Bela and Makran to Pakistan is the reason of his taking up arms. If this letter (which is reproduced in Inayatullah Baloch's book) is genuine, it is perhaps the first ever clear manifestation of a sentiment against the "Punjabi fascism."[71]

> From whatever angle we look at the present government of Pakistan, we will see nothing but Punjabi Fascism. The people have no say in it. ... There is no place for any other community in this government, be it the Baluch, the Sindhis, the Afghans or the Bengalis, unless they make themselves equally powerful.[72]

It is quite difficult to ascertain the authenticity of this letter. More so, the letter was written on 28 June 1948. From August 1947 to June 1948, when Pakistan was

80   *Centre–Province relations post-independence*

mostly ruled by migrants that included Quaid-e-Azam Muhammad Ali Jinnah and Liaquat Ali Khan, how much of Punjabi domination was there in Pakistan at that time remains a question. Like Dr. Marri, Selig Harrison has claimed that the Khan supported Prince Karim's action because it might help him to reassert his power in Kalat.[73] The former Foreign Minister of Kalat Fell, in his interview with Inayat Baloch, refuted this.[74]

During Prince Karim's armed resistance, a certain narrative was developed and used by the propaganda team of the resistance. This narrative persisted beyond Prince Karim's armed resistance. The resonance of this narrative exists even today. The narrative claimed:

> Quaid-e-Azam Muhammad Ali Jinnah and his grand colleagues in whose hand the English have given the government, wish to enslave us, and to have our dear homeland (Balochistan), every inch of which was secured by our forefathers at the cost of blood, inhabited by foreigners. We are not prepared to be unworthy sons of our ancestors. We are to fight for every inch of our home land to maintain its freedom. … Quaid-e-Azam Muhammad Ali Jinnah and other colleagues of this shameless person intend to liquidate our Baluch culture, so that we may not be able to call ourselves as Baluch in future, shall not be able to speak our mother tongue and neglecting our modest customs, shall follow their shameful ways. We are determined that we will save our culture and will not give up our mother tongue while living and will defend our honor to the last.[75]

Several factors such as Prince Karim's failure to win support from Afghanistan and USSR coupled with internal differences especially on what strategy to follow and Ahmad Yar Khan's indecisiveness or doublespeak resulted in Prince Karim's return to Balochistan and seeking a negotiated settlement with the government of Pakistan. Douglas Fell met him at Harboi to convey to him Ahmad Yar Khan's message that if he surrendered, he would be pardoned. It is not clear what exactly this message implied. Does this meant that Ahmad Yar Khan would forgive him for taking up arms without his consent or the government of Pakistan assured the Khan of Kalat Ahmad Yar Khan that Prince Karim would not be put to trial. Whatever was the case, Prince Karim surrendered unconditionally. He was arrested and a jirga sentenced him to ten years of imprisonment. Baloch nationalists argue without providing any concrete evidence/proof that Prince Karim surrendered after he was assured that no harm would come to him. Yet he along with his followers was arrested. This act, according to the Baloch nationalists, was Pakistan's first act in a series of betrayals and broken promises.

Balochistan States Union (BSU)

From 1948 when Kalat, Makran, Kharan and Las Bela became part of Pakistan till 1951, different departments of the government of Pakistan continued to debate how best to deal with Balochistan. Despite Quaid-e-Azam Muhammad Ali Jinnah's commitment of personal interest, Liaquat Ali Khan's reform committee on Balochistan, the government more or less failed to work out a feasible and workable plan to deal with Balochistan. What was compounding the problem was the existence of states of Kalat, Kharan, Las Bela and Makran. The agent to Governor General in February 1951 questioned the rationale of keeping these states and suggested their merger into one administrative unit to end this administrative dilemma.

After intensive discussion among various departments of the government of Pakistan, in March 1952, it was decided that these four states (Kalat, Kharan, Las Bela and Makran) will be merged into a BSU. An agreement was signed by the rulers of Kalat, Kharan, Makran and Las Bela. All of them accepted the integration of their territories into a single state union with a common executive, judiciary and legislature. Another important development which took place and is often ignored by Baloch nationalists' account of events is that the rulers of Kalat, Kharan, Makran and Las Bela, on 11 April 1952, also signed supplementary instruments of accession. According to these instruments of accession, this state union was acceded to Pakistan. According to Wilcox, the rulers of Kalat, Kharan, Makran and Las Bela were handsomely paid for doing this and their annual allowances were increased.[76] Ahmad Yar Khan, the former Khan of Kalat, viewed the establishment of the BSU and his appointment as the head of it[77] as the restoration of his right to be the legitimate ruler of Balochistan[78] and revived his dream of being the king of a unified Balochistan. Under this illusion, he approached the Marri and Bugti sardars and suggested that they should apply to the government of Pakistan for inclusion of their territories into the BSU.[79] However, the BSU failed to achieve any of the stated objectives. The council of rulers comprising Khan of Kalat (head of the council) and rulers of Las Bela, Kharan and Makran could not reach an agreement on any/every issue and constantly remained at loggerheads. The proposed elections for the legislative body of the BSU never took place, and due to this, the cabinet never reached its full strength.[80] Some positive developments did take place in the improvement of law and order, health and education.[81] Saeed Dahwar argued that soon after the establishment of the BSU, people like Chaudhry Muhammad Ali started advocating the establishment of a One Unit (joining all territories of then West Pakistan into a single administrative unit to counter the East Pakistan's majority status) which ultimately nailed the BSU experiment down.[82] Awan pointed out another important reason for BSU's less than adequate performance. According to Awan, BSU lacked the financial resources to achieve any meaningful progress even if the rulers of the states had reached an agreement on any of the issues. This financial handicap restricted BSU till it was finally dissolved.[83] In February 1954, during the Sibi darbar, a petition was submitted by a number of Baloch sardars to dissolve the BSU and merge the territories under BSU into the Chief Commissioner's Balochistan. Views on whether it was a genuine move or a doctored one persist even today.[84]

Keeping with the fact that the government of Pakistan was, at that time, already working on its One Unit scheme and that within four months of the filing of this petition, the government dissolved BSU and merged it with Balochistan on 16 June 1954 indicate that the government might have been already working on it

82   Centre–Province relations post-independence

and would have done it with or without this petition. Ahmad Yar Khan's dreams and hopes were shattered once again, and he accused the government of betrayal and, for the first time, threatened the government of Pakistan of violence. In a lost vein and an act of frustration and without any legal justification, he asked for the return of the leased areas. The government of Pakistan, however, brushed away his rants.[85]

Despite his claim of betrayal, in January 1955, the Khan of Kalat along with rulers of Kharan, Makran and Las Bela signed an agreement, according to which:

> His Highness the Khan-e-Azam hereby cedes to the Government of the Dominion of Pakistan his sovereignty and all his rights, authority and powers as President of the council of Rulers of the Union, together with all his territories, including territories known as the leased areas, and having been duly authorized to that end by members of the Council of Rulers, that is to say the Rulers of Makran, Las Bela and Kharan, their sovereignty and all their rights, authority and powers as such Rulers together will (i.e. with) all their territories … The Government of the Dominion (of Pakistan) shall exercise all powers, authority and jurisdiction for the governance of the said union and territories in such manner and through such agency as it may think fit.[86]

The BSU was officially terminated on 14 October 1955 and soon after became part of the One Unit. According to the article 6 of the Balochistan State Union Merger Agreement, all previous agreement and accession agreements signed between the four states and the government of Pakistan became invalid and obsolete. It resulted in the permanent dissolution of the states. The rulers of the four states were provided hefty pensions, an increase in annual allowances and a number of other entitlements.[87] Baloch nationalists, however, claim that all this was done without the approval of Ahmad Yar Khan and most of the Baloch sardars.[88]

One Unit and Balochistan

The challenges faced by Pakistan at the time of its creation in 1947 pushed its ruling elite to emphasize on its security at the expense of state cohesion. Soon after 1947, serious differences between the East and West Pakistan emerged. The politico-military elite belonging to West Pakistan distrusted the ethnically Bengali East Pakistan, which was the majority in terms of population.[89]

To end this disparity and counter the Bengali majority, the politico-military elite of West Pakistan decided to merge all provinces and former princely states into a unified administrative unit called One Unit. The policy of One Unit failed to achieve the desired objectives. The East–West Pakistan differences persisted and ethnic rivalries surfaced among various ethnic groups (Pathan, Baloch and Sindhis) and anti-Punjab sentiment rose as Lahore (the capital of Punjab) was made the capital of West Pakistan.[90]

The government of Pakistan, at the time of appointing the representative for Balochistan in the One Unit administration, demonstrated a total lack of

Independence of Pakistan 83

understanding and learning about the dynamics of Baloch society and politics and appointed Dr. Khan sahib, a pashtun from the NWFP province, as the representative for Balochistan. Baloch, who had been historically averse to travelling beyond their borders and were used to getting their jobs done in their tribe or at the maximum in Quetta during the British rule, now had to travel to Lahore. More so, the appointment of an outsider to represent the Baloch was considered an insult.

Rise in resentment against the abadkars (settlers) in Balochistan

The abadkars (settlers), the majority of them ethnically Punjabi, settled in Balochistan, mostly in Quetta, at the time of partition in 1947 were not as affected as the Baloch by this development. The perception among the Baloch was that due to their ethnic and blood relations in Punjab, this change was actually beneficial for the settlers. The resentment against the abadkars was on the rise even before this change as the abadkars were in greater number in government jobs as well as dominating the business sector. According to a study conducted by Dr. Robert Wirsing, by 1958, only 10 per cent of the government officials in Balochistan were locals and were 20 percent of the total police force in Balochistan.

Ahmad Yar Khan initially supported the One Unit. However, when the opposition and protest against the One Unit grew, Ahmad Yar Khan revised his position and started struggling for the restoration of his state. According to Awan, now Ahmad Yar Khan focused his energy on campaigning for the establishment of a province of Balochi-speaking areas, including Dera Ghazi Khan and Jacobabad districts. He organized several anti-One Unit demonstrations and urged the government of Pakistan to establish a single province for Balochi-speaking people.[91] According to a fellow sardar, Sardar Sherbaz Khan Mazari, Ahmad Yar Khan aspired to be the king of a Greater Balochistan.[92] It was precisely this self-centred approach that resulted in the failure of the largest ever gathering of the Baloch sardars in October 1957.

Ahmad Yar Khan and 35 Baloch sardars including Sherbaz Khan Mazari, Nawab Khair Bakhsh Marri, Nawab Akbar Khan Bugti, Nawab Ghous Bakhsh Raisani and Mir Jafar Khan Jamali held a meeting in Karachi, ostensibly to protest against One Unit and to decide the future course for Baloch politics in Karachi.[93] During the meeting, Ahmad Yar Khan not only demanded the dissolution of the One Unit but demanded the creation of a new Baloch province. However, by the time the proceedings of the meeting were taking place, the enthusiasm of most of the people present had already veined. This happened due to a conversation which took place earlier that day between the then President of Pakistan Iskander Mirza and Ahmad Yar Khan. According to Sherbaz Mazari, on the day of the meeting of the Baloch sardars, Iskander Mirza invited the participants of the meeting for tea at the presidential residence. In the presence of the most prominent Baloch sardars: Akbar Bugti, Khair Bukhsh Marri, Ghous Bakhsh Raisani, Mir Jafar Khan Jamali and Sherbaz Mazari, Iskander Mirza asked Ahmad Yar Khan:

84 *Centre–Province relations post-independence*

"Why are you trying to mislead these sardars…", were the words he used to begin. Then scathingly, he continued, "These days you are opposing the One Unit and talking about the new linguistic province, but when that same One Unit was created you were making long gushy speeches in its favour. What you really hanker for, is the recreation of your old Kalat State. All the rest is merely eye-wash. You now just want to fool these people into supporting you." The Khan looked embarrassed and remained silent. We finished our tea and left quietly. At the conference the enthusiasm ebbed. Later when some of the leaders belonging to the old Kalat state demanded the break-up of the One Unit scheme and the restoration of Kalat, the majority of the other Sardars left the gathering in protest.[94]

Return of Gwadar to Pakistan

In the meanwhile, Gwadar continued to be under Oman's control. As it has been pointed out in the previous chapter, Sultan Saeed backtracked on its commitment with the Khan of Kalat Mir Nasir Khan and refused to return Gwadar once he found the circumstances favourable to return to Muscat. Since then, Gwadar remained under Oman's suzerainty. Gwadar's strategic significance was evident throughout this period and was reinforced since the Cold War began in the mid-1940s. It was believed that USA was eying Gwadar as a potential military base.

For Pakistan, Gwadar "was an alien enclave in Pakistan on the Makran coast."[95] Displaying rare strategic foresight and acumen, the then Prime Minister of Pakistan Feroz Khan Noon, utilizing British facilitation, bought Gwadar from Oman on 6 September 1958 for 3 million pounds sterling, a price which many at the time believed was too high.

First martial law in Pakistan and Nauroz Khan's armed resistance in Balochistan

The political instability, increasing gulf between the political leadership of West and East Pakistan and the political ambitions of the President of Pakistan Iskander Mirza resulted in a military coup in Pakistan, which turned out to be the first in a series of martial laws in Pakistan. Professor Ishtiaq Ahmed, a leading expert on Pakistan, argued that by 1958, there was a widespread resentment and sense of alienation from the centre among the minority ethnic groups. This resentment and alienation manifested in Ahmad Yar Khan's alleged attempt to once again secede from Pakistan in 1958.[96] It was alleged that Ahmad Yar Khan approached the Shah of Iran for a possible inclusion of Balochistan in Iran[97] and sought Afghanistan's support in a Baloch armed rebellion[98] and that Ahmad Yar Khan raised the old state of Kalat flag.[99] Shuja Nawaz, one of the most authoritative historians of Pakistan Army, also believed that Ahmad Yar Khan was planning to secede.[100] However, Shuja Nawaz also stated that General Ayub Khan believed that President Iskander Mirza instigated Ahmad Yar Khan to plan to secede. The reason behind this, according to Ayub Khan, was that President Iskander Mirza wanted to use this to stage his coup.[101] Ayub Bakhsh Awan (A.B. Awan), who served as the Director of the Intelligence Bureau and also as Home Secretary in the government of Pakistan also highlighted the role President Iskander Mirza played in this incident.[102] According to Awan, Ahmad Yar Khan stayed with Mirza as his guest. Ahmad Yar Khan, on his return from Karachi, redoubled his efforts to regain the pre-independence status of Kalat and publically claimed that President Iskander Mirza had assured him of his support in this regard.[103] Ahmad Yar Khan in his autobiography gave a much more detailed and colourful account of this episode. According to Ahmad Yar Khan, President of Pakistan Iskander Mirza asked for Rs. 500,000 to allow Kalat to secede from One Unit.[104]

A closer look at Ahmad Yar Khan's political career thus far clearly indicates that he lacked the resolve and determination to take up arms against his opponents, in this case the government of Pakistan. He was an expert of drawing room/ armchair politics and court intrigues but was not a man of action. Whatever was the case, Pakistan Army took action against Ahmad Yar Khan. Although the alleged force preparing for armed resistance could not be found, Ahmad Yar Khan was arrested and taken to Lahore. Sherbaz Khan Mazari stated in his book that the act caused a wave of anger among the Baloch and further compounded the existing ill-will which had been caused by an incident that had occurred the previous year by an act of administrative insensitivity.[105] After his arrest, Ahmad Yar Khan was ripped off of his titles and his son Agha Daud Jan was appointed as his successor by a presidential order. On 7 October 1958, President Iskander Mirza abrogated the constitution of Pakistan, dismissed the central and provincial governments, proclaimed martial law and appointed General Ayub Khan as the Chief Martial Law Administrator. General Ayub in turn, with Mirza's approval, imposed martial law throughout the country from midnight 7–8 October. This coup was a classic case of a reform coup as defined by Samuel P. Huntington.[106] Ironically, after a few days, Iskander Mirza was thrown out by the Pakistan military and General Ayub also appointed himself the President of Pakistan in what General Ayub called a revolution.

Nauroz Khan's armed resistance against the Pakistan Army

As the events unfolded, the theory that Ahmad Yar Khan was used by Iskander Mirza to stage a coup got credence. The way Ahmad Yar Khan was arrested angered the Baloch, regardless of their views about Ahmad Yar Khan. It was the dishonouring of the Baloch honour which was the main issue for the Baloch. To rub salt on injury, the government of Pakistan ordered the Baloch tribesmen to hand over their weapons to the police. More so, security forces patrolled different areas. Nauroz Khan of the Zarakzai, the legendary old lion who was a proud symbol of resistance against the British colonizers and twice escaped from British captivity in 1926 and 1927,[107] in an old age of eighty years took up arms against the dishonouring of the Baloch.[108] A band of around 1,000 men under the leadership of Nauroz Khan took to the hills and started targeting government forces.[109]

86   Centre–Province relations post-independence

They demanded the release of Ahmad Yar Khan, dissolution of the One Unit and a guarantee to maintain and respect Baloch honour and the tradition.[110]

This is a classical Baloch way of negotiating where all the demands are packaged together to take a strong bargaining/negotiating position. In 1960, the representatives of the Pakistan Army and Narouz Khan met and discussed the disarming of the guerrillas and restoration of peace.[111] Selig Harrison claimed that this meeting was inconclusive as no agreement was reached. Baloch nationalists argued that an agreement was reached. Nauroz Khan agreed to disarm and disband his guerrillas in return of a general amnesty and rehabilitation. Nauroz Khan's nephew Sardar Doda Khan Zehri Zarakzai, carrying a Quran, assured Nauroz Khan that the Pakistani authorities have accepted all their demands. On this, Nauroz Khan and his guerrillas returned from the hills. Pakistani security forces, denying that they made any such pledge, arrested Nauroz Khan and his guerrillas. They were tried in a military court and were sentenced to death. Later, Nauroz Khan's death punishment was converted into life imprisonment.[112] Nauroz Khan's son Batay Khan and five others were hanged in July 1960.[113]

Though the details about the actual happening of this event never came out, soon a number of stories and legends started to circulate among the Baloch. These stories raised the status of the bravery and gallantry of these martyrs to mythical proportions. According to such accounts, all six cried "Long Live Balochistan" before being hanged.[114] These heroes were immortalized in the poetry of Gul Khan Naseer, a famous and nationalist Baloch poet. These legends continue to inspire the Baloch nationalists even today. Sherbaz Mazari mentioned one such legend in his book:

> Is this one your son? An army officer cold-heartedly asked Nauroze Khan as he pointed to the body of the elderly warrior's son. Nauroze Khan stared at the soldier for a moment then replied quietly, "All these brave young men are my sons." Then looking at the faces of the dead supporters, he noticed that the moustache of one of them had dropped in death. He went over to the dead body and tenderly curled the moustache upwards while gently admonishing, "Even in death, my son, one should not allow the enemy to think, even for one moment, that you have despaired".[115]

Due to the treatment extended to Nauroz Khan and his men after their surrender and arrest and by allegedly backing off from its pledge of general amnesty to these men, according to Baloch nationalist accounts, it was once again proven that the government of Pakistan does not honour its commitment with the Baloch. Baloch nationalists argued that after what they did to Prince Karim and his men in 1948, the treatment the government of Pakistan extended to Nauroze Khan and his men indicated that Pakistan treated Balochistan as a colony.

Basic Democracies system in Balochistan

The Ayub regime's first attempt at political institution building was the establishment of the system of local bodies known as the Basic Democracies. Ayub Khan

Independence of Pakistan 87

was of the view that parliamentary democracy was not suitable for Pakistan. His concept was that the people should elect their representatives locally, who would then constitute an electoral college that would elect the chief executive. Consequently, 80,000 directly elected Basic Democrats, 40,000 from each wing (East Pakistan and West Pakistan) of the country, constituted the lowest level of a tiered system of decision-making. The lowest unit was the union council. Each union council comprised ten elected members and five appointed members, all called Basic Democrats. Union councils were responsible for local community development and the maintenance of law and order. The system formed a sort of pyramid, with the union councils at the bottom and the divisional councils at the top. The most important were the union councils; the most important members were the 80,000 elected Basic Democrats assigned the central role of electing the president. In 1960, they voted to confirm Ayub Khan as president.

The introduction of the Basic Democracies system coincided with the construction of cantonments in Balochistan. Although these two developments were not linked, Baloch nationalists viewed both of these developments as encroachment on their rights and power. An important effect of this system's introduction in Balochistan was that it brought to the fore a new generation of the Baloch leadership. Sardars Khair Bakhsh Marri, Attaullah Mengal, and Ahmed Nawaz Bugti were elected to the office. Ironically though, at that time, a number of Baloch nationalists viewed them as representative of the government of Pakistan's encroachment on the political autonomy of the local and regional governments.

Ayub Khan's regime was also not happy with the election to office of sardars Marri and Mengal. Soon, the Ayub government replaced Sardars Attaullah Mengal, Khair Bakhsh Marri, and Akbar Bugti from their positions of the sardars of their tribes in an attempt to limit their political and tribal clout and appointed new sardars. This was obviously not acceptable to the Baloch who viewed it as an intrusion and violation of the Baloch tribal code. A new wave of violence started with the murders of the government-appointed sardars. This time, the violence was carried out by the Parari[116] under the command of a firebrand and committed Marxist, Sher Muhammad Marri, popularly known as General Sherof. He, using classical guerrilla warfare methods, established more than twenty training camps in various parts of Balochistan. Parari guerrillas were well trained and organized and focused on military and governmental target such as military conveys, trains and army camps. Despite this organized violence, the main voice of the Baloch viewpoint remained the political leadership of Balochistan that was now operating under the banner of the NAP.[117]

CONCLUSION

This chapter covered perhaps one of the most important part of the Baloch nationalist narrative: Kalat's accession with Pakistan. This chapter analysed this narrative by detailing every step of the process. The chapter covered the political developments of the first two decades of the centre–Balochistan relations.

88   Centre–Province relations post-independence

The developments of the first two years of this interaction, especially the way Kalat's accession took place, created a distrust and contempt for the state of Pakistan in Baloch eyes, which got worse with the passage of time. Ill-conceived policies of the centre further complicated the situation. For the first two decades of Pakistan's history, the centre's main worry was how to address the Bengali problem. This one-point agenda and the policies which were made due to this created further problems for the centre and its relations with the smaller provinces and ethnic groups of Pakistan. Pakistan's policy makers perused the same policy towards Balochistan that was followed by the British. The policy debates about how to or not introduce reforms in Balochistan which took place among the Pakistani policy circles were not very different from how the British administration viewed this issue. In the last chapter, we have discussed how the British policy makers viewed Balochistan's tiny population, huge geography and lack of education as the reasons why it is not financially viable to introduce large-scale reforms in the area. This chapter detailed the same arguments made by Pakistani policy makers, especially during the deliberations of the reform committee on Balochistan.

Further analysing the Baloch narrative, this chapter argued that the Khan of Kalat Ahmad Yar Khan also played a negative role during this period. His personal ambitions overshadowed his judgement about what is good for the people of Kalat and Balochistan. During his meetings with Quaid-e-Azam Muhammad Ali Jinnah, he repeatedly stated that he cannot decide the future of Kalat and that this decision can only be made by people's representatives. However, it must be noted that Ahmad Yar Khan in 1946, while discussing the return of the leased areas with the British authorities, clearly stated that the people inhabiting the leased area must not be consulted. Was it because he suspected that the Baloch living in relative ease under the British rule might not approve the return of the leased areas to the Kalat state? However, in the case of Kalat's accession with Pakistan, he insisted on the people's verdict through their representatives due to the fact that he was sure that the House of Commons dominated by the members of the Kalat State National Party (KSNP) would never approve accession of Kalat with Pakistan.

The way he manoeuvred for gaining an independent status for Kalat at the time of independence, then shifting sides and supporting the centre especially when the policy of One Unit was adopted and then once again going against it, and aspiring for a Greater Balochistan with himself as the Khan-e-Azam of Greater Balochistan are clear indications of his dubious role.

Ayub Khan's regime was equally disastrous for the centre–Balochistan relations. The way the Ayub government handled the Baloch issue created a number of problems for the state, which have over the years been further strengthened. However, it was during this period that a *new generation* of Baloch nationalist leadership such as Attaullah Mengal, Khair Bakhsh Marri and Akbar Bugti emerged on the political landscape.

Another important player in this game which emerged during this period is the armed Parari movement under the leadership of Mir Hazar Khan, which initiated

Independence of Pakistan   89

a guerrilla struggle against the state of Pakistan. This Marxist-Leninist guerrilla movement played the most important role during the most violent and serious Baloch insurgency which took place in the 1970s. It will be discussed in detail in the next chapter.

Notes

1 Ishtiaq Ahmed, *Pakistan The Garrison State Origins, Evolution, Consequences, 1947–2011* (Karachi: OUP, 2013).
2 Ibid.
3 Ibid.
4 Ibid., 679–80.
5 Ibid., 837.
6 Ibid., 40.
7 Emerson, *From Empire to Nation*, 92.
8 Geertz, *Old Societies.*
9 Joseph R. Strayer, "The Historical Experience of Nation-Building in Europe," 25.
10 Emerson, *From Empire to Nation*, 92.
11 Quaid-e-Azam Muhammad Ali Jinnah once in an interview stated that the relations of India and Pakistan would be similar to USA and Canada. Quaid-e-Azam Muhammad Ali Jinnah wanted to live his retired life in Bombay, whereas Gandhi had reportedly expressed a desire to live his last days in Pakistan.
12 Ali, *Emergence of Pakistan*, 376.
13 Talbot, 64.
14 Syed Iqbal Ahmed, *Balochistan Its Strategic Importance* (Karachi: Royal Book Company, 1992).
15 Ibid.
16 A former civil servant and the deputy commissioner of Nawab Shah, Sind.
17 M. Rafique Afzal, *Selected Speeches and Statements of Quaid-e-Azam M. A. Quaid-e-Azam Muhammad Ali Jinnah*, 415–16.
18 PS-54, Minutes of Viceroy's Twentieth Miscellaneous Meeting, R/3/1/166, 135.
19 *New York Times*, August 12, 1947.
20 Dr. Abdul Rehman Brahui, *Balochistan aur Pakistan, Ailahaaq ke kahani, Haquaq ke Zubani*, 21.
21 Brahui, 95; and Khan, *Tahrik*, 97.
22 Brahui, 95.
23 Awan, *Baluchistan*, 205.
24 Axmaan, *Back to the Future*, 178.
25 Ibid.
26 Inayat Baloch, *The Problem of Greater Baluchistan, A Study of Baluch Nationalism* (Stutgrat: GMBH, 1987), 172 quoting Government of Kalat, Hakumet-e-Kalat ka Elan, 1–7.
27 Ibid.
28 For details, see Axmann, *Back to the Future*, 227.
29 Axmann, *Back to the Future*, 227–28.
30 Baloch, *The Problem of Greater Baluchistan*, 182.
31 Axmann, *Back to the Future*, 227–28.
32 Ibid.
33 Inayatullah, *The Problem of Greater Baluchistan*, 181–82.
34 Ibid.
35 Inayatullah, *The Problem of Greater Baluchistan*, 182. According to Mr. Fell, Khan was of the view that "independence of Kalat required a powerful backer."

90 *Centre–Province relations post-independence*

36 Brahui, 72.
37 Mir Ahmad Yar Khan Baluch, "Partition of India, Its effect on Kalat State," unpublished, 12–13 as quoted in Baloch, *The Problem of Greater Baluchistan.*
38 Inayatullah, *The Problem of Greater Baluchistan.* I. Baloch claims that both Ahmad Yar Khan and Fell gave copies of this draft treaty to him.
39 Brahui, 73.
40 Ibid.
41 Brahui, 74.
42 Ibid.
43 Brahui, 77.
44 Brahui.
45 Brahui, 94; and Ahmed Yar Kahn, *Mukhtasar Tahreekh-e-Khoum Baloch-wa-Khawanian Baloch*, 92.
46 Ibid.
47 Brahui, 94.
48 Baloch, 185, quoting Khan, "The Partition of India," 17–18, unpublished paper.
49 Ibid.
50 Although at the time of these developments, Karachi was the capital of Pakistan, I am using Islamabad to avoid any confusion.
51 Baloch, op.cit., 186–87.
52 Baloch, 187.
53 PS-133, Ministry of Foreign Affairs to Geoffrey Prior, Telegram, F. 20-GG/13, 17 March 1948, *Quaid-e-Azam Muhammad Ali Jinnah Papers*, 228.
54 Baloch, 187, quoting IOR.L/P+S/13/1847.
55 *Daily Bolan*, April 2, 1948, 187.
56 Baloch, 187, Ch. Muhammad Ali, *Emergence of Pakistan*, 282, IOR.L/P+S/13/1847.
57 Baloch, 105.
58 Baloch, 188, IOR.L/P+S/13/1847.
59 Ahmed Yar Khan, 159.
60 Baloch, 162.
61 M. Sardar Khan Baluch, *History of Baluch Race and Baluchistan*, 125–26.
62 Rizwan Zeb, "Kalat and the Radio," *The Friday Times*, August 19, 2016, www.thefridaytimes.com/tft/kalat-and-the-radio/.
63 Ibid.
64 Ibid.
65 Ibid.
66 Inyatullah Baloch, Gul Khan Nasir, to name a few.
67 Akbar S. Ahmed, *The Thistle and the Drone*, 139.
68 Baloch, 190.
69 Ibid.
70 Abdul Waheed Kurd, 41, 307.
71 Baloch, op.cit., 192, quoting Prince Abdul Karim's letter to the Khan of Kalat in Prince Abdul Karim versus Pakistan state, unpublished.
72 Ibid. Akbar S. Ahmed's quotes from this letter in the chapter Musharraf's Dilemma in his book *The Thistle and the Drone*, 139.
73 Selig Harrison, *In Afghanistan Shadow*, 26.
74 Baloch, 193.
75 Baloch, quoting Prince vs Pak, 194.
76 Baloch, 150–51.
77 Awan, 215.
78 Wilcox, 151.
79 Awan, *Balochistan*, 214–15.
80 Ahmed, *Balochistan*, 151.

Independence of Pakistan 91

81 Dehwar, *Contemporary Importance*, 334; and Wilcox, 151.
82 Dehwar, 334.
83 Awan, 215–16.
84 Ibid.
85 Awan, 216–17.
86 Wilcox, 240–42.
87 Ibid.
88 Dehwar, 336.
89 Wayne A. Wilcox, "Problems and Process of National Integration in Pakistan," *The Pakistan Student*, March–April 1967, 12 as quoted in Rounaq Jahan, *Pakistan*, 24.
90 Talukdar Maniruzzaman, "Crises in Political Development and the Collapse of the Ayub Regime in Pakistan," *The Journal of Developing Areas* (1971): 221–38 as quoted in Rounaq Jahan, *Pakistan*, 15.
91 Awan, 220.
92 Sherbaz Khan Mazari, *Disillusionment*, 83.
93 Ibid., 82.
94 Ibid.
95 Syed Iqbal Ahmad, *Balochistan Its Strategic Importance* (Karachi: Royal Book Company, 1992), 172.
96 Ishtiaq, 109.
97 Mazar, 83.
98 Harrison, 27–28.
99 Wilcox, 240–42.
100 Shuja Nawaz, *Crossed Swords Pakistan, Its Army, and the Wars Within* (Karachi: OUP, 2008).
101 Ibid.
102 A. B. Awan, *Balochistan: Historical and Political Processes* (London: New Century Publishers, 1985), 223.
103 Ibid.
104 Ahmed Yar Khan, *Inside Balochistan*, 174.
105 Sherbaaz Mazari in his book wrote that in 1957, a Baloch woman accused of adultery had been murdered by members of her husband's family. Ignoring the precedents of the local jirga law, the authorities had insisted on sending the dead woman's clothing for forensic tests to Lahore. A post-mortem was also carried out much against the wishes of the family. This affair had incensed the tribal community in every part of Kalat. It was generally viewed among the locals to be a calculated insult and a degradation of Baloch honour and traditions.
106 S. P. Huntington, "Patterns of Violence in World Politics," in *Changing Patterns of Military Politics*, 32–40. According to Huntington (p. 33), in a reform coup "a combination of military and civilian groups seizes power intending to make reforms in the political, economic or social structure. They usually do make some reforms, though they do not instigate a convulsive revolutionary process." As quoted in Rounaq Jahan, *Pakistan: Failure of National Integration* (New York: CUP, 1972), 51.
107 Axmann, 286.
108 Ibid.
109 Mazari, 84.
110 Axmann, 286.
111 Awan, 228–89.
112 Ahmed, *Strategic Importance*, 169.
113 Ibid.
114 Harrison, 28–29.

92 Centre–Province relations post-independence

115 Mazari, *Disillusionment*.
116 Parari is a Baloch word used to describe a person or persons whose grievances cannot be solved through talk.
117 Parari is significant not only because its military force would grow to over a thousand during the 1960s but also because it would be responsible for establishing a parallel government in many areas of Balochistan that built schools and provided medical services.

4 Centre–Balochistan relations (1969–77)

INTRODUCTION

This chapter covers the developments in Centre–Balochistan relations from 1969 to 1977. The chapter argues that for Balochistan, the decade of 1970s started with a positive note as General Yahya Khan accepted an important Baloch demand and granted Balochistan the status of a province. Another positive development for Balochistan was the 1970 election in which, for the first time, Baloch people were given the chance to elect their representatives. Sardar Ataullah Mengal, Akbar Bugti and Khair Bakhsh Marri who emerged as the political leaders of Balochistan in 1960s sided with the NAP in the 1970 elections.

In the 1970 election, in NWFP and Balochistan, the two provinces bordering Afghanistan, the NAP emerged as the majority party. The vote was fragmented along tribal lines, and the NAP did not have the same overwhelming support in NWFP and Balochistan that the Awami League had secured in East Bengal. During the civil war in erstwhile East Pakistan, General Yahya also banned the NAP for allegedly conspiring to start an insurrection in West Pakistan. This was the historical and psychological baggage that the state of Pakistan carried along with it when Bhutto emerged as the leader of and struggled to stabilize the *new* Pakistan. Bhutto was a *Bonapartist*,[1] and this factor also played a huge role in the political developments which took place in the decade of 1970s.

The developments that took place during the decade of 1970 played an important and significant role in the Baloch narrative. Two developments or events hold the most important positions in this narrative: the accession of Kalat under duress and the military action of the Pakistan Army in Balochistan during this decade. The 1970s also witnessed the dismissal of the first elected government of Balochistan and the most serious insurgency in Balochistan. These developments became the most important and commonly mentioned grievances in Baloch nationalist literature.

This chapter argues that the lack of political acumen of the Baloch leadership, Bugti and Mengal–Marri rivalry, tribal feuds in Balochistan, Bhutto's unwillingness to share power and accept the existence and the mandate of the NAP, state's

94   *Centre–Province relations post-independence*

security perception in the wake of the 1971 war and the separation of East Pakistan were the main reasons for the political instability in Balochistan during the 1970s.

Pakistan under General Yahya Khan

After the nationwide demonstration against his government and spiralling political unrest in Pakistan, President Ayub Khan resigned as the President of Pakistan and handed the helm of affairs of the country to the then Chief of the Army Staff, General Yahya Khan, who became the martial law administrator and president of Pakistan on 25 March 1969. After assuming the presidency, Yahya aimed at resolving the constitutional dilemma faced by the country and the increasing ethnic rivalry between the eastern and western wings of Pakistan. To address the grievances of East Pakistan, General Yahya doubled the quota for East Pakistan in the armed forces. He dissolved the One Unit and restored the provinces of West Pakistan as they were in 1955 when the One Unit was established to achieve parity against the majority of the Bengali-dominated East Pakistan.

He also granted Balochistan the status of a full-fledged province of Pakistan. General Yahya also declared that the first direct, based-on-adult-franchise elections will be held in Pakistan in December 1970. He promised these elections to be free and fair. In keeping with the political trends and past experience, a number of observers have argued that General Yahya was under the impression that these elections would result in a hung parliament and that he would be able to continue his role of a power broker between the political leadership of the country. According to the estimates of his team of experts, in the forthcoming 1970 election, the Awami League would get 80 seats in the National Assembly, whereas Qayyum League and Daultana Muslim League would get 70 seats each, the National Awami Party (NAP) would get 35 seats and the Pakistan Peoples Party (PPP) would get 25 seats.[2] This generally accepted interpretation was challenged by G.W. Choudhury, who stated that Yahya knew beforehand that the Awami League would win majority seats in the elections and that Mujib assured him that the six-points would be modified.[3]

1970 elections and Balochistan

For Balochistan, General Yahya Khan's decision to grant provincial status to Balochistan was a welcome development. Although a group led by Ahmed Yar Khan advocated the restoration of the Balochistan States Union or a province to be based on this, it was ignored. The new Baloch leadership comprising Ghaus Bakhsh Bizenjo, Nawab Khair Bakhsh Marri, Sardar Ataullah Mengal, and Nawab Akbar Bugti who rose to prominence during the Ayub regime also decided to participate in the forthcoming elections. Barring Bizenjo, who had a long political career and understanding, Nawab Marri, Nawab Bugti and Sardar Mengal only aimed at safeguarding the Baloch identity and rights. According to Sardar Sherbaz Mazari, they believed in the concept of Balochiyat to the fullest.[4] After

Centre–Balochistan Relations (1969–77) 95

some deliberations, the three decided to join the National Awami Party (NAP), a decision in which Bizenjo played the most important part. During the election campaign in Balochistan, Bizenjo, Marri, Mengal and Bugti spearheaded the election campaign of the NAP.[5]

In the 1970 elections, out of the overall 300 seats for the National Assembly, the Awami League won 160 seats, the Peoples Party won 81 seats, Pakistan Muslim League (Qayyum) won 9 seats, and independent candidates won 16 seats. The remaining seats were won by a mix of smaller, regional and religious parties such as Jamaat Islami, Jamiat Ulema-e-Pakistan, etc. The pattern was repeated in the provincial assembly elections. The Awami League won 228 seats from East Pakistan. The Peoples Party won 113 in Punjab, 28 in Sind, and 3 in NWFP. The National Awami Party managed to win 13 in NWFP and 8 in Balochistan.[6]

In 1970, Balochistan had four seats in the National Assembly of Pakistan. Out of these four seats, Bizenjo and Marri won each, Abdul Hayee Baloch, the president of the Baloch Students Organization, won the third seat. The fourth seat from the Pashtun constituency was won by JUI. As a result of these elections, for the first time in Balochistan since the creation of Pakistan in 1947, just like elsewhere in the country, people were given the opportunity to elect their own representatives. For the first time, the people of Balochistan were represented by the leaders of their own province.[7]

As it turned out, the NAP was able to emerge as the majority party in two provinces: NWFP and Balochistan. In Balochistan, in the house of 20, the NAP had won 8 seats, whereas five seats were won by independent candidates and three seats were won by Qayyum League. Therefore, it became quite clear that the NAP would make the government in Balochistan.

1970 national elections and the separation of East Pakistan

Despite all estimates and claims, as the election day approached, it became obvious that the main contestants in the election were Mujibur Rahman-led Awami League (AL) and Bhutto-led Pakistan Peoples Party (PPP). In East Pakistan, the Awami League managed to win all the seats, whereas the PPP emerged as the majority party in West Pakistan. As the Awami League had won 160 seats as compared to the second best 81 seats won by the PPP, it became obvious that the numbers were favouring the Awami League and that AL would be forming the next government.

However, Yahya and Bhutto dragged their feet and started applying delaying tactics. This agitated the East Pakistanis as they viewed this as a deliberate attempt to deny the Awami League its right to establish the national government and Mujibur Rahman to become the Prime Minister. The resultant political unrest got violent on occasions. General Yahya adopted a militaristic approach to solve the problem and ordered a military crackdown to restore law and order and establish the government's writ in East Pakistan. On 25 March 1971, Operation Searchlight was launched and law and order was soon restored in East Pakistan as most of the activists either were arrested, were dispersed or went underground. This

96 *Centre–Province relations post-independence*

crackdown, however, widened the already existing gulf between the two wings of the country. Soon, the activists resurfaced and the political agitation elevated into an insurgency. The insurgents were trained, equipped and fully supported by India. Soon, the situation deteriorated to such an extent that India attacked Pakistan on the eastern front which resulted in the creation of Bangladesh in December 1971. More than 90,000 Pakistanis including 20,000 women and children became Indian prisoners of war (PoWs). The Indians also captured 5,795.64 square miles of Pakistani territory on the western front.[8]

Academics are still divided on who is responsible for the dismemberment of Pakistan. One group blames Yahya, another blames Bhutto, whereas a third group considers it an Indian conspiracy in which Mujibur Rahman acted as an Indian proxy.[9]

PAKISTAN: PICKING UP THE PIECES

In the wake of the fall of Dhaka, two developments in Pakistan were significant: one, after the secession of East Pakistan and creation of Bangladesh, Punjab's significance increased immensely as other than the political clout it enjoyed since 1947, it was now ethnically the majority province of Pakistan. Second, although initially General Yahya had no plans of stepping down, under intense pressure from the Pakistani Armed Forces, especially the junior officers of the Pakistan Army, General Yahya stepped down and handed the power over to the chairman of the PPP, Zulfikar Ali Bhutto.

Professor Ishtiaq Ahmed in his magnum opus, *Pakistan The Garrison State, Origins, Evolution, Consequences*, stated that after the separation of the East Pakistan, Punjab became the most populated province of Pakistan. According to him, the share of Punjab in the overall Pakistani population was 58%, Sindh had 21.6%, NWFP 16.7%, Balochistan 2.4%, and the tribal areas 1.3%.[10] He further claims that after the separation of East Pakistan, the Pakistan Army had 70% Punjabis, 20% Pashtuns and a mix of Mohajirs, Sindhis, Kashmiris and Baloch comprising the remaining 10%. In officer corps, there were 68 to 70% Punjabis, 15% Pashtuns, 10% Mohajirs and 5–7% Sindhis and Baloch.[11]

Bhutto took over at a time when Pakistan was going through its most tragic phase of history. The country was dismembered; the army had to face the humiliation of surrendering to India and accept defeat in East Pakistan. It was believed that only Bhutto had the qualifications and credentials to revive the national spirit and rebuild the country.

Bhutto at the time of assuming power delivered a highly emotional speech and pledged that he would pick pieces, very small pieces, but will make a new Pakistan. Ian Talbot, commenting on Bhutto as the leader of the new Pakistan and the potential problems he would face, stated:

> He also possessed the experience of representing Pakistan on the wider world stage. Aside from his own sense of destiny, no Pakistani politician was in fact better placed to rebuild the machinery of government and national morale

shattered by the Bangladesh debacle. Its tangible consequences were equally serious and involved the loss of the foreign exchange brought by jute and tea exports and of an assured market for up to 40 percent of the products of West Pakistan's manufacturing base. Although the breakaway of the eastern wing dramatically altered the context of Pakistan's politics, Bhutto faced the same dilemmas which had defeated his predecessors, namely how to assert the authority of the elected institutions of the state over the military and bureaucracy establish a functioning federal system and resolve the role of Islam in constitutional theory and practice.[12]

Bhutto became the martial law administrator and President of Pakistan. He also held portfolios of defence, foreign affairs, internal affairs and inter-provincial coordinator for himself and appointed a 12-member cabinet.[13]

He also appointed his loyalists and party members as governors of the four provinces.[14] Among the first decisions he took was the release of the Sheikh Mujibur Rahman and allowed him to return to what was now Bangladesh.[15] He also lifted the ban on the NAP, political ally of the Awami League in the 1970 elections.

Political reconstruction and the constitutional debate: The PPP and the opposition

Among the first challenges Bhutto faced after assuming the leadership of Pakistan was to develop a political consensus among different political parties so that a new constitution could be prepared. He met with Khan Abdul Wali Khan, the leader of the National Awami Party (NAP), and Mufti Mahmud, the leader of the religious political party Jamiat-e-Ulema-e-Islam (JUI). In the emerging political set-up, these two parties were the main opposition parties and majority parties in the provinces of NWFP and Balochistan, and it was clear that they were heading towards establishing coalition governments in these provinces.[16] As a gesture of goodwill and to ensure a congenial political environment, Bhutto formally offered the NAP and JUI to join the government and offered them two cabinet slots.[17] Both the NAP and JUI declined the offer. The main points of difference between the PPP, the NAP and JUI were the martial law and appointment of governors in NWFP and Balochistan, where the NAP and JUI were the majority parties. While Bhutto favoured a gradual restoration/return of democracy, arguing that the martial law provided him the powers to implement and ensure the effectiveness of the reforms. Opposition parties, especially the NAP and JUI, disagreed. The NAP demanded that the martial law should be lifted immediately and a session of the National Assembly be called as soon as possible.[18]

The NAP also demonstrated its street power by organizing rallies to protest the appointment of governors in NWFP and Balochistan without consulting the NAP.[19] Although the government managed to contain the fallout of such political hyperbole,[20] the political atmosphere got charged and the goal of political reconciliation seemed to be unattainable. Under such circumstances, the leaders of the PPP, the NAP and JUI met for a second round of talks in March 1972. After

98   Centre–Province relations post-independence

intense negotiation, an agreement was finally reached between the three parties on 6 March 1972.[21] As per the agreement, the PPP acknowledged the constitutional right of the NAP and JUI to establish provincial governments in NWFP and Balochistan and have their nominees appointed as the governors of NWFP and Balochistan. In exchange, the NAP–JUI agreed to withdraw their opposition to the martial law till 14 August 1972.[22] All parties also agreed on the main points of an interim constitution which would be endorsed in a National Assembly session in April. It was agreed that the session of provincial assemblies will take place on 21 April. It was decided that a committee would be established which would prepare the draft constitution of Pakistan.[23]

However, the political goodwill achieved through this agreement proved to be short-lived. The PPP's political stratagem in NWFP and getting into alliance with the Mazdoor Kisan Party (MKP) and Qayyum Muslim League (QML), both political rivals of the NAP, and the appointment of Qayyum Khan, the head of QML, as the interior minister[24] was taken by the NAP as a deliberate attempt on the part of Bhutto to curtail the NAP's political standing and clout in NWFP.

When the National Assembly session took place, Bhutto surprised everyone by announcing that the martial law would be lifted on 21 April 1972.[25] He expected that the interim constitution should be adopted by the house for the smooth functioning of the state. The opposition accepted this, and the interim constitution was adopted on 17 April.[26]

As per the agreement reached between the PPP, the NAP and JUI, on 29 April, Ghaus Bakhsh Bizenjo and Arbab Sikander were appointed the governors of Balochistan and NWFP, respectively. Sardar Atuallah Mengal and Mufti Mahmud became the chief ministers of Balochistan and NWFP, respectively.

By looking at these developments, one can argue that the political climate in Pakistan was neither frosty nor too warm. While the ruling party and the opposition parties had serious differences, they managed to implement the March Accord. Another explanation for this could be Bhutto's foreign and regional policy compulsions. Pakistan–India negotiations at Simla regarding the PoWs, lands under occupation and other contentious issues were coming up. Bhutto, in keeping with Wali Khan's warning that Bhutto would be representing only half of Pakistan, if he went to Simla without taking the governments of NWFP and Balochistan on board,[27] wanted to ensure that the political waters in the country should not boil.

Barring Jamaat Islami and few other minor opposition parties who accused Bhutto of succumbing under Indian pressure and of a sell-out, generally the Simla Accord was welcomed by the political leadership of the country including the NAP and JUI.

In October, an all-party meeting took place to reach a consensus on the principles and main points of the constitution of Pakistan. Major political parties who attended the meeting included: the NAP, JUI, JI, QML, Council Muslim League (CML) and Jamiat-e-Ulema-e-Pakistan (JUP). An accord was signed on 20 October. As Wali Khan was in London for a medical check-up, Ghaus Bakhsh Bizenjo and Arbab Sikander signed the accord on his behalf. Despite the fact that Bhutto personally would have preferred a *de Gaulle style*, presidential system,[28] the

Centre–Balochistan Relations (1969–77) 99

accord stated that the future constitution of Pakistan would follow a federal parliamentary system.

Political scientist Khalid Bin Sayeed has described the urge to establish personal control over the state as Bonapartism. According to him, Bhutto was primarily motivated by *animus dominandi*, that is, the aggrandizement of his own power base and by making it subservient to his will and power.[29]

On 10 April 1973, the draft constitution was passed and approved by the National Assembly. One hundred and twenty-five votes were cast in favour of the draft constitution.[30] Nawab Khair Bakhsh Marri and Mir Ali Ahmed Talpur were two noted naysayers. As per the newly adopted constitution, Bhutto was sworn in as the Prime Minister of Pakistan on 14 August 1973.

CENTRE–BALOCHISTAN RELATIONS

In March 1972, when Bhutto was holding talks with the opposition parties, he invited Nawab Khair Bakhsh Marri and Sardar Ataullah Mengal to Islamabad as the leaders of the NAP Balochistan to discuss the political situation of Balochistan. This turned out to be a very difficult meeting. According to the accounts available of the meeting, Nawab Marri acted as a senior sardar dealing with a minor wadero.[31] According to Rafi Raza who attended the meeting, "sardar Marri was throughout abrasive. I do not recall anyone else speaking in this tune to ZAB, nor ZAB being so restrained."[32]

One of the most important points of discussion was the governorship of Balochistan. Sherbaz Mazari in his memoirs has detailed how this decision was made during the meeting. Initially, Bhutto offered Nawab Marri to accept the position. According to Sherbaz Mazari, the Marri sardar coldly turned his face aside without bothering to comment.[33] Bhutto then offered the position to Sardar Mengal who as per the Baloch tradition and manners responded that he would rather have Nawab Marri have it. Nawab Marri, responding to Bhutto's second request, "arrogantly turned his face away from him and haughtily announced that Attaullah should have it."[34] While this political ping pong was going on, Ghaus Bakhsh Bizenjo, who was attending the meeting uninvited, jumped in and said to Bhutto, "they are sardars. It is beneath their dignity to accept such an office. Give it to me instead."[35] Bizenjo was appointed the Governor of Balochistan.

Bhutto, however, made it clear that he has only agreed to appoint a governor who is neither a ruling party's member nor an apolitical person, to achieve national unity and that the governor would stay in his position as long as he enjoyed his support.[36]

Major events during the NAP government in Balochistan

The NAP government in Balochistan was unique in a number of ways. For the first time, Balochistan was to be ruled and governed by elected representatives. Ataullah Mengal and others were nationalists who faced prison terms and were considered anti-state during the previous Ayub regime. The provincial government

100 *Centre–Province relations post-independence*

expressed its intention of promoting democratic values, improving law and order and addressing concerns regarding basic human needs in the province. The provincial government also expressed its willingness and desire to work closely and in collaboration with the central government. Sardar Ataullah Mengal, after assuming the chief ministership of Balochistan, promised to make Balochistan a shining Balochistan.

However, soon, the provincial government started taking decisions which were taken as hostile by the centre. Among the very first decisions the Mengal administration took was to repatriate 5,500 (mostly Punjabis) civil servants from Balochistan. Out of these 5,500 civil employees, 2,880 were serving in the police force.[37] According to the Mengal government, out of the 12,000 government employees, only 3,000 were Baloch. Ninety percent of the personnel of the Frontier Force (FC) were outsiders. The Mengal government created a new police force, Balochistan Dehi Muhafiz (BDM).

Another bone of contention was the Mengal government's refusal to allow the Coast Guards, a federal force, to patrol the Makran coast. While these decisions by the provincial government were creating a rift between the centre and the province, Marri and Mengal tribesmen attacked the Punjabi abadkars (settlers) in the Pat Feeder area. In Quetta, armed Bugti tribesmen besieged the provincial secretariat and demanded that Ahmad Nawaz Bugti resigned from its ministership from Mengal's cabinet.[38] If all this was not enough, on December 26, a tribal war started between the Jamotes and Mengals when the Mengal lashkar (tribal force) attacked the Jamotes. Forty-two people were reported killed in the attack. The provincial government failed to restore law and order. Cynics argued that as the Mengal tribe was involved, the Mengal government was a party in the tribal clash. Eventually, the federal government intervened and sent in Army troops to restore law and order. It was believed that the Governor of Balochistan, Bizenjo had requested the federal government to intervene, but Bizenjo later stated that he only asked for security forces and not the army. The Mengal government and the NAP leadership sharply criticized the federal government's intervention into the provincial matters. Bizenjo openly accused the federal interior minister, Qayyum Khan, as the man behind the whole incident. According to him, it was Qayyum who encouraged the Jam of Lasbela to go on this path.[39] The NAP leadership claimed that the main reason behind this episode was the refusal of the Jamotes to implement reform measures introduced by the Mengal government in their areas.[40] Wali Khan in a statement declared the federal government's action as a breach of the constitutional right of the provincial government and interference in the internal affairs of Balochistan.[41]

The London plan

An important issue which had adverse effects on the centre–province relations was the so-called London plan. According to several reports, in 1972, a number of Pakistani politicians, mostly from the opposition parties, particularly the NAP, visited London for various reasons.[42] It was claimed that during the same time,

Sheikh Mujibur Rahman, the leader of the Awami League and now the founding father of Bangladesh, was also present in London. This prompted the newspapers of Pakistan, mostly belonging to the government-owned National Trust Newspapers to report that these politicians have met with Sheikh Mujibur Rahman and were planning to overthrow the Bhutto government and dismember the state of Pakistan. This, according to these media outlets was the so-called London plan.[43] The NAP leadership declared these allegations as baseless and denied the existence of any such plan. The NAP leadership accused the central government of making all these allegations up to malign the Mengal government in Balochistan. While this tug of war was going on between the Bhutto administration and the leadership of the NAP, on 10 February, the federal security forces found a cache of Russian-made ammunition, when it raided the Iraqi embassy in Islamabad. It was claimed that these weapons were for the Baloch insurgents in their so-called struggle against the state of Pakistan.[44] Responding to this development, the Bhutto government, using its constitutional rights, dismissed the Mengal government and a thirty-day presidential rule was imposed upon Balochistan. On 16 February, a number of NAP leaders including Bizenjo, Mengal, and Marri and score of NAP workers were arrested. Several cases were registered against the leaders of the NAP, especially Bizenjo, Marri, and Mengal. These charges and filed cases included charges of running smuggling gangs, possession of arms, raising private militias and misuse of public funds. The Mengal government was accused of providing government ammunition to its own private force which mostly comprised Mengal tribesmen. It was also charged that these three leaders were running guerrilla training camps. Bhutto appointed Nawab Akbar Bugti and Aslam Khattak as the governors of Balochistan and NWFP, respectively.

Was the Bhutto regime correct about the London plan?

While the reports about the London plan made headlines during the Bhutto regime and were widely used by his team as a proof of the NAP's anti-Pakistan agenda, it was never proved. Many argued that even the Bhutto regime never went beyond using it as a point-scoring measure against the NAP. Was it just a political propaganda against the NAP as it was the Awami League's partner during the 1970 elections? or was there any credence to this? Was there ever a London plan? If so, what it was?

Former Indian diplomat Sashanka Banerjee[45] who was stationed at London during the time of the alleged meeting between Sheikh Mujibur Rahman and the NAP leadership, has in a recently published article shed light on the issue.[46] According to Banerjee, "on the day Pakistan surrendered to India at Dhaka, Bangladesh's foreign minister-in-exile advised Baloch, Pakhtoon, and Sindhi nationalists to launch a joint liberation struggle against Pakistan with Indian help."[47] According to Banerjee, Khan Abdul Wali Khan, Nawab Akbar Khan Bugti, Nawabzada Khair Bakhsh Marri, Ataullah Mengal, and a representative of G. M. Syed attended the meeting at the Charing Cross Hotel near Trafalgar Square in London.[48]

102 *Centre–Province relations post-independence*

According to this account, it was not Sheikh Mujibur Rahman but his foreign minister Abdus Samad Azad who was holding the meeting with them. Azad offered:

> … given the ground realities of the evolving unsavoury political situation in Pakistan – that there was need to forge a joint front of liberation struggle among the ethno-sub-national peoples in Pakistan aimed at breaking away from Pakistan and becoming sovereign independent nation states as Bangladesh had done, would they approve of it. Pakistan in defeat was in disarray, the Indian Army had reached the gates of Lahore, therefore this was the most opportune moment to strike. And if they agreed, Bangladesh was capable of helping them set up the entire infrastructure of struggle and extending wholehearted support and succour including political, diplomatic and most importantly material back up to such an unified movement.[49]

However, an understanding could not be reached. According to Banerjee who was briefed by Azad soon after the meeting,

> … the talks failed. It was apparent that the secret plan of action was chalked out in haste. There were no prior consultations. The uncertainty over the outcome of the war was certainly the main reason why the idea was brought up in the secret confabulations so late in the day.[50]

Banerjee also claimed that in 1973, Sheikh Mujib confirmed to him that he was aware of this meeting and that "It was unfortunate, he said, that the Baloch people missed their historic opportunity for freedom because of the hesitation of their leadership."[51]

Balochistan under Akbar Bugti's governorship

Soon after assuming the governorship, in a total reversal of the NAP government's policy, Nawab Akbar Bugti asked the centre to send on deputation a few officers from the central pool to assist the Balochistan government. He also sacked a few local officials who he considered too close to the previous provincial government. Bugti's style of governance was that all decisions were made by a single authority, Akbar Bugti himself. He exercised total control over the executive, financial and political matters related to Balochistan. During his tenure, nothing ever got approved without his consent. Stanley Wolpert wrote, "whether it was allotments of tractors and bulldozers, construction of new tube wells, or electricity connections, permits or licenses nothing could go to the chief minister unless the governor i.e. Nawab Akbar Bugti first approve or reject it."[52] Wolpert also points to another interesting aspect of Akbar Bugti's governorship. According to Wolpert, Nawab Akbar Bugti at times sent detailed reports to Bhutto about the political and security situation in Balochistan solely based on his own view. One of these so-called situation reports stated:

Centre–Balochistan Relations (1969–77) 103

Counter insurgency forces are in ... disarray. Bhutto ... has not yet realized the situation. He is still dreaming his dreams of one party government. His love for whole and sole power blinded him to the danger of not
sharing power. ... Bhutto is convinced that sooner or later Bugti will turn
against him. ...Bugti knows this and so a situation of mistrust prevails. ...
the national leadership does not support Bugti. ...The People's Party press
gives him no build up. ... So Bugti is unable to give the people what they
want. ... if affairs continue to move as they are moving today, Balochistan
is lost to Pakistan.[53]

Nawab Bugti resigned from Governorship of Balochistan on 31 October 1973.
According to Bugti, he accepted the position of governor with the hope that he
could be able to help the people of Balochistan in improving their condition, but
despite his best efforts, a number of factors impeded his several attempts to achieve
this objective.[54] Bhutto accepted Bugti's resignation and appointed Khan-e-Baloch, Mir Ahmad Yar Khan as the new governor of Balochistan.[55] An important
aspect of this time period in Balochistan was that the provincial administration
could not perform well as the governor and the chief minister and his cabinet did
not see eye ball to eye ball. The main reason for this was their tribal differences
and the fact that the only reason they were together in the provincial administration was their opposition to the NAP leadership of Balochistan. Bhutto dismissed
the chief minister and his cabinet and imposed federal rule in the province in
December 1975.[56] Governor, as the representative of the federal government in
Balochistan, was made incharge of the province. Ironically though, all members
of the dissolved cabinet including the chief minister were appointed advisors to
the governor.

In April 1976, while visiting Balochistan, Bhutto announced to officially abolish the sardari system in Balochistan.[57] This decision was ironic in the sense that a
number of sardars were closely supporting him and his policies in Balochistan and
the biggest sardar, Ahmed Yar Khan, was his governor in Balochistan.

Bhutto understood that nothing in Balochistan would change unless its financial and developmental issues were addressed. He was also aware that this
backwardness was the biggest tool which the Baloch nationalists and insurgents use to justify their struggle. To address the Baloch economic grievances, Bhutto embarked upon a massive development plan for Balochistan.
He increased federal fund for Balochistan. As per the official data, the federal
fund for Balochistan increased almost hundred percent in one year. In the year
1972–73, it was Rs. 120 million, whereas in 1974 it was Rs. 210 million.[58] During his government, according to official sources, the revenues of the province
increased from Rs. 88 million to Rs. 226 million in one year (1974–75). This
was achieved by providing the province with the royalty money and excise
duty for the Sui gas. A number of new development projects were also started.
Special attention was given to improving the communication network, construction of roads, hospitals, schools, banks, technical institutions as well as
health facilities.[59]

104 *Centre–Province relations post-independence*

The Baloch insurgency

The dismissal of the Mengal government and the subsequent arrest of Sardar Ataullah Mengal, Nawab Khair Bakhsh Marri and Ghaus Bakhsh Bizenjo and others, was taken as an attack on the Baloch honour. Due to this, a number of Baloch rose against the central government. According to Selig Harrison,

> The Ryvaj, the traditional code of honor, requires the true Baloch to fight, if necessary, to defend his personal and tribal honor, and the overwhelming majority of Baloch tribal leaders regarded Bhutto's action as a deliberate insult to all Baloch, requiring military redress.[60]

Six weeks after the ouster of the Mengal government, Baloch insurgents were targeting army conveys.[61] Most significant of these attacks took place on 18 May 1973 at Tandoori in which the Baloch insurgents targeted a team of Dir Scouts patrolling the area, killing all of them and taking away their weapons.[62] In a different attack which took place on the same day, the Baloch insurgents targeted the Additional Deputy Commissioner of Kalat.[63]

As it was stated in the previous chapter, the Pararis decided not to completely dismantle and keep their network intact despite agreeing to a ceasefire in the late 1960s. Bhutto's breach of Baloch honour provided the Parari leadership reason enough to restart their militant activities. As it happened, the Pararis under the leadership of Mir Hazar played a significant role in the Baloch insurgency during the Bhutto regime.[64] Selig Harrison stated that

> The authority of the guerrillas was largely unchallenged in the Marri area, where they enjoyed the active, albeit covert, support of the tribal sardar and received food and other necessities from the Baloch populace. Here, in particular, the Pararis hoped to establish a 'liberated' zone of base area, comparable to Mao's Yenan, in the event that the Baloch embarked on a full-scale struggle for independence from Pakistan.[65]

The militant presence was particularly strong in Sarawan, Jhalawan and Marri-Bugti areas. The Baloch guerrillas had an elaborate command structure. The prominent commanders of the Baloch insurgents included Mir Hazar Khan, Lauang Khan, Ali Muhammad Mengal, Zafar Khan, Khair Jan Bizenjo, Suliman Khan Ahmadzai, and Mir Alsam Khan Gichki.

By July 1974, the casualty figure of the security forces was on the rise. The Baloch insurgents managed to control most of the roads and highways and almost cut the province off from the rest of the country. This resulted in the occasional disruption of the rail links and supply of coals to Punjab. The insurgents also regularly targeted and almost halted any oil and gas exploration and further drilling and surveying.

This changed with the battle at Chamalang which lasted for six days. At present, the battle at Chamalang occupies a significant place in Baloch narrative of

Centre–Balochistan Relations (1969–77) 105

injustice and atrocities committed against them by the centre. Every year, during the summer, the Marris used to relocate to the valley of Chamalang. In 1974, while most of the Marri men were engaged in fighting with the Pakistan Army, women, children and the elderly came to the valley with their flocks of animals. According to various accounts, the Pakistan Army decided to use this as a tool to lure the Baloch insurgents into a decisive battle.[66] The plan worked and a number of minor skirmishes took place between the Baloch insurgents and the Pakistan Army. On 3 September 1974, the Pakistan Army, supported by the Pakistan Air Force, attacked the 1,500-strong Baloch insurgent force. Around 125 insurgents were killed and 900 were captured, although most of the important guerrilla leaders managed to escape. Baloch insurgents claimed that they killed 446 Pakistan Army soldiers. Although the Baloch insurgents at the time claimed that they inflicted heavy losses on the Pakistan Army, it became obvious that the battle of Chamalang proved disastrous for the Baloch insurgents as they never fully recovered from the losses they suffered in the fighting. Although the violence continued sporadically, the momentum of the insurgency was lost. Another indication of this fact is that in 1974, more than 5,000 Marri tribesmen surrendered and handed over their arms to the government in exchange of full pardon.

After the surrender of the Baloch guerrillas, Bhutto in a statement claimed that the insurgents have been defeated and the writ of the state has been restored.[67]

In 1978, the government released a report in which it was stated that 70,000 strong forces were deployed to quell the insurgency in Balochistan. According to official estimates, the Baloch insurgents numbered 55,000 which included cells and groups with proper command and control structure as well as loosely organized guerrilla groups. During the insurgency, more than 340 engagements took place between the two sides in which 5,300 Baloch insurgents and 3,300 Pakistani security force personal lost their lives.[68]

The insurgency of 1970s was the bloodiest insurgency in Baloch history till the time, and what differentiated it from the earlier insurgencies (1948 and 1958) was the direct involvement of two of the most prominent tribes: Marri and Mengal and their sardars, Nawab Khair Bakhsh Marri and Sardar Ataullah Khan Mengal in it.[69] Another unique feature of this insurgency was the presence of a group of revolutionaries belonging to the elite class families of Punjab and studying in various British educational institutions including Cambridge University and the London School of Economics.

The London Group

Most of the details about this group are still not available, but as per what is now publically available, the known members of this group included Najam Sethi, Ahmed Rashid, Dalip Johny Das, Asad Rehman, Rashid Rehman, and Muhammad Ali Talpur.[70] According to A.B. Awan, the members of the London Group received military training at PLO camps in Jordan and a few of them were trained in India.[71] This assertion is strongly denied by the members of the group. It was reported that the members of the London Group were involved in

106 *Centre–Province relations post-independence*

the logistical side and motivational training of the insurgents. A.B. Awan, claimed that "Most of them came back without making any contribution, except that of providing some amusement for the tough Baloch fighters."[72] As true Marxists and those who strived for a Marxist revolution in Pakistan, the members of this group had a fundamental difference with the Baloch insurgents. The Baloch insurgents were fighting for their rights and a few of them for the Baloch independence and not for an ideological revolution, something which eventually resulted in the parting of ways between the two. However, the known members of the group, for instance leading Pakistani journalist Najam Sethi and Muhamad Ali Talpur, are still considered authority on the Baloch problem in Pakistan and regularly express their views on national and international media.

WHAT WENT WRONG? CENTRE VERSUS BALOCH NARRATIVE

Centre's narrative

Despite a promising start in which both sides expressed their desire and willingness to work together, the rift in relations between the centre and the province started to appear very soon. The Mengal government's decision regarding certain issues already discussed in an earlier section that involved federal government and/or issues that required the approval and consent of the federal government irritated the Bhutto administration. The decision to send all non-Baloch civil servants back to their provinces of domicile, taking over and restructuring of the police and not allowing the Coast Guards to operate were decisions which were taken without consulting or discussing their implications and ramifications with the federal government. This clearly irritated Bhutto.[73] The Bhutto regime viewed these policies as an attempt by Ataulah Mengal and other like-minded sardars to ensure that the sardari hold of the province continued[74] and that Bhutto's agenda of modernization which included abolishing of the sardari system was not implemented which clearly went against their interest in the province.

Bhutto was of the view that the Mengal administration was preparing the ground for secession from Pakistan. The decision to send all non-Baloch government employees back to their home provinces, according to the Bhutto regime, was a deliberate attempt to create an administrative vacuum. The new changes in the structure of police and the creation of the Balochistan Dehi Muhafiz (BDM) were taken as a deliberate attempt to induct its own people in the security forces which would then be used to fulfil this agenda.[75]

As the memory of the East Pakistan debacle was fresh, the regime also believed that the Baloch sardars have external support in their alleged plan to secede from Pakistan. The reason the Mengal administration did not allow the Coast Guards to operate, according to this view, was to ensure that they receive arms and equipment from their regional foreign supporters without any hindrance. The seizure of a large cache of arms from the Iraqi embassy which was destined for the Baloch insurgents was considered a clear proof of this outside support.[76]

Centre–Balochistan Relations (1969–77)   107

Regarding the tribal feuds, especially between the Mengal and the Jamotes, the centre was of the view that the Mengal government was totally involved in this and the Chief Minister Ataullah Mengal led the tribal lashkars from Mengal, Bizenjo and almost nine other tribes including the Balochistan Dehi Mufiz (BDM) forces, against the Jamotes and killed, looted and plundered the Jamotes. During the fight, a number of Jamotes were killed and a large number of them had to seek refuge in the nearby hills where they were besieged by these tribal forces. As the provincial government was involved in this, the centre had no option but to intervene to restore law and order in the province. This is exactly why the Pakistan Army was sent in to take control of Lasbela on 9 February 1973. Bhutto also clearly stated that the Pakistan Army has a constitutional obligation to ensure national security and that was what it did in Balochistan.[77]

Bhutto was particularly proud of the fact that he introduced land reforms in the country. He believed that these Baloch sardars were one of the major hindrances in its implementation. Speaking in the parliament, he stated:

> We introduced land reforms on national scale but the sardars of Baluchistan, thinking themselves to be above the law, did not file the forms required. They threw out these forms contemptuously and said: "We would like to see who will come into our territory to implement the land reforms. We are the masters of all that we survey. In our jurisdiction, nobody will dare". In their manifesto, they had a provision for land reforms, but when it came to implementation, they refused to even comply with the first step which was to make a declaration of their land holdings. This is how true they are to their word. This is how faithful they are to the pledge which they had given to the people of Baluchistan.[78]

Bhutto, speaking in the parliament, gave another reason why he thinks that *these* sardars (Mengal and Marri) are the trouble makers. He mentioned a meeting which took place in Murree which was attended by a large number of political leaders from all major parties of Pakistan such as Ataullah Mengal, Khair Bakhsh Marri, Ghaus Bakhsh Bizenjo, Maulana Mufti Mahmud, and Professor Ghafoor Ahmed. A number of issues were discussed related to the political stability of Pakistan. An important issue under discussion was the political developments in Balochistan.

> We made certain tentative proposals. I said, "Now in two days I am going to the United States; let me come back and we will pick up these negotiations and hold discussions". Everyone agreed, each and every one of them agreed. While they were getting up to go, Sardar Mengal asked them to sit down. Everyone sat down. He said, "No, I am breaking this tentative agreement. We will continue to fight; our man will be in the hills, we will not tell our men to come down; our men will resist government of Pakistan, our men will resist you. We will waylay and burn the buses; we will not stop until we come to the final agreement." I said, sardar sahib, what are you saying? If you do that, the whole thing will escalate. You will fight but do you think we will stand by

108 *Centre–Province relations post-independence*

and watch? You will waylay buses and set fire to villages and shall we take it lying down? Why do you want to do that? Can't you wait for a few days? I am returning soon. All of you agreed only a few minutes earlier." He said, "Now I am a man of 'Ghairat'. I do not believe in all this talk and negotiations. This is all rubbish. I am a man of action". I said, "Do you realize the consequences? This is going to escalate. You will fight, we will have to resist. Your men will go into the hills; we will have to follow them. They will burn villages; we will have to take action. This thing will get out of hand, out of the political domain". He said: "that we know. We realize it but we have always been fighters; we have fought in the past and we will fight in the future until the final agreement is reached on our terms. Now this is the position they take in negotiations that until the final agreement comes on their terms, they will continue the fight.[79]

Bhutto's lack of trust of the Baloch political leaders (sardars) was so great that despite the fact that Nawab Akbar Bugti sided with him against the Mengal government and other NAP leadership (Khair Bakhsh Marri, Ghaus Bakhsh Bizenjo), Bhutto did not trust him. While Bhutto used him as a tool against the other Baloch sardars and to quell the Baloch insurgency, yet his biggest worry was what would happen if Nawab Bugti decided to side with the other Baloch sardars.[80]

Government of Pakistan's white paper on Balochistan

The government of Pakistan issued a white paper on Balochistan on 19 October 1974. This was an important document as it clearly stated how the centre viewed the situation in Balochistan and who, according to the government of Pakistan, was responsible for the violence and political unrest in Balochistan. According to the white paper, the situation worsened because of two reasons: firstly, the threat to the status quo or the position of these sardars due to the development policies of the centre, and secondly, the objective of succeeding from the federation.[81] According to this document, the sardars, especially Ataullah Mengal and Khair Bakhsh Marri, were anti-development as they saw it as something which would minimize their hold on the people and the land. Therefore, these sardars strongly opposed the modernization policies for the province.[82]

The white paper also clearly stated that the Baloch insurgents had regional and international support. The document cited a number of examples as proof of the existence of such active support. This, according to the white paper, was the reason why the Mengal government did not allow the coast guards to operate in the strategic Makran coast area as this would have exposed their supply line.[83]

Regarding the insurgents and their training and equipment, the whitepaper stated that most of the insurgents encountered by the Pakistani security forces were well trained and had no shortage of arms and ammunition. Establishing a link with the coup in Afghanistan, the white paper alleged that since the coup in Afghanistan, the militant activities in Balochistan also intensified.[84] The white paper also elaborated in detail the role of the regional players, especially Afghanistan in Balochistan.[85]

Centre–Balochistan Relations (1969–77) 109

Regarding the ultimate objective of the Baloch insurgents, the white paper stated that the final aim was the creation of a Greater Balochistan.

Baloch narrative

Baloch narrative of why all this happened is totally different. According to this narrative, Bhutto had no intention of handing over the powers in the province to the elected representatives of the NAP. This was clearly illustrated in his decision to appoint Ghous Bakhsh Raisani as the Governor of Balochistan. However, the people's demonstrations on the streets and the fact that the situation at the borders was still not totally under his control and that the numbers were not in his favour in the Balochistan assembly, made him realize that he was not in a position to have another confrontation with the NAP.[86] The moment he managed to achieve his objectives of getting the constitution passed from the parliament and politically felt his feet on firm grounds, he started moving against the NAP government in Balochistan. The centre under his leadership took every step to make the day-to-day functioning of the provincial government of Balochistan almost impossible.

Regarding the Mengal government's decision to send all non-Baloch government employees back to their provinces of domicile, the Baloch narrative or Mengal government's position was that most of these civil servants belonged to Punjab and Punjab cadre of the bureaucracy.[87] The PPP government in Punjab instructed these civil servants to put every possible obstruction in the Balochistan provincial government. As these government employees were more concerned about their jobs, they completely ignored the instructions of their relevant ministers in the Mengal administration and followed the instruction of the centre. They were also given the impression that the NAP government is there for a short while and they should not destroy their careers by complying with the orders of the Mengal government in Balochistan.[88] It was this administrative paralysis inflicted upon the Mengal government by the centre that pushed the Mengal government to raise its own rural police, the Balochistan Dehi Mufiz (BMD). According to Bizenjo, the centre was onboard on the decision of the establishment of the BMD, yet, after its establishment, it strongly objected to this force and called it a private army of the NAP.[89] Ironically though, once the Mengal government was dissolved, the PPP government retained this force after sacking its chief, Colonel Sultan Muhammad Mengal, and changing its name to Balochistan Reserved Police. In 1981, Sardar Mengal in conversation with Tariq Ali said; "When we tried to correct the balance in the Police force, Bhutto and his Punjabi aide Khar organized a police strike against our government."[90] The governor of Punjab, according to Sardar Mengal, was following a plan to create problems for the Mengal government in Balochistan. It was Khar, according to Sardar Ataullah Mengal, who withdrew the Punjabi civil servants from Balochistan and not the Mengal government. By doing this, he wanted to create an administrative vacuum in the province which would have made the Mengal government's functioning very difficult, if not impossible. This decision was followed by the police strike,[91] which according to Mengal was again instigated by Bhutto and his aide Khar.

110 *Centre–Province relations post-independence*

Ataullah Mengal's stance on this whole issue conveniently ignores the fact that sending the non-local government servants back to their provinces was an electoral promise of NAP Balochistan.

According to this narrative, the law and order problem in the Pat Feeder area and in Las Bela was instigated by the PPP government in the centre.[92] The NAP leadership also accused Bhutto of being the mastermind behind the Jamote uprising against the Mengal government. Ghaus Bakhsh Bizenjo in a speech in March 1973 stated:

> The Lasbela incident is there for everyone to see. In Lasbela, the Muslim Leaguers led by Qayyum Khan paid the Jamote bribe money and provided weapons so that they could rise against the Baloch government and Governor Rule could be imposed in the province. I issued warrants against the miscreants but they were not implemented. When we asked the provincial militia to apprehend the miscreants, the centre did not allow the militia to do so. Thus, the only option left for us was to call upon our people to suppress the rebellion. The people were successful but even then the democratic government of Balochistan was dismissed.[93]

Ghaus Bakhsh Bizenjo further alleged that the aim of this move was to put Balochistan under the governor rule. When the BDM and other provincial resources came in to resolve the situation, the federal government intervened. Despite this, the Mengal government was able to eliminate the problem,[94] but then it was accused of instigating a civil war in the province.[95]

The NAP leadership in Balochistan also questioned how the PPP, which had no elected representative in the Balochistan assembly in 1970,[96] managed to have a majority in 1974[97] despite the fact that no elections took place during this period. This was achieved, according to them, by unconstitutional means such as use of force, blackmail and political and monetary bribes. The appointment of Jam Ghulam Qadir as the Chief Minister of Balochistan was made by breaching almost every clause of the constitution.[98]

The NAP leadership in Balochistan also accused Bhutto of double standards. Bhutto, according to them blamed the sardars of being the main reason behind the Balochistan crisis and the backwardness of the province as they do not want to lose their grip on the province. However, all his supporters and allies in Balochistan were sardars.[99] Jam of Lasbela, Jam Ghulam Qadir, sardar of Zarakzais, Sardar Doda Khan Zarakzai, sardar of the Bugtis, Nawab Akbar Khan Bugti and Khan-e-Baloch, Mir Ahmed Yar Khan were in Bhutto's camp. The NAP leader, Wali Khan, in an interview stated that: Bhutto claimed that he is against the sardari system. According to him (Bhutto), Bizenjo was removed because he was a sardar – which he was not. But then he replaced Bizenjo with Akbar Bugti – a really big sardar. Akbar Bugti was a bigger sardar than Bizenjo, and now, of course, he has the Khan of Kalat, the Khan of all sardars put together, and yet Mr. Bhutto claims that he is totally against the sardars and the sardari system.[100]

Centre–Balochistan Relations (1969–77)   111

The rivalry between Nawab Bugti and Bizenjo, Sardar Mengal and Nawab Marri also was a factor in the developments which took place in Balochistan. According to Bizenjo, Bhutto had been all too willing to believe the exaggerated stories Akbar Bugti fed him about a guerrilla army being raised in Balochistan. Bugti's motivation was thwarted ambition, according to Bizenjo, since the NAP had refused to make him the governor under the deal they had struck with Bhutto for the formation of the NAP–JUI government in Balochistan. Akbar Bugti was duly rewarded for his anti-NAP activities by being made the governor after the NAP government was dismissed.[101]

As regards the discovery of the arms cache from the Iraqi embassy, the Baloch narrative was that it was all a set-up. It was part of a conspiracy against the NAP government in Balochistan.[102] No proof that these arms were for the Baloch insurgents were ever found, not even after the arrest of the NAP leaders and the Hyderabad trial, or later under General Zia.[103]

Baloch nationalists also argued that the Shah of Iran was also part of the conspiracy against the nationalist government in Balochistan. According to this line of reasoning, the Shah of Iran assumed that a nationalist government in Pakistani Balochistan would encourage the Iranian Baloch to stir up trouble in their area. According to Harrison,

> Bhutto told me in 1977 interview that the Shah had been very insistent, even threatening, and he promised us all sorts of economic and military help, much more than we actually got. He felt strongly that letting the Baloch have provincial self-government was not only dangerous in itself, for Pakistan, but would give his Baloch dangerous ideas.[104]

Sardar Ataullah Mengal in particular and the national Baloch leadership in general also opined that another reason for the illegal sacking of the NAP government in Balochistan was the fact that the people were witnessing how in the two provinces, namely NWFP and Balochistan, where the NAP was in control, educational, land and labour reforms were taking place and things were improving as compared to the two provinces, Punjab and Sindh, where the PPP was ruling, everything was a mass.[105] The NAP Balochistan leadership categorically rejected the claim that the Baloch insurgents were fighting for independence or separation of Balochistan from Pakistan.[106] All they wanted was a province in which they have full provincial autonomy and control of their wealth and a federal system in which the centre would only take care of defence, foreign affairs, communication and currency.[107]

WHY THE BALOCH LEADERSHIP FAILED?

The 1970 election was the first opportunity the Baloch leadership got to run their province. As political affiliations and allegiances were based on tribal loyalties, there was no solid political base, and the promises made during the election

112 *Centre–Province relations post-independence*

campaign were rather emotional than grounded in socio-economic realities of the area. Barring Bizenjo, the NAP leadership in Balochistan had no political training and lacked any administrative experience. A closer look at the dynamics of the Baloch political landscape of the 1970s indicate that the NAP Balochistan government suffered from four weaknesses and these weaknesses played a paramount role in its downfall.

Tribal feuds

The Baloch society is primarily a tribal society and the leadership of NAP Balochistan included Sardar Ataullah Mengal and Nawab Khair Bakhsh Marri, two of the most prominent Baloch sardars. The NAP Balochistan leadership could not rise above the tribal level. The Pat Feeder incident, which made headlines during the NAP government as a conflict between the locals and non-locals, was actually a result of a long-standing tribal rivalry. What is ironic is that it was a Baloch sardar, Sardar Ghous Bakhsh Raisani, who projected it as a conflict between the locals and the non-locals.[108]

The differences between the Mengals and the Zehris and Zarakzais, who had been close to Islamabad since the days of General Ayub Khan,[109] culminated into Doda Khan Zarakzai establishing a parallel government in the Jhalawan area.[110] When Governor Bizenjo accused Nabi Bakhsh Zehri of providing arms and ammunition to Doda Khan and declared that the provincial government would soon take steps against Doda Khan, Doda Khan responded with a promise of a bloodbath if the provincial government moved against him.[111]

The fact that the insurgent violence during the 1973–77 took place and mostly remained limited to a certain area was a clear indication of the fact that a number of Baloch tribes and tribal leaders were not supportive of the Baloch cause as postulated by the Baloch nationalists.

NAP leadership's lack of political acumen

Barring Ghaus Bakhsh Bizenjo, who started his political career as a student activist during his stay at the Aligarh University, the other two prominent leaders of NAP Balochistan; Sardar Ataullah Mengal and Nawab Khair Bakhsh Marri, were pure and simple tribal sardars without any political training. Another thing which both had in common was their hatred for Bhutto which they never tried to hide, which in itself was an indication of their lack of political acumen.

Bizenjo in a meeting with Sherbaz Mazari expressed his helplessness in this regard. He told Mazari that he tried his utmost to resolve the political crisis in Balochistan, but all his efforts failed because Ataullah Mengal and Nawab Khair Bakhsh Marri who following their sardari mentality, according to which one should never negotiate when one is weak, had such an obstinate attitude towards this.

Bugti–NAP differences

Nawab Akbar Bugti was one of the most prominent members of the new generation of Baloch leaders that emerged during the 1960s. Despite the fact that he could not participate in the 1970 elections due to a legal complication, he was an active member of the NAP Balochistan and not only funded the NAP, but it was mostly because of his influence that the NAP managed to get a respectable presence in the provincial assembly. The first sign of disagreement emerged when the NAP decided not to accept Nawab Bugti's nomination for a reserved seat for women.

However, the differences spiked when Bugti was asked by a junior member to leave the NAP's provincial working committee meeting as he was not a member and Sardar Mengal and Nawab Khair Bakhsh remained silent.[112]

Bizenjo claimed that Bugti wanted to be the Governor of Balochistan, and when the NAP leadership could not comply with his wish, he went against the Mengal government and was rewarded with the governorship by the Bhutto regime.[113]

Bhutto factor

Bhutto also played an important role in the downfall of the NAP government in Balochistan. Bhutto wanted to make the Pakistan Peoples Party the ruling party in the whole country, and the NAP's governments in Balochistan and NWFP were a total abomination to him. His opponents believed that the whole episode of the discovery of weapons from the Iraqi embassy allegedly to be handed over to the Baloch insurgents was a plan prepared by Bhutto himself to use it to discredit and eventually dismiss the NAP government in Balochistan. He was aided in his designs by Sardar Doda Khan Zarakzai, Jam Ghulam Qadir of Lasbela, Nawab Akbar Khan Bugti and Ahmed Yar Khan.

Mengal and Marri's attitude towards Bhutto added to this. According to Sherbaz Mazari:

> I suggested that he seek a rapprochement with the Baloch leaders of NAP. Surprisingly Bhutto now revealed his growing state of despondency. He said, "Who should I talk to?" He then pointed out that Attaullah Mengal openly used "the filthiest of language" against him, adding that it was not just directed at him, 'but also on my office, as after all I am the President of Pakistan." Then he criticized Khair Bakhsh Marri. The Marri sardar, he said, 'is so arrogant that when I talk to him he turns his face away. I find his behavior intolerable.[114]

He did not even trust his one-time ally Nawab Akbar Bugti. After Bugti's resignation from governorship, Bhutto in an interview stated, "(He)... is suffering from schizophrenia. He's frightened now because he betrayed his old friends. 'Politics is a game of chess', 'and Bugti played his chess badly.'"[115]

114 *Centre–Province relations post-independence*

THE ROLE OF REGIONAL COUNTRIES (AFGHANISTAN, IRAN AND USSR)

Pakistan–Afghanistan relations had been problematic since 1947. In keeping with the historical affinity between the Baloch tribes and Afghanistan, that was where they had always sought refuge and support when required. Prince Karim, after declaring mutiny, crossed over to Afghanistan in 1948. Although its support for Pashtunistan is well documented, however, what exactly was Kabul's position on Balochistan was not clear. Despite this lack of clarity, Kabul provided full support to the Baloch insurgents.

After the fatal battle of Chamalang, most of the members including the top leadership of the Parari movement relocated to their safe heavens in southern Afghanistan. Under the patronage of the Daud regime, the Pararis were facilitated. According to Selig Harrison, the Daud regime also paid salaries to Mir Hazar's men.[116] For quite some time, the Pararis used their sanctuaries in Afghanistan as resting places after conducting raids against Pakistani Army positions and conveys.[117] Here, Mir Hazar Ramkhani, leader of the Pararis, revised his strategy, worked out a new plan of action, and renamed the group Baloch People's Liberation Front (BPLF).[118]

Apart from fully supporting the Baloch insurgents, Kabul also warned Islamabad of a war if it continued to target the Baloch guerrillas.[119] Afghan deputy foreign minister Waheed Abdullah in a statement stated that "a number of Baloch refugees have already fled into Afghanistan" and that an increase in the flow "would cause grave problems, not just for Afghanistan, but for the region and the world".[120] If this was not enough, there were some reports that Kabul also tried to get Bhutto assassinated. According to Sherbaz Mazari, a leading Pakistani parliamentarian and a Baloch sardar;

> In August 1974 a BSO student named Majid died in a grenade explosion during a failed attempt to assassinate Bhutto in Quetta. I was to later learn that the Afghans had trained a team of Baloch extremists to kill Bhutto during his visit to the province.[121]

It was a generally held view, especially among the Pakistani scholars that Afghanistan was supporting the Baloch insurgents with the full support and encouragement of the USSR, yet a number of scholars believed that USSR actually never showed much interest in aiding the separatist struggle in Balochistan.[122]

During this phase, the interest, involvement and the role of Iran in Balochistan is often not only mentioned but at times exaggerated by the Western as well as the Baloch scholars. Iran had a Baloch population of its own and Tehran closely observed the development in the Pakistani Balochistan as it was under the impression that the developments in Pakistani Balochistan could have implications for the Iranian Balochistan. This worry could be considered misplaced as the Iranian Baloch were far less organized and strongly under the control of Tehran.[123]

Centre–Balochistan Relations (1969–77) 115

Baloch scholars and writers go to the extent of claiming that Bhutto started the whole operation against the Baloch on the whims of the Shah of Iran and was in fact acting on his behalf. They argue that Iranian pilots flew Iranian helicopters to crush Baloch insurgency during the civil war, and these helicopters provided the key to victory in a crucial battle at Chamalang.

However, many knowledgeable analysts have questioned this assertion.[124] The Bhutto–Shah relationship, their rivalry for presenting themselves as the regional leader and what Bhutto has written about Shah in his writings point to the fact that they were perhaps not as close as this group believed them to be. For instance, Bhutto wrote: "There was an uncomfortable perversity about him," he could be jealous and mean in small things... unrelentingly ruthless and disparaging about personalities... in their absence. ... he could tell a big lie without blinking. He spoke disparagingly about almost all his neighbouring countries and their leaders. ... he had a complex towards me. He respected and feared my capabilities." "Bhutto noted that the Shah was intensely envious of him and even more revealingly, perhaps, of his own fall-that his grandiose designs and fanciful ambitions... contributed in no small measures to his ruin. ... He lost touch with reality."[125]

CONCLUSION

Yahya Khan ended the One Unit and granted Balochistan the status of a province. The general perception is that just like in the rest of the country, the election in Balochistan was free and fair and the Baloch people were given the opportunity to elect their own leaders. The election in Balochistan was contested on tribal lines; hence, it became very clear that there was no chance of any unified Baloch leadership emerging out of this election. The nationalist sardars or leaders of Balochistan (Mengal, Marri along with the seasoned Baloch politician Bizenjo) were part of the National Awami Party (NAP). Their election campaign was more emotional than practical. They promised too much too soon, and that became a source of huge embarrassment for them once they came into power. For instance, they promised in their manifesto that they will abolish shishak and the sardari system. Both of these election promises were impractical, in keeping that the NAP leaders in Balochistan were all sardars and the sardari system was their only source of power and political clout. Same is the issue of shishak. Once they came into power and failed to fulfil their promises, there were violent protests in the province.

The developments that took place during this decade added to the Baloch nationalist narrative which continued to evolve since Khan of Kalat joined Pakistan. Contrary to what actually happened (detailed in the relevant chapter), Baloch nationalists claimed that Pakistan actually occupied Kalat and the Khan of Kalat signed the accession document under duress; the developments of the 1950s, especially the treatment of Nauroz Khan and the arrest of Khan Ahmed Yar Khan, added to the Baloch narrative of injustice and grievances. In the Baloch narrative, the decade of 1970s further added to this narrative of injustice. The

116   *Centre–Province relations post-independence*

1970s is the decade of bloodshed and Islamabad's brutal military action against the Baloch masses and whatever they held dear. This Baloch narrative expediently ignores that this is also the decade, as amply demonstrated in this chapter, when the Baloch leadership failed to perform. The Baloch nationalist narrative claimed that the NAP or Baloch elected leadership was unsuccessful because the Punjabi establishment, the Pakistan Army and the federal government created problems for them. This claim has the echo of Prince Karim Khan's rationale for taking up arms against the state of Pakistan in 1948.

In this narrative, there is no mention of the infighting, tribal feuds, and miscalculated and impractical decisions made by the Baloch/NAP leadership. The differences between Ataullah Mengal and Akbar Bugti and how Bugti sided with Bhutto against his own fellow Baloch sardars played an important role in the events which followed. The tribal feuds and the clashes between the Jamotes and Mengals, the role of the Zehri brothers and the tribal way Mengal as CM reacted to all these problems by mobilizing a Mengal lashkar against them are cases in point.

There is no denying the fact that Bhutto also contributed to the problems the NAP faced. He wanted the PPP to be the single power in the country and Pakistan to be a single-party country; however, most of his partners in all what he did were Baloch sardars: Raisani, Akbar Bugti and none other than Ahmed Yar Khan.

The NAP government in Balochistan took decisions which were untimely and unwise. For instance, the decision to send all the non-Baloch government servants back to their parent departments or provinces was not a wise decision, especially when they knew that they do not have the trained manpower in Balochistan.

The same happened with their armed struggle. It collapsed primarily under the weight of its internal contradictions. The goals of the Baloch movement also remained inconsistent, ranging from provincial autonomy to the demand for an independent Balochistan. The Baloch Peoples Liberation Front (BPLF), the Baloch Students Organization (BSO) and the NAP remained divided on both the means and ends of the struggle. The BPLF and the BSO epitomized the militant face of the Baloch movement and engaged in guerrilla warfare against the state, while the NAP represented the moderate side of the struggle and stood for greater autonomy for the Baloch within the constitutional framework of Pakistan. While these factors stood to weaken the movement at one level, they also simplified the task of the federal agencies in overcoming the Baloch resistance.

At the national level, the situation in Balochistan and Bhutto's decision to send the Pakistan Army there undermined his own attempt to establish civilian supremacy. Bhutto's handling of political developments in Balochistan has been regarded by a number of writers as representing the Achilles heel of his regime. His dispatch of around 80,000 troops into the sparsely populated province of fewer than 5 million people to deal with the tribal/autonomist insurrection of 1973–76 returned the army to a political role. Many viewed this heavy handed use of force carrying echoes of Yahya's ill-conceived actions in erstwhile East Pakistan.

One can conclude that it was Bhutto's Balochistan policy which contributed in his downfall. General Zia, in a peaceful coup dubbed Operation Fair Play

Centre–Balochistan Relations (1969–77) 117

overthrew Bhutto government, suspended the constitution and dissolved the parliament. Thus began a new era in Pakistan's history which forever transformed the country. This would be discussed in the next chapter.

Notes

1 Khalid bin Sayeed, *Politics in Pakistan: The Nature and Direction of Change*, 91.
2 Macsarenhas, *The Rape of Bangladesh* (New Delhi, 1971), 56.
3 Choudhury, *The Last Days of United Pakistan*, 128.
4 Sherbaz Mazari, *A Journey to Disillusionment* (Karachi: OUP, 1999), 243.
5 Ibid., 242.
6 Ian Talbot, *Pakistan: A Modern History* (London: Hurst, 2005).
7 Mazari, *A Journey to Disillusionment*, 174–75.
8 Nawaz, *Pakistan Army*, 329.
9 G.W. Choudhury, *The Last Days of United Pakistan* (London: Hurst, 1974); Lawrence Ziring, *Pakistan in the Twentieth Century: A Political History* (Karachi: OUP, 1997); Sisson and Rose, *War and Secession*, 275; Ayesha Jalal, *The State of Martial Rule: The Origins of Pakistan Political Economy of Defence* (Cambridge, 1992), 310; and Hasan Zaheer, *The Separation of East Pakistan*, 147.
10 Ishtiaq Ahmed, *Pakistan The Garrison State, Origins, Evolution, Consequences 1947–2011* (Karachi: OUP, 2013), 203–4.
11 Ibid.
12 Talbot, 216–17.
13 The two non-party members of Bhutto's cabinet were Bengalis, Nurul Amin and Raja Tridev Roy, who were elected to the National Assembly from East Pakistan in 1970. Their inclusion in the cabinet was intended to emphasize Bhutto's refusal to recognize the secession of East Pakistan. See *Keesing's Contemporary Archives*, February 5–12, 1972, Vol. 18, 25091.
14 Ghulam Mustafha Khar, Hayat Mohammed Sherpao, Rasul Baksh Talpur, and Ghaus Baksh Raisani were appointed governors of Punjab, NWFP, Sindh and Balochistan, respectively.
15 *Outlook*, April 29, 1972, 7.
16 *Pakistan Times*, December 23, 1971.
17 *Kessing's Contemporary Archives*, February 5–12, Vol. 18, 25091.
18 *Dawn*, December 25, 1972.
19 *New York Times*, December 30, 1971.
20 *Pakistan Times*, December 29, 1971.
21 *Dawn*, March 7, 1972.
22 *Kessing's Contemporary Archives*, July 8–15, 1972, Vol. 18, 25359.
23 *Dawn*, April 12, 1972.
24 *Outlook*, April 15, 1972, 4.
25 *Outlook*, April 22, 1972.
26 The Interim constitution of the Islamic Republic of Pakistan 1972; *Pakistan Times*, April 18, 1972.
27 *Pakistan Times*, June 23, 1972.
28 Hafeez Malik, "The Emergence of the Federal Pattern in Pakistan," in *Contemporary Problems in Pakistan*, ed. W. J. Korsin (Lieden: J. Brill, 1974), 52.
29 Sayeed, 91.
30 Ishtiaq, 213.
31 According to the tribal hierarchy, Khair Bakhsh Marri was a superior sardar. However, Bhutto was not only a minor wadero, but also the head of the state.
32 Rafi Raza, *Zulfikar Ali Bhutto* (Karachi: OUP), 153.

118 *Centre–Province relations post-independence*

33 Mazari, 243–44.
34 Ibid.
35 Ibid.
36 Government of Pakistan, *White Paper on Balochistan* (Rawalpindi: Government of Pakistan, October 1974), 9.
37 *Outlook*, November 11, 1972.
38 *Outlook*, December 9, 1972.
39 *Dawn*, January 27, 1973.
40 *Dawn*, January 28, 1973.
41 *Dawn*, February 10, 1973.
42 A. B. Awan, *Balochistan: Historical and Political Process* (London: New Century Publisher, 1985).
43 *Dawn*, Karachi, September 11, 1972; Farhan H. Siddiqi, *The Politics of Ethnicity in Pakistan* (London: Routledge, 2012), 65.
44 *Dawn*, February 11, 1973.
45 On 20 October 2013, Bangladeshi Prime Minister Ms Shaikh Hasina Wajid awarded Sashanka S. Banerjee the Friends of Bangladesh Liberation War Award. He is author of *India, Mujibur Rehman, Bangladesh Liberation & Pakistan: A Political Treatise* (Createspace Publishers, 2011).
46 Sashanka S. Banerjee, "As Bangladesh Became Free on December 16, 1971, a Secret London Conclave Mooted Balochistan's Liberation," *The Wire*, December 16, 2016, https://thewire.in/87253/bangladesh-1971-balochistan-india-london/.
47 Ibid.
48 Ibid.
49 Ibid.
50 Ibid.
51 Ibid.
52 Wolpert, *Zulfi Bhutto of Pakistan*, op.cit.
53 Anonymous report on Baluchistan, enclosed by Governor M.A.K. Bugti in his letter of 3 August 1973 to President Z.A. Bhutto held in BFLA, as quoted by Wolpert.
54 Wolpert, 225.
55 Ibid., 230.
56 *Dawn*, January 1, 1976.
57 *Dawn*, April 9, 1976.
58 *White Paper on the Performance of the Bhutto Regime*, Misuse of the Instruments of State Power, (Islamabad: Government of Pakistan, 1979); Islamic Republic of Pakistan, *An Amnesty International Report Including the Findings of a Mission to Pakistan 23 April–12 May 1976* (London: Amnesty International, 1977), 41; and Khalid B. Sayed, *Politics in Pakistan: The Nature and Direction of Change* (New York: Praeger, 1980), 134.
59 Ibid.
60 Harrison, 36.
61 Ibid.
62 *White Paper*, 23.
63 *Dawn*, Karachi, May 19, 1973.
64 Harrison, *In Afghanistan's Shadow*, 33–34.
65 Ibid.
66 Ibid., 38.
67 Baluchistan Revolt over, Bhutto says, *Washington Post*, October 17, 1974.
68 Selig S. Harrison, "Nightmare in Baluchistan," *Foreign Policy*, no. 32 (Fall 1978): 138–39.
69 *White Paper*, 25.
70 Shuja, 333.

Centre–Balochistan Relations (1969–77) 119

71 Ibid., 334.
72 A. B. Awan, *Balochistan: Historical and Political Processes* (London: New Century Publishers, 1985), 229–300; and Shuja, 335.
73 Taj Muhammad Breseeg, *Baloch Nationalism Origin and Development* (Karachi: Royal Book Company, 2004).
74 *White Paper.*
75 Prime Minister Zulfikar Ali Bhutto's Speech in the parliament, Situation in Baluchistan, April 26, 1976, Ministry of Information and Broadcasting, Directorate of Research, Reference & Publications, Government of Pakistan, Islamabad.
76 Ishtiaq, 214.
77 Ibid.
78 Prime Minister Zulfikar Ali Bhutto's Speech in the parliament, Situation in Baluchistan, April 26, 1976, Ministry of Information and Broadcasting, Directorate of Research, Reference & Publications, Government of Pakistan, Islamabad.
79 Ibid.
80 Stanley Wolpert, *Zulfi Bhutto of Pakistan His life and Times* (New York: OUP, 1993), 217.
81 *White Paper*, 2.
82 Ibid., 136.
83 Ibid., 15.
84 Ibid., 25.
85 Ibid., 41–42.
86 *Friday Times*, April 18–24, 1997.
87 M. M. S. Dehwar, *Contemporary History of Balochistan*, 390.
88 Ibid.
89 Ibid.
90 Tariq Ali, 117–18.
91 Zainab Rizvi, *The Last Warrior*, 24.
92 Janmahmad, *Essay on Baloch National Struggle in Pakistan*, 301–2.
93 T. Bizenjo, *Bab-e-Balochistan: Statements, Speeches and Interviews of Mir Ghous Bux Bizenjo* (Quetta: Sales and Services, 1999), 75.
94 Ibid.
95 S. Mahmud Ali, *The Fearful State*, 145–46.
96 Talbot, 200.
97 *People's Front*, 2, no. 6–7 (1975).
98 Sardar Muhammad Ishaq Khan, ed., *The Constitution of Islamic Republic of Pakistan* (Lahore, 1973); and *People's Front*, London, 2, no. 6–7 (1975).
99 Ibid., 39.
100 *People's Front*, 2, no. 1 (1974): 4.
101 Breegs, 325.
102 Harrison, 35.
103 Dehwar, 399.
104 Harrison, 97.
105 *People's Front*, 3.
106 Breegs, 336.
107 Aziz Bugti, *Tarikh-e-Balochistan*, 126–30; and Breegs, 337.
108 *Dawn*, December 7, 1972.
109 Awan, 268.
110 Ibid.
111 "Militia Goes into Action Against Baluchi Tribes," *Dawn*, Karachi, December 3, 1972.
112 Mazari, 240–41.
113 Breegs, 325.

120 *Centre–Province relations post-independence*

114 Mazari, 308–9.
115 Ibid., 327, also see; *Christian Science Monitor*, December 14, 1973.
116 Mazari, 81.
117 Harrison, *In Afghanistan's Shadow*, 39.
118 Ibid.
119 Lewis M. Simons, "Afghans Give Warning to Pakistan on Baluchistan," *The Washington Post*, September 24, 1974.
120 Ibid.
121 Mazari.
122 Henry S. Bradsher, *Afghanistan and the Soviet Union* (Durham, NC: Duke Press Policy Studies, 1983), 254–55.
123 Janmahmad, *Essays in Baluch National Struggle in Pakistan: Emergence, Dimensions, Repercussions* (Quetta: Gosha-e-Adab, 1989), 389.
124 Harrison, "Baluch Nationalism and Superpower Rivalry," *International Security* 5, no. 3 (1980–81): 154. Robert Wirsing had questioned the accuracy of this depiction by Harrison and maintained that Iranian-piloted Chinook helicopters played a very minor role in the fighting. R.G. Wirsing, *Pakistan's Security under Zia: The Policy Imperatives of a Peripheral Asian State* (Basingstoke, 1991), 105–6.
125 Wolpert, 210.

5 Balochistan and the peace interval (1977–99)

INTRODUCTION

This chapter covers the longest and the only peace interval in centre–Balochistan relations. The previous chapter detailed the developments which took place during the 1970s after Balochistan was granted the status of a province, and the nationalist leadership managed to establish the provincial government, *though short lived*, in Balochistan. The dismissal of the provincial government and a number of other developments resulted in the bloodiest phase of Baloch history in recent times. However, this period was followed by a peaceful period which lasted for almost 23 years (1977–99).

During the peace interval in Balochistan, hardly anything changed for the common Baloch and the province of Balochistan, yet it remained peaceful. There are a number of reasons for this: divisions in the political and militant leadership of the Baloch nationalist movement, two of the three Baloch nationalist leaders left Balochistan and started living in London, the Soviet invasion of Afghanistan and the Afghan war. As a result, the Pakistan Army concentrated more on Balochistan because it was considered a possible target of the Red Army. During the second phase of the peace interval, Pakistan went through its decade of democracy (1988–99). Baloch leaders participated in the political activities in the country, and a number of Baloch sardars and politicians such as Akbar Bugti, Bizenjo and Zafarullah Khan Jamali emerged as national-level politicians and played a significant role in the Pakistani politics. The Baloch nationalist narrative is silent on these developments. Instead, it focuses on the influx of the Afghan (Pashtun) refugees during the Afghan war and the change in population figures in Balochistan. Regarding the second part of the peace interval, the narrative claims that the centre continued to interfere in provincial matters because of which the Baloch elected representatives could not perform. In this narrative, no mention is made of why, for instance, Akhtar Mengal not only continued to contest elections but became the chief minister of the province, why a number of prominent Baloch politicians were participating in politics at the national level and the absence of nationalist/insurgent violence in Balochistan.

This chapter argues that although Zia-ul-Haq channelled in a lot of money into Balochistan in the shape of developmental projects, his main concerns was strategic

122 *Centre–Province relations post-independence*

as he could not afford any trouble in Balochistan in the wake of the Soviet presence in Afghanistan. During the decade of democracy, Balochistan was never a major issue for the central and/or the Baloch provincial governments which continued to conduct business as usual. During this phase, a number of elections took place in which the Baloch leaders fully participated. Nationalist leaders and their sons actively participated and supported their candidates in the elections and became chief minister of the province (Akhtar Mengal is a case in point). A number of Baloch politicians for the first time in Pakistani history participated in the politics at the national level. This all happened without any significant change in the lives of the Baloch people, and they continued to follow the same system of governance. The only reason which explains the absence of violence and Baloch participation in politics is that during this period the centre decided not to follow a policy of confrontation and pursued a policy of engagement. Hence, there was no sparking or triggering event using which the Baloch leader could continue or start a new wave of violent conflict. Another point which proves this point is that a number of projects and developments that later became contributing reasons for the return of insurgency in Balochistan actually started during this period, but no major violence took place.

The chapter is divided into two parts: the first part looks at the Zia era and the policies pursued by him and the decade of democracy and the political development which took place during this period and the trends that emerged in the evolving political culture of Pakistan; the second section, which is the main body of the chapter, details the strategic and political developments in Balochistan during this time.

ZIA AND PAKISTAN

When Bhutto appointed General Zia-ul-Haq as the Chief of Army Staff superseding five senior generals, his main consideration was to have a Chief of Army Staff he could trust and who would support his policies. In other words, Bhutto wanted another General Tikka Khan. Apparently, General Zia had all the qualities Bhutto was looking for. General Zia, however, could not fulfil Bhutto's expectation and, in the midst of a political crisis in Pakistan, took over the helm of affairs of Pakistan on 5 July 1977, in a coup d'état code-named Operation Fair Play. Initially, General Zia claimed that he or the army had no intention of staying in power and that elections in Pakistan would be conducted within 90 days. As the political parties and political activities were not banned, political parties including Bhutto's Peoples Party started their campaign. Bhutto who was arrested when his government was toppled on 5 July 1977, in an unprecedented move, was released by the army on 29 July 1977. Bhutto immediately started his campaign and soon regained his lost popularity among the Pakistani people. During the campaign, he repeatedly stated that after making the government, he would ensure that all those who staged the coup against his government were punished. This alarmed General Zia and his fellow coup makers. General Faiz Ali Chishti famously told General Zia that it is either Bhutto's neck or our neck (Army Generals, the Coup makers).

Balochistan and the peace interval (1977–99) 123

This led Zia to change course. Zia now claimed that without accountability, elections in the country would be meaningless. Zia also claimed that his government has found out that the Bhutto regime had committed a number of irregularities and have abused power and used it to silence the political opposition in the country. Zia's new position was supported by the Pakistan National Alliance (PNA) leadership, especially Asghar Khan. After witnessing the resurgence of public support for Bhutto, PNA leadership was not much optimistic about its election prospect.

Zia's view of Pakistan and Pakistani politics

Zia was a practicing Muslim and ideologically close to the Deobandi school, although for some time, he was considered a Jammat Islami sympathizer. General Zia belonged to a middle-class migrant family from Jalandhar in the Indian Punjab and strongly believed that Islam was the only binding force that could keep Pakistan together and that Pakistan can only survive as an Islamized Pakistan. Throughout his regime, he ensured that the centre should hold most of the powers. He used the constitution of 1973 to this advantage and granted tremendous powers to the centre including dismissing a provincial government, a power which Bhutto used to dismiss the NAP government in Balochistan.

Zia was of the opinion that Pakistan was created on the two-nation theory and to establish a state in which Islamic system would be introduced and implemented. Islam, according to Zia, would be and should be the force that would lead the Pakistani state towards national integration.[1] To achieve this objective, Zia believed that a holistic program of Islamization of Pakistan should be devised and implemented. For Zia, the success of the Pakistan National Alliance (PNA)'s political agitation movement against election rigging in Pakistan depended on its use of the language of Islam. The PNA used religious slogans to put its point across. A movement that started as a reaction to the Bhutto government's election rigging in 1977, culminated into demanding Nizam-e-Mustafa (system of Mustafa, another word for Islamic system) for Pakistan. General Zia in his maiden speech stated that this (use of Islam to galvanize the people by the PNA leadership) proved that in Pakistan, only Islam can save the country and the people of Pakistan. For this reason, Islamization of the country's administrative system should be a priority.[2]

He started his process of Islamization with the Pakistan Army and sought to transform it into an Islamic fighting force.[3] At the same time, General Zia claimed that to preserve Islam and the freedom of Pakistan, the Pakistan Army has a vital role to play.[4] Islam now elevated from an ideology for the state of Pakistan to the *raison d'etre* of its existence. Now the propagation of any other ideology would be considered not only treason but also a deliberate attempt to jeopardize the existence of the state of Pakistan.[5] Under the PLO, the advocacy of any secular ideology was prohibited.

Zia in one of his statements stated: "Pakistan and Islam are the names of one and the same thing and any idea or notion contrary to this would mean hitting at the very roots of the ideology, solidarity and integrity of Pakistan."[6]

124 Centre–Province relations post-independence

In a speech in 1980, General Zia emphasized the vital role of Islam in Pakistan's national integration:

> Pakistan was achieved in the name of Islam, and Islam alone could provide the basis to run the government of the country and sustain its integrity...The present government would provide the opportunity to others to serve the country after it had achieved its objectives...(but) no un-Islamic government would be allowed to succeed the present regime.[7]

The emphasis on the role of Islam in Pakistan and the Pakistan's freedom struggle implied that there was no room for ethnic, linguistic and sectarian groups propagating their own views. General Zia once echoed Field Marshal Ayub Khan's (ironically, perhaps the most irreligious and secular of all rulers of Pakistan by that time) words: "One God, one Prophet, one Book, one Country, one system – no discussion."[8]

Political opposition to Zia's regime

General Zia's approach towards Pakistan's politics resulted in the emergence of a number of challengers. The most serious challenger was the Movement for the Restoration of Democracy (MRD), which was established in February 1981. The MRD compromised the Pakistan Peoples Party (PPP), Pakistan National Party (PNP), the Pakistan Democratic Party (PDP), Jamiat-e-Ulema-i-Islam (JUI-Fazlur Rehman group), Qaumi Mahaz-i-Azadi (QMA), Khaksar Tehrik (KT), Muslim League (Malik Qasim group), the Awami National Party (ANP) and the Pakhtoonkhwa National Awami Party (PNAP).

The MRD's leadership, especially from the three smaller provinces: Sindh, NWFP and Balochistan, considered General Zia's policies as another ploy to establish the hegemony of Punjab over the three smaller provinces of Pakistan. Punjab, being the largest province in terms of population was dominating two of the most important institutions of the state of Pakistan. The Pakistan Armed Forces, especially the army and the civil bureaucracy. General Zia's Islamization policy had the largest number of supporters in Punjab as compared to other provinces. This so-called Punjabization of Pakistan, according to this group of political leaders, would have an adverse effect on the national integration of Pakistan.[9]

For quite some time, the MRD posed a serious challenge to General Zia's regime. As a group of different political parties belonging to various sides of the political divide, the MRD had only one uniting factor: opposition to General Zia's regime. However, the MRD soon got bogged down with internal rivalries and political jealousies. Almost all other member political parties in the MRD were suspicious and jealous of the Pakistan Peoples Party's mass following and its leadership's motivation and policies. The PPP's mass following and popularity was larger than all other MRD's political parties put together. The smaller parties were worried that the PPP would overshadow them. Air Marshal (Retired) Asghar Khan-led Tehrik-i-Istiqlal, which was most active and vocal against Bhutto's government against

Balochistan and the peace interval (1977–99) 125

Bhutto's government during the PNA agitation, was the PPP's biggest critic within the MRD. At times, both parties seemed to be struggling against each other than against General Zia's regime. Asghar Khan's approach to this indicated that he considered the PPP as the main obstacle to his rise as a political leader.[10] Therefore, it came as no surprise that Tehrik-i-Istiqlal parted ways with the MRD and applied for the registration of the party as per the Political Parties Amendment Act, 1985.[11]

The MRD's other major problem was its lack of consensus on its demands. When the creation of the MRD was announced in 1981, it demanded the restoration of 1973 constitution. However, Khan Abdul Wali Khan considered the 1973 constitution redundant and demanded that a new constitution that ensured the rights and interests of the smaller provinces should be framed.[12] The heart of the problem was that the MRD's leadership was sharply divided on almost everything, especially on issues like provincial autonomy. It also lacked a clear vision and understanding about the steps required to convert the MRD into a real political alliance with a proper organizational set-up and manifesto.[13]

Therefore, it came as no surprise when the MRD ran out of steam. Apart from the factors mentioned above, lack of popular support, especially in Punjab and NWFP, contributed to its failure.

The Sindhi–Baloch–Pashtun Front (SBPF)

On 18 April 1985, a London-based political party, the Sindhi–Baloch–Pashtun Front (SBPF), was created. It included a member of Peoples Party's stalwarts Hafeez Pirzada who was Bhutto's cabinet minister and a member of the team negotiating with the PNA team during the final days of Bhutto regime and Mumtaz Bhutto, a former Governor and Chief Minister of Sindh. Baloch section of the front was represented by Sardar Ataullah Mengal, a former Chief Minister of Balochistan, whose government was sacked by the Bhutto government. Afzal Bangesh, a Marxist leading a political party, the Mazdoor Kisan Party (Workers Peasants Party), represented the Pashtun section of the front. These four leaders were considered the main pillars of the SBPF.

The SBPF's one-point agenda was to make Pakistan a confederation on the model of the United Arab Emirates (UAE). According to the SBPF, unless this objective is achieved, Pakistan would continue to be dominated by the Punjabis. The SBPF leadership claimed that to end this Punjabization of Pakistan, Pakistan must revert back to the principle laid out in the 1940 Lahore Resolution.[14] Just like Khan Abdul Wali Khan, the SBPF leadership also believed that the 1973 constitution could no longer serve as the constitution of the country as it has failed to ensure the rights and interests of the three smaller provinces of Pakistan. The SBPF argued that in the new political and administrative set-up of the country, the centre should only exercise its control on defence, foreign policy, communications and currency. It should also have arbitration powers in disputes between the states. According to the SBPF, all states should have a right to raise their own militias and security forces.[15] The President of the Confederation, according to

126   *Centre–Province relations post-independence*

the SBPF, would be elected through an alphabetic rotation among the states. The SBPF also strongly argued to keep a check on the armed forces of this proposed confederation. During peace time, defence expenditure would not exceed 3 percent of the GDP.

The SBPF failed to make much impact on ground, and its struggle remained an intellectual endeavour.

Controlled democracy under Zia

To provide some sort of legitimacy to his regime, General Zia in 1984 held a referendum to be elected as the President of Pakistan for the next five years. If the majority of the voters elected Zia as the president for the next term, it would imply that they have also endorsed his Islamization policy. In fact, the question which the voters were asked to answer in a yes or a no was not whether they elect General Zia as the President of Pakistan, but whether they (the voters) endorsed the Islamization policy. A yes answer implied a vote for Zia's next term as President. Official estimates claimed that the voter turnout was 64 percent. Out of this, 96 percent voted a yes. Reuters, on the other hand, claimed that the turnout was close to 10 percent.[16]

As a next step, national and provincial elections were held in 1985. These non-party elections were solely contested on ethnic, business, tribal, class and clan linkages. General Zia appointed Muhammad Khan Junejo as the Prime Minister.[17] Three years later, on 29 May 1988, General Zia dismissed the Junejo government and dissolved the national and provincial assemblies. General Zia once again promised elections within 90 days.

DECADE OF DEMOCRACY (1988–99)

After the death of General Zia in a plane crash on 17 August 1988, the top brass of the Pakistan Army under the leadership of General Mirza Aslam Beg, who assumed the post of COAS, decided that the civilian set-up would continue to function. Ghulam Ishaq Khan, the Chairman of the Senate of Pakistan at the time, was asked to take over as the President of Pakistan. It was also decided that general elections would not be postponed, and 19 November 1988 was announced as the election date.

Soon, political activities and campaigning gained momentum throughout the country. More so, it became quite clear during the election campaign that the real contest would be between Benazir Bhutto-led PPP and Nawaz Sharif and like-minded politicians who established a political alliance, the Islamic Jamhoori Ittehad (IJI).[18] These elections marked the beginning of the decade of democracy (1988–99) in Pakistan. This decade long era of democracy ended with General Musharraf's coup against the Nawaz Sharif government in October 1999.

Although a number of restrictions were imposed on the politicians and certain guarantees were sought before inviting Benazir Bhutto to form a government after the PPP emerged as the victorious party in 1988 election, yet according to many

Balochistan and the peace interval (1977–99) 127

this was the beginning of the journey towards democracy and the two-party system started in Pakistan. Both Benazir Bhutto and Nawaz Sharif served two terms as the Prime Minister of Pakistan. However, both could never finish their terms in office as their governments were sacked.

Return of democratic practices and political musical chair (1988–99)

The PPP won 94 out of 217 National Assembly seats in the 1988 election. After the members for tribal areas, minority groups and women members (from a specified quota of seats for women in the National Assembly of Pakistan) joined the PPP, the figure rose to 122.[19] This made the PPP the single largest majority party in the National Assembly. After some reluctance and intense negotiation, President of Pakistan Ghulam Ishaq Khan invited Benazir Bhutto to form the central government in Pakistan. On 2 December 1988, Benazir Bhutto took oath as the first Muslim woman Prime Minister of Pakistan and the world.[20]

On 6 August 1990, President Ghulam Ishaq Khan, using his power under the article 58 (2-B) of the constitution, dismissed Benazir Bhutto's government.[21] President Ghulam Ishaq Khan accused the Benazir government of abuse of power and corruption. It was widely believed that General Aslam Beg, the then Chief of Army Staff supported President Ghulam Ishaq Khan's decision. In the next election, Nawaz Sharif became the Prime Minister of Pakistan. President Ishaq Khan once again using his presidential power under the article 58 (2-B) of the constitution of Pakistan sacked the Nawaz government on 18 April 1993. Nawaz Sharif went to the Supreme Court of Pakistan against this decision. In an unprecedented move, the Supreme Court restored Nawaz Sharif's government on 26 May 1993.

However, the political crisis continued. General Abdul Waheed Kakar intervened and, instead of imposing martial law, settled the matter with both Ghulam Ishaq Khan and Nawaz Sharif resigning from their posts.[22] The election that followed once again brought Benazir Bhutto at the helm of affairs in Pakistan. Benazir Bhutto managed his confidant and old Bhutto loyalist, Farooq Leghari, to be elected as the new President of Pakistan. Ironically, Farooq Leghari, using the same article 58 (2-B) sacked Benazir Bhutto's government. In the following elections, Nawaz Sharif-led Muslim League won a two-third majority in the National Assembly. Although Farooq Leghari continued as the President of Pakistan, with 165 members supporting the Nawaz government and an understanding with Benazir Bhutto, Nawaz Sharif got the thirteenth amendment to the constitution passed from the parliament which ripped off the President of Pakistan of the power to dismiss a democratically elected government from office. Soon, the Nawaz Sharif government passed another amendment (fourteenth amendment). This amendment subjected the members of the parliament to strict party discipline. This eliminated the chances of removing the prime minister through a no-confidence motion.

128 *Centre–Province relations post-independence*

The emerging trends of political culture of Pakistan during the decade of democracy

During the decade of democracy, certain trends in Pakistan's political landscape emerged. Politics in Pakistan became a zero-sum game in which both ruling and opposition parties, instead of agreeing on rules of the game and strengthening democracy in Pakistan, continued to undermine each other. It was fairly common during this period that political figures were accused of being foreign agents, especially American and Indian agents, and of working against the ideology of Pakistan. Hardly any meaningful legislation took place in the parliament throughout this period. Most of the legislation was done through Presidential ordinances.[23]

Decade of democracy confirmed a number of long-held perceptions about Pakistani politics. Punjab, the most populated province of Pakistan, held the largest number of seats in the National Assembly. Whoever wins the election in Punjab would play the dominant or king-making role in the parliament. The MQM, which was created during General Zia's regime to counter the influence of religious politics in urban Karachi, continued to be the dominant political force in Karachi. In Balochistan, political leadership continued to be in the hands of the tribal sardars. In Pashtun-majority areas of Balochistan, Jamiat-e-Ulema-e-Islam (Fazlur Rehman's group) emerged as the dominant force. Overall, politics and politicians in Pakistan were clearly divided on clan, family, class and ethnic lines, instead of national issues. Due to these factors, national questions during Pakistan's decade of democracy remained unresolved.[24]

During the decade of democracy, due to continued political rivalries between the ruling parties, not much was done to uplift the economy of Pakistan. As a result, the economic bubble which was created during General Zia's era due to the massive aid money coming in during the Afghan jihad busted and Pakistan's economy started showing signs of fatigue.[25] Observers of Pakistani politics are still divided on what caused the failure of the democratic regimes to perform: *lack of grass root political institutions, nature of the society and state of Pakistan, law and order problems, imbalance between institutions and limited powers of political leadership and the struggling economy of Pakistan.*[26]

Balochistan remained part of this political musical chair. A number of provincial governments were changed along with the national governments. Baloch politicians, especially representing opposition, continued to complain about centre's continuous and persistent intrusion into provincial affairs.[27]

During the decade of democracy, three political trends with regard to Balochistan emerged: *first*, politicians in Balochistan, regardless of their party affiliation, demonstrated their eagerness to stay in power. At times in Balochistan, parties that were opposing each other in the National Assembly were coalition partners in the provincial assembly of Balochistan. On occasions, all members of the ruling party in the provincial assembly were ministers; or all members of the provincial assembly were in government. *Second*, a number of prominent Baloch politicians such as Nawab Akbar Bugti, Zafarullah Khan Jamali and Ghaus Bakhsh Bizenjo emerged as national-level politicians and actively participated in the national politics of Pakistan. *Third*, sons of staunch nationalist leaders Sardar Ataullah Mengal and Nawab Khair Bakhsh Marri, with their fathers' approval, actively participated in Balochistan politics. Sardar Akhtar Mengal served as the Chief Minister of Balochistan.

BALOCHISTAN DURING THE PEACE INTERVAL (1988–99)

General Zia's approach and policy towards the Baloch issue

General Zia had a particular vision for Pakistan in which there was no room for ethnic differences. For him, Pakistan could only be united under the banner of Islam. For him, the only identity that should matter in Pakistan was Muslim. Zia believed that if Pakistan were to become a strong, unified Pakistan, then the people of Pakistan must abandon their differences and should stand united as a nation. He believed that the One Unit policy provided the best solution to Pakistan's national integration. He, however, also made it clear that for the sake of national unity, he would not reinvent the wheel and alter the constitution of 1973. He also rejected suggestions to amend the constitution so that the central government could not dismiss the provincial government. He was of the view that making any changes to the constitution would be opening a Pandora's box.

As regards the political crisis and insurgency in Balochistan, General Zia believed that both Zulfiqar Ali Bhutto and Baloch nationalist leaders Nawab Khair Bakhsh Marri, Sardar Ataullah Mengal and Ghaus Bakhsh Bizenjo were at fault. Bhutto could not accept the fact that the NAP, not the PPP, was the majority party in Balochistan, and the NAP leadership, on the other hand, lacking any political experience, acted as ruling their tribal fiefdom. They ignored the fact the Balochistan was part of Pakistan. They insisted on over-stepping their constitutional rights and obligations and insisting on having their own policy, openly providing arms to their tribesman and blocking federal/central government's departments' and forces' access to Balochistan. Despite all this, General Zia was of the view that the problem of Balochistan was primarily a political problem and should have been addressed/resolved using political means.

Bhutto, in General Zia's view, infact used NAP's Baloch leadership's lack of political acumen and outsmarted them. Therefore, according to General Zia, it was not the constitution that was lacking or that it did not provide enough rights to the province. He was quoted as saying that if something is not implemented properly, you should not blame the system.

According to Selig Harrison, General Zia in several conversations with him between 1978 and 1980 detailed his views about Balochistan. General Zia, according to Harrison, differentiated between Balochistan as a geographic entity and the Baloch, the people of Balochistan.[28] According to Selig Harrison, Zia believed that Balochistan was strategically and militarily too important for Pakistan. It had ample energy and mineral resources that the whole Pakistan required. Balochistan's total population equals the population of Lahore, in Punjab. Baloch are citizens of Pakistan and can go anywhere in Pakistan to work.

130   *Centre–Province relations post-independence*

Baloch problem, according to General Zia, was the threat of a possible Soviet invasion into Balochistan.[29]

General Zia's approach and policy towards Balochistan was visibly different from Bhutto's policy. However, with hindsight one could argue that other than the difference in approach about how to deal with Balochistan, General Zia's policy regarding Balochistan was based on its geo-strategic significance. This multiplied with the possibility, though remote, of a possible Soviet invasion of Balochistan.

Releasing the Baloch prisoners and general amnesty to the insurgents

General Zia considered Bhutto's heavy-handed approach towards Balochistan counterproductive. Bhutto, on the other hand, claimed that it was General Zia who stopped him from withdrawing the army from Balochistan. He claimed that General Zia argued that after sacrificing so much, if the army withdrew without achieving the objective, it would have adverse effect on the morale of the soldiers.

However, soon after taking over the helm of affairs, General Zia adopted a cautious and visibly more accommodative policy towards Balochistan. He released Sardar Ataullah Mengal, Sardar Khair Bakhsh Marri and Ghaus Bakhsh Bizenjo. General Zia also ordered the release of almost 6000 Baloch prisoners held captive in Kohlu and Loralei prisons. Going one step further, in January 1978, General Zia declared general amnesty for all Baloch insurgents and dissolved the infamous Hyderabad Tribunal investigating treason charges against the NAP's top leadership: Khan Abdulwali Khan, Ghulam Muhammad Balore, Ghaus Bakhsh Bizenjo, Sardar Khair Bakhsh Marri, and Sardar Ataullah Mengal, among others. All charges and cases against them were dropped. A score of other political prisoners were released.[30] According to some reports, he also decided to withdraw army from Balochistan.

General Zia also tried to establish direct contacts with the Baloch leaders and started pouring developmental funds into Balochistan. He tried to convince the Baloch leaders that the army never favoured military action in Balochistan, and General Zia personally tried to convince Bhutto that he should resolve the Baloch problem through political means.

Zia's initial contact with Ataullah Mengal and Khair Bakhsh Marri

After Ataullah Mengal, Khair Bakhsh Marri and Ghaus Bakhsh Bizenjo were released by General Zia in 1977, General Zia was hopeful that he would be able to reach a mutually agreeable understanding with them. However, it seemed that the Baloch sardars have not learned any lessons from the events that took place in Balochistan in the last four years (1973–77) and talked in absolute terms. They insisted on the removal of Raja Ahmed Khan, Chief Secretary of Balochistan, a Punjabi, from this position. General Zia refused to accept this demand. To accommodate the Baloch leaders, he appointed Lt. General Rahimuddin Khan as the new Governor of Balochistan. This was considered inadequate by Sardar

Balochistan and the peace interval (1977–99) 131

Ataullah Mengal and Khair Bakhsh Marri. They believed that despite this change, Balochistan would continue to be ruled by Punjabi officers.[31]

As a consequence of this inflexibility demonstrated by the Baloch leaders, especially Sardar Ataullah Mengal and Nawab Khair Bakhsh Marri, the talks were halted and eventually failed in 1978.

Finding other allies in Balochistan

After the failure of General Zia's dialogue with Marri–Bizenjo–Mengal trio in 1978, General Zia started his search for new political allies in Balochistan. General Zia was aware of the tribal feuds and rivalries and also that a number of other Baloch sardars do not share Sardar Ataullah Mengal and Nawab Khair Bakhsh Marri's political views and would be more accommodating and forthcoming with the centre. Such tribes were the Zarkzai and Jamali. Doda Khan Zarkzai had been a supporter of centre's policy towards Balochistan and had been close to Islamabad.[32] The Jamali were also considered close to the centre and were willing to support General Zia's effort in Balochistan.

After initial contacts were maintained and an understanding reached, General Zia visited Quetta on 29 July 1979. During this visit, he met with various Baloch notables. It was reported that almost all of these Baloch notables urged General Zia to remain in office.[33]

At the time, especially in Balochistan, it was rumoured that General Zia, Sardars Ataullah Mengal, and Khair Bakhsh Marri have reached a secret understanding. Under the secret deal, General Zia had permitted Nawab Khair Bakhsh Marri, Ataullah Mengal and General Sharoff to leave the country.[34] It was also believed by some Baloch political activists that General Zia had also cultivated contacts with the Baloch Student Organization (BSO). According to this line of reasoning, Balochistan government's recent attempts to provide jobs to Baloch graduates and students were part of this understanding.[35]

Pakistan and the Soviet Union's invasion of Afghanistan

On 27 December 1979, Soviet forces invaded Afghanistan. Pakistani defence planner's worst nightmare scenario and long-held fear had materialized. Pakistan was now sandwiched between two enemies: India and USSR. This event had significant implications for global peace and the USA, which was engaged in the so-called Cold War with the USSR. Villanova University Professor Hafeez Malik summed up Pakistan's dilemma:

> the consolidation of the Soviet hold on Afghanistan, along with the Indo-Soviet treaty of friendship would enable the two powers to crush Pakistan in their future pincer movement; Afghanistan, with the accretion of Soviet protection and support for its armed forces, would become unmanageable for Pakistan; ideologically Pakistan would become vulnerable to a socialist revolution.[36]

132   Centre–Province relations post-independence

Pakistani security policy makers just like their Western, especially the American, allies believed that the Soviets wanted to reach the warm waters of the Indian Ocean. Pakistan's defence planners worked out three possible routes of an invading Soviet Army. Two of these passed through Balochistan: from Khjoak and Bolan passes to Sukkur and Karachi or Quetta to Karachi via the RCD highway.

Pakistan's threat perception was not totally ill-founded. Being a member of the American block, it has been threatened of grave consequences by top Soviet leadership in the past.[37] The USSR has, in the past, blown both soft and hard by signalling open hostility and by helping Pakistan in its economic and industrial activities.

Balochistan has been of particular interest to the USSR. Mir Ahmed Yar Khan as early as 1948 warned that the Soviets were eyeing the Gwadar area in Makran coastal area of Balochistan. Interestingly, in the 1960s, the issue of Soviet interest in Gwadar re-emerged. This time it rang alarm bells in India. A few members of the Lok Sabha (the Indian parliament) raised the question of Soviet Union's naval presence in the Gwadar area and that the USSR is building a naval base in Gwadar. These members were particularly concerned about the implication of this development on India, an ally of the Soviet Union. The Indian government in response to these questions stated that the USSR, according to reports was only helping the development of the port. In 1969, with visible improvement in Pakistan–Russia relations, one of the projects which were discussed between Islamabad and Moscow was a highway linking Chaman to Makran Coast. The USSR also offered to build a port at Gwadar.[38]

According to another report which is mostly contested by observers of Pakistan's foreign policy and politics, Zulfiqar Ali Bhutto, who by the end of his era (1972–77) became increasingly suspicious of the Americans and suspected American hand in the political agitation against him and his government, reached a deal on Gwadar with the USSR.[39] The deal included Soviet Union's pledge to support Pakistan in its dispute with India on Kashmir, help resolve the Pashtunistan problem and that the USSR would arm the Pakistan Armed Forces. Eventually, Pakistan would join the Soviet bloc. Even after the fall of Bhutto, the USSR renewed its offer to General Zia who declined the offer.

Balochistan in the wake of Soviet invasion of Afghanistan

A huge set of literature is available on the implications of Pakistan's extensive involvement in Afghanistan.[40] Pakistan not only hosted more than three million Afghan refugees, Islamabad's continued involvement in the Afghan jihad adversely affected Pakistan's society. Most affected with this huge Afghan refugee influx were the provinces of NWFP and Balochistan. The influx of Afghan refugees, most of them ethnic Pashtuns, adversely affected the demographics in Balochistan. Pakistan received huge amounts of aid during the Afghan jihad against the Soviet Army. The uneven distribution of this aid money further widened the rift between Punjab and the smaller provinces, especially Balochistan and the NFWP. Late Khan Abdul Wali Khan summed up this resentment by comparing

Balochistan and the peace interval (1977–99)   133

the Afghan refugees with a cow. According to Wali Khan, the Frontier (NWFP) was holding the horns of the cow while Punjab its teats.[41]

Baloch nationalists also observed the Soviet invasion of Afghanistan and their options. Sardar Ataullah Mengal was willing to support and accept the Soviet ingress into Pakistan from Afghanistan:

> Punjabi domination...means tens of thousands of them coming in civil servants and army fellows telling you what to do, people from Lahore buying up our farms, buying the best lands in Quetta, more and more of them crawling all over us, annihilating us. We Baloch must choose, ... between losing our identity at the mercy of the Punjabi or stretching our hands to others. If the Russians came, he said, If it comes to that conclusion, we might at least have some kind of conditional freedom. They may send their technocrats and their soldiers, but they would not send a whole population to occupy Balochistan as the Punjabis are doing, step by step. Russia is too far away. They might do some good things, they might educate our children. What "freedom" do we have to lose?...we know there is a difference getting freedom and changing masters. But would the Americans be better?...and would no doubt insist on having military bases, perhaps the Americans would be satisfied if they could just keep the Russians out. They might not be as bad.[42]

The Americans realized Balochistan's strategic significance even before the creation of Pakistan. After the Soviet invasion of Afghanistan, this strategic significance of Balochistan multiplied. Zbigniew Brzezinski, the then American National Security Adviser, believed that the Soviets would soon advance towards Balochistan and would be in a position to control maritime movement in the Indian Ocean. To counter such an eventuality, Admiral Thomas Moore, US Naval Chief suggested building a naval base in Gwadar.[43]

Centre's economic and development policy towards Balochistan

It was noted in the previous chapter that Bhutto time and again took pride in the fact that he had invested heavily in the development of Balochistan and done more for Balochistan than any previous government of Pakistan. His government's particular emphasis was on the construction of new roads. General Zia's government, however, claimed that until 1977 not much was done in this regard and what little has been done was due to Pakistan Army's efforts.

Throughout General Zia's period, especially due to Balochistan's reinforced strategic significance, Balochistan's economic and developmental share expanded. For the first time since gas was discovered in the 1950s, it was supplied to Quetta, the airport was updated with facilities to handle more and large flights, and a TV station was established. Due to the changed circumstances in the wake of the Soviet occupation of Afghanistan, apart from Pakistan's regular five-year plan, in 1980, a Special Development Plan for Balochistan was announced. The Special

134   *Centre–Province relations post-independence*

Plan alluded to the urgent need to uplift the living and social condition of the Baloch. The plan emphasized the construction of new and the improvement of existing infrastructure and transportation routes. It did not hide the fact that some of it might be used to strengthen Pakistan's defence along its Afghanistan border.[44] Once again, as was the case in the past, road construction in Balochistan was among the top priorities of the central government. Makran and its coastal routes received special attention.

As per the new plan in which Rs. 82,972 million (4.6 million US dollars) was allocated for improving and building new transportation and communication infrastructure in Balochistan, Liyari to Ormara–Karachi–Pasni–Gwadar highway was to be improved. Rs. 742 million was allocated for the construction of a Kohlu–Kahan road. Going through the Marri territory, this road, according to the central government would play an important role in the economic uplift of Balochistan by facilitating the oil exploration in Balochistan. During General Zia's era, a number of foreign governments and donor agencies also contributed to several projects in Balochistan.[45] Mahnaz Isphani in her book mentioned the financial aid provided by the Kuwait Fund for Arab Economic Development (KFAED).[46] KFAED provided a loan of $17.5 million for the construction of a gas pipeline. According to media reports, KFAED also expressed its willingness to invest $400 million in several other projects ranging from irrigation to electricity.[47] The Americans also provided huge financial aids for projects in Balochistan. The Americans were particularly interested in the development of the Makran area. The Americans provided $40 million for a road project linking Las Bela to Turbat. USAID, the organization responsible for handling all such aids, also considered funding a highway construction project from Karachi via the Makran coast to the Iranian border.

Throughout this period, one area that stood out was the Makran coastal area, especially Gwadar. Both the Americans and Pakistan believed that the Soviets were eyeing the Gwadar area for further expansion into the Indian Ocean. Experts now considered Gwadar ideal not only for a naval base but also as a hub of maritime trade activity. How the Baloch viewed this economic development and how it affected the common Baloch? While all this economic activity was good it could not trickle down to improving the Baloch masses. The Baloch needed basic human needs, in particular clean drinking water, hospitals and schools, etc. In these sectors, much was left to be desired.

Baloch nationalist movement during the peace interval

By the end of the 1970s, the Baloch nationalist leadership started to fall apart. It became visible that Khair Bakhsh Marri and Ataullah Mengal saw little logic in continuing political activities. Baloch political leadership in general demonstrated no keenness in joining the MRD; not because they supported the military regime, but because of what happened to the Baloch during the Bhutto's era. They still doubted the PPP's intention and saw hardly any point in getting rid of one Punjabi-dominated government to get another Punjabi-dominant government. Mir Ghaus Bakhsh Bizenjo, who was now heading the Pakistan National Party

Balochistan and the peace interval (1977–99) 135

(PNP), joined the Movement for Restoration of Democracy (MRD). Within the MRD (as we have seen in an earlier section), the views were divided on the issue of centre–provincial relations and provincial autonomy. Bizenjo argued that in Pakistan four identity groups live. According to Bizenjo, solution to Pakistan's national integration problem was in recognizing and accepting the existence of these ethnic groups and to establish a loose federation. Such a loose federation, in its essence, according to Bizenjo would be closer to the Lahore (Pakistan) resolution of 1940.[48] Bizenjo was convinced that only the formula of a loose federation could save the country from disintegration. Ironically though, he was also convinced that the Punjabis would not allow this to happen.

There were many in Balochistan, especially the Baloch militants and student groups, who considered Bizenjo to be a political fraud. They believed that Bizenjo would have reached an understanding with General Zia in return of some petty benefits, had he not been stopped by the Sardars Mengal and Marri. Bizenjo haters even disputed his Marxist–Leninist credentials, arguing that his political career was backed by Akbar Musti Khan, a Baloch businessman.[49]

Moscow, according to Selig Harrison, treated Bizenjo as a possible future head of the Sate of Pakistan.[50] Aziz Bugti argued that after witnessing the insurgent violence and Pakistan security force's response, Bizenjo as a Baloch political leader vowed that he would do as much as he can politically before pushing his fellow Baloch into another round of violence. His whole political strategy during the 1980s revolved around this realization.[51]

Nawab Khair Bakhsh Marri, who was considered to be the staunchest Baloch nationalist among the trio of Mengal–Bizenjo–Marri, was not convinced that they should negotiate with General Zia. Before any discussion, Khair Bakhsh Marri demanded that General Zia must withdraw Pakistan Army from Balochistan and pay the Baloch who suffered during the four years (1973–77) of violence.[52] In 1981, he went to Afghanistan and met with Mir Hazar Ramkhani, the commander of the Balochistan Liberation Front.[53]

He saw no point in negotiating with the Punjab or Punjabi-dominated Pakistan government. According to him, Punjabis would never give the Baloch their due rights.[54] According to Harrison:

> When I (Harrison) suggested that a settlement with Pakistan would be preferable to achieving independence under Superpower tutelage, he responded... that if Punjabis or the Pakistani state are prepared to talk to us in a mature way, with some kind of realism and some understanding of how our people feel, we are prepared for a settlement, as we have always been. But there is no use wasting time talking of minor matters. They must be prepared to talk in terms of a national status to us, of a relationship with us based on that status. I must confess that I cannot ever remember a Punjabi talking in such terms.[55]

The third member of the trio of Baloch nationalist leadership, Ataullah Mengal considered General Zia's actions such as end of the military operation, release of political prisoners and general amnesty to the Baloch guerrillas inadequate.

136 *Centre–Province relations post-independence*

Mengal stated that in many areas of Balochistan, the army was still present and patrolled those areas.[56] Mengal argued that General Zia's actions have reinforced the feeling among the Baloch that the Baloch are second-class citizens of Pakistan. He informed Selig Harrison that the younger generation of the Baloch are convinced that they have no future in Pakistan.[57] These young Baloch believe that in keeping with them so few in number, the Baloch would never get due rights in a democratic Pakistan. For them (the younger generation of the Baloch), the only solution to all Baloch suffering was independence.[58] Just like Nawab Marri and Bizenjo, Ataullah Mengal was convinced that the Punjabi-dominated establishment (bureaucracy and the army) would never let General Zia reach a meaningful understanding with the Baloch.[59] According to Mengal, this group of Punjabis pressurized General Zia not to accept Baloch nationalist leadership demand to replace the Punjabi Chief Secretary of Balochistan.[60] Speaking with Lawrence Lifschultz, Mengal stated that "this group of Punjabis takes the attitude that the Baloch have to prove their patriotism. This would not happen *anymore* as we had had enough." According to Mengal, from now onwards, they have to come to the Baloch. He further stated that "if he was called a traitor by this Punjabi group, this would mean that I (Attalullah Mengal) am loyal to my people."[61]

By mid-1979, both Sardar Marri and Sardar Mengal decided to continue their political activities from abroad. Both left the country for medical treatment.[62]

Sardar Ataullah Mengal continued to alter his position on a settlement with the State of Pakistan. Up till 1978, he was ready to accept the Bizenjo formula of a loose federation.[63] By 1980, he argued that the Baloch, in keeping with their less numbers in the federation, could only feel secure if the federation followed the formula of parity among its federating units regardless of the population ratio.[64] To support this position, Mengal argued that the Punjabi-dominated (then) West Pakistan opted for the parity formula through the establishment of One Unit to counter the majority of the East Pakistan. They (the Punjabis) according to Mengal (at the time) insisted that the Bengalis should sacrifice for the sake of the unity of the country. Now according to Mengal, it was time for the Punjabis to sacrifice.[65]

Going a step further in 1983, Sardar Ataullah Mengal issued a declaration of independence of Balochistan. At the time of issuing this declaration, Mengal emphasized the timing of this declaration. According to Mengal, a crucial turning point[66] has been achieved in the Balochistan problem. He has issued the declaration for independence because the situation has reached the point of no return. What exactly he meant by the crucial turning point or why he thought that the relationship between Islamabad and Balochistan had reached a point of no return, he did not elaborate. However, he stated that the present government (of General Zia) is not fundamentally different in its treatment of and approach towards the Baloch. Mengal argued that all governments in Islamabad want to colonize Balochistan and plunder its wealth and resources. That is the only constant in Islamabad–Quetta relations.[67]

Mengal further stated that the only purpose of Pakistan is to provide its army with all privileges. As it happened in 1971, as soon as an ethnic group decides

Balochistan and the peace interval (1977–99)   137

to challenge thearmy's supremacy, it suffers the fate Bengalis faced.[68] The only solution to this for the Baloch according to Ataullah Mengal was independence:

> If the Baloch are to survive, then we must struggle for an independent Balochistan, outside the framework of Pakistan. We are conscious of ourselves as a national entity. If the present situation is allowed to prevail, then that entity will be lost. Efforts are being made in Pakistan at the moment to drown us with an influx of refugees and immigrants. The authorities in Pakistan want to outnumber the people of Balochistan by bringing settlers from outside Balochistan into the province as labourers, peasants and businessmen. The goal is to bring people in and force the Baloch out... it is my firm belief now that the Baloch will never realise their rights within the framework of Pakistan.[69]

Again Mengal blamed Punjab for this. According to Mengal, Punjab's population was rising and this population needed to be employed. Balochistan provided an ideal place, with its vast land, resources and wealth. Balochistan could accommodate thousands of people, according to Mengal.[70] Punjab was doing exactly that and in the process was destroying the Baloch.[71]

> If you give the gun to the Punjab and at the same time you designate 56 percent of the seats in a National Assembly to the Punjab, then how can there be any safeguards for provincial rights? Now all three provinces together could not beat the Punjab in such an Assembly. When there was East Pakistan the votes would have been overwhelmingly against the vested interests of the Punjabis. In this sense we constituted a clear majority in the country. It is precisely for this reason that the Army would not abide by the 1970 elections and kicked East Pakistan out of the federation. Now all the guns lie with the Punjab. The Army and the civil service are overwhelmingly Punjabi.[72]

The decline of the Baloch nationalist movement

The decade of 1980s witnessed a gradual decline of the Baloch nationalist movement. General Zia's policy of accommodation and reconciliation played an important role in it. Though most of the thorny issues remained unresolved and the common Baloch continued to survive under similar conditions as in the past, Balochistan and Baloch politics became more restive and peaceful.

With the Pakistan Army taking the helm of affairs, Baloch leadership considered the Pashtun element within the NAP becoming accommodative to the centre. This led to a split in the NAP. Bizenjo's Pakistan National Party (PNP) was banned within months. By the early 1980s, the Balochistan Peoples' Liberation Front also started showing signs of fatigue. Views got divided on the outcome or ultimate objective of the struggle. One group led by Mir Hazar and Khair Bakhsh Marri wanted independence of Balochistan, whereas another, comprising mostly of BPLF's non-Baloch members, wanted to expand the struggle into Pakistan.

138 *Centre–Province relations post-independence*

A number of vocal and vibrant Baloch leaders and workers, especially belonging to the Baloch Students Organization (BSO), were arrested which robbed the movement of its grassroots workers and second and lower tier of leaders and activists.

Perhaps the most important factor was the parting of ways of the trio of Bizenjo, Marri and Mengal. Bizenjo, through his PNP and later as a national-level leader of Pakistan, opted for peaceful political struggle and focused his energies on the issue of greater provincial autonomy within the framework of the federation of Pakistan. Ataullah Mengal and Khair Bakhsh Marri left the country to continue their struggle for independent Balochistan. However, it never became clear what exactly was the stand of the Baloch nationalist leaders, especially Sardar Ataullah Mengal as he navigated from one position to another swiftly as it has been detailed in an earlier section. From 1978 to 1983, he navigated for advocating a loose federation to issuing a declaration of independence of Balochistan.[73] He once again changed his position when he returned to Pakistan in the 1990s and allowed his son to participate in provincial politics of Balochistan, contest elections and become the Chief Minister of Balochistan. General Zia also found a number of Baloch sardars more than willing to help him. Doda Khan Zarakzai, a lifelong Muslim leaguer and pro-centre sardar, extended his full support to General Zia. Moinuddin Baloch, the younger brother of Ahmed Yar Khan, and Zafarullah Khan Jamali joined General Zia's cabinet. Another important Baloch who supported General Zia was the marble king of Balochistan, Mir Nabi Bakhsh Zehri.[74] Due to these factors, the Baloch nationalist movement faced a gradual decline.

Political activities in Balochistan during the decade of democracy

When General Zia appointed Junajo as the Prime Minister of Pakistan, Bizenjo's PNP joined the Junajo government. In the 1988 elections, the PNP won only two seats in a house of 45 in Balochistan. Bizenjo who was widely respected in Balochistan and was called the father of Balochistan also lost in the 1988 elections.

The beginning of the decade of democracy in Balochistan was marked with a political crisis in Balochistan. On the advice of the Chief Minister Mir Zafarullah Khan Jamali, Governor of Balochistan General (retired) Mohammad Musa dissolved the Balochistan assembly on 15 December 1988. The rationale behind this decision was that no party or alliance had a majority to form a government in Balochistan.[75] Jamiat-e-Ulema-i-Islam (JUI) and the Balochistan National Alliance (BNA) eventually reached an understanding and established a coalition government in Balochistan in which Nawab Akbar Bugti became the Chief Minister of Balochistan. However, when the PPP government initiated the developmental projects under the banner of People's Programme worth Rs. 2 billion, differences appeared between the central and provincial governments. The program was aimed at providing and improving basic human needs (drinking water, health facilities, education) to the people of Pakistan. Bugti government considered the program against the provincial autonomy.[76]

Balochistan and the peace interval (1977–99) 139

New political parties in Balochistan

In the 1970s, Balochistan had only one political party, the National Awami Party (NAP). When the NAP was banned by the Bhutto government, Baloch politicians such as Bizenjo started political activities under the Pakistan National Party (PNP). With the restoration of democratic practices in Pakistan, a number of new political parties and groupings emerged in Balochistan.

Bizenjo's PNP continued to participate in provincial politics. The PNP, like most of the political parties in Pakistan, aspired to remain in power and supported the Muslim League led by Nawaz Sharif and the Pakistan Peoples Party led by Benazir Bhutto. Just before the 1988 elections, the PNP was part of the interim government. After the PPP won the 1988 election, the PNP established an alliance with the PPP. In the 1990 elections, it switched sides and got into an alliance with the Muslim League. The 1993 elections were most devastating for the PNP as only one of its members managed to win his seat. Even that was because of his tribal connection. At one point, while the PNP was in alliance with the Muslim League in Balochistan, at the national level it supported the PPP's (rival political party of the ML) candidate for the slot of prime minister.[77]

From within the PNP emerged the Balochistan National Youth Movement (BNYM). Dr. Abdul Hayee Baloch, former BSO president, established this youth-focused group in the PNP to ensure smooth transition of Baloch student activists into the PNP via the BNYM. Bizenjo disagreed with this approach and charged Dr. Hayee of violating the party rulers and expelled Dr. Abdul Hayee and his group from the PNP.

Dr. Abdul Hayee Baloch now established the BNYM as an independent and proper political party. The BNYM had a number of inherent advantages: most of its cadre including the leadership came from the Balochistan Student Organization (BSO). The current BSO automatically served as a support group among the Baloch youth. More so, the BNYM was able to secure the support of Nawab Bugti and Ataullah Mengal.

The BNYM was part of the BNA–JUI alliance which established the government in Balochistan after the 1988 election. In 1989, the leadership of the BNYM decided to expand the BNYM's political focus and decided to drop the Y (youth) and rename it the Balochistan National Movement (BNM). Though the BNM is credited to be the only Baloch political party representing the middle class, it had a number of sardars in its cadre. Prime amongst them were Akhtar Mengal and Muhammad Arif Hasani.

The alliance between the BNM and the BNA turned out to be shortlived as the BNM and Akbar Bugti differed on the issue of no-confidence motion against the then Prime Minister Benazir Bhutto. While Bugti was actively campaigning for this no-confidence motion to succeed, the BNM decided that it would vote against the motion.

Eventually in 1990, the BNM left the provincial government of Balochistan. The BNM suffered another setback just before the 1990 elections, when a group led by Akhtar Mengal left the BNM. The BNM could not perform in 1990 elections and

140 *Centre–Province relations post-independence*

managed to win only two provincial assembly seats in Balochistan.[78] For the 1993 elections, the BNM followed the seat-to-seat adjustment formula. When Nawab Magsi became the Chief Minister of Balochistan, four BNM provincial assembly members joined the Magsi cabinet.[79]

Jamhoori Wattan Party (JWP)

Akbar Bugti was one of the most prominent Baloch sardars and politicians. His critics considered him to be a self-centred, egotistic and a strict sardar. He was also a pro-Pakistan and pro-federation Baloch politician who stayed in Balochistan throughout the Zia period.[80]

Since the restoration of democratic practices in Pakistan, Nawab Akbar Bugti argued that there is a need for a new political party in Pakistan. On 16 August 1990, Akbar Bugti announced the establishment of a new political party: the Jamhoori Wattan Party (JWP). As its creation almost coincided with the election, the JWP had organisational issues and its set-up was delayed. However, as it was widely believed that the JWP would form the next government in Balochistan, a large number of Baloch politicians, who did not share Akbar Bugti's political ideas, joined the JWP.[81]

After the 1990 elections, the JWP emerged as a strong party and could have formed the government, had the IJI (Islamic Democratic Alliance) decided to align with the JWP, its electoral ally. But the IJI, PPP, PNP, JUI, and BNM established a coalition government in Balochistan. The JWP became a very strong and vibrant opposition party in the assembly. This also provided Akbar Bugti the time to focus on organizational and other party issues. The biggest problem with the JWP was that it was Akbar Bugti's party. He was the leader, the political ideologue, the political worker and the decision-maker of the JWP. Another incident which hampered the evolution and progress of the JWP as a political party was the murder of Salal Bugti. This sad incident not only gave rise to tribal infighting between the Bugti sub-tribes, but also resulted in Akbar Bugti's decision to confine himself to Dera Bugti. These factors hindered the emergence of the JWP as the third force in the Pakistani politics as envisaged by Akbar Bugti.[82]

Balochistan and Pakistan's Central Asian Dream

The decade of 1990s began with the triumph of the West in the Cold War. The fall of the Berlin Wall marked the end of the Cold War. Soon, the USSR was dissolved. This resulted in the emergence of a number of new states including the energy-rich (oil and gas) Muslim Central Asian Republics (CARs). As the CARs were landlocked, and in the case of Uzbekistan, the largest of the CARs, double landlocked, these states were keen to find alternative routes to transport oil and gas to the outside world. This search also aimed at finding alternative routes from and reliance on Russia.

Pakistan reached out to CARs leadership and revived and expanded the Economic Cooperation Organization (ECO). Pakistan's prime ministers and

Balochistan and the peace interval (1977–99) 141

federal minsters frequently visited the CARs. The significance of Gwadar, which was repeatedly emphasized by the American and other Western analysts during the Soviet invasion of Afghanistan, was reinforced as it was the closest outlet to the sea for the CARs. Both Nawaz Sharif and Benazir Bhutto offered the CARs leadership to avail Pakistan and Gwadar as their gateway to the outside world via the Indian Ocean. Nawaz Sharif in 1992 stated that *Pakistan would be a gateway to Central Asia*. Pakistan also signed an agreement with Turkmenistan to build a pipeline transporting gas from Daulatabad gas facility of Turkmenistan to Afghanistan to Pakistan. The pipeline was Turkmenistan–Afghanistan–Pakistan pipeline (TAP). In 2006, India also joined this project and the pipeline was renamed TAPI.

During the decade of democracy, Pakistani leadership initiated a number of projects in collaboration with the Central Asian states. Pakistan started the construction of the Gwadar Port. Pakistan also initiated the ambitious plan of constructing extensive road and railway and pipeline networks linking Gwadar with the rest of the country. Pakistan's leadership was optimistic that due to these economic projects and region-based activities Pakistan would not only be projected as the energy corridor, it would immensely improve Pakistan's economic situation. More so, it would integrate Afghanistan, Pakistan and the Central Asian states into an economic partnership. However, continued political uncertainty in Pakistan, unending civil war in Afghanistan and continued competing regional interests halted the progress on the Gwadar Port project and other such projects. When General Musharraf took the helm of affairs in 1999 and tried to move forward on the Gwadar Port and related projects without taking the Baloch political leadership on board, Balochistan was inching towards the end of its peace interval in its relations with Islamabad. This would be discussed in the next chapter.

CONCLUSION

Balochistan went through a peace interval which lasted for almost 23 years (1977–99). This peace interval is largely missing from the Baloch nationalist narrative. The most plausible explanation for this is that it does not fit into the narrative of enduring injustice against the Baloch and Balochistan.

During this period, the strategic significance of Balochistan was reinforced after the Soviet invasion of Afghanistan. Soviet interest in reaching the warm waters of the Indian Ocean and their long-term interest in Balochistan, especially Makran and its port (though undeveloped at the time) Gwadar, made General Zia, the President of Pakistan at the time, focus more on Balochistan.

Zia, a strong believer in making Pakistan an Islamic state and a strong opponent of a multiethnic and multicultural Pakistan, followed a policy of reconciliation in Balochistan even prior to the Soviet invasion of Afghanistan. He withdrew the army from various parts of Balochistan, dissolved the Hyderabad tribunal, declared amnesty for Baloch insurgents and provided them compensation money. However, after the Soviet invasion of Afghanistan and the emergence of an American–Pakistani–Saudi–Chinese alliance to support the Afghan resistance,

142 Centre–Province relations post-independence

Balochistan gained a strategic position for the Pakistani and American decision-makers as it was Balochistan which provided the USSR its shortest and most viable outlet to the warm waters of the Indian Ocean. Zia poured in a lot of money to build roads, airport, gas supply and other developmental projects which, other than being visible development projects, were also strategically important in case of a Soviet invasion of the area.

During the decade of democracy, Baloch politicians participated in Pakistani politics. Akbar Bugti, Zafar Jamali and Bizenjo played important roles in the national politics. A new generation of Baloch politicians emerged and actively participated in politics. This group included people like Akhtar Mengal, Abdul Hayee Baloch, Abdul Malik, and a number of others.

Throughout this period, it became clear that Baloch politics was still conducted on tribal lines and the sardars play the key role in Baloch politics. This was despite the emergence of a number of political parties in Balochistan, but every Baloch political party sought the patronage of a sardar. Baloch National Movement, which is led by Dr. Abdul Hayee Baloch, representing the Baloch middle class, only became a significant political player in Baloch politics when it got the support of Akbar Bugti and Ataullah Mengal.

After the disintegration of the USSR and the emergence of the Central Asian Republics, Balochistan, especially Gwadar, once again became the focus of attention, this time due to economic reasons. All governments during the 1990s projected Pakistan as an energy corridor and an outlet for the landlocked Central Asian states.

Throughout this period, Balochistan was peaceful and the Baloch leadership was fully participating in the political activities in the province and the country. Akbar Bugti was projecting his Jamhoori Wattan Party as the third political force in the country. These were positive signs for Balochistan, Pakistan and centre–province relations. This, however, soon changed and insurgent violence returned to Balochistan. This would be discussed in the next chapter.

Notes

1 The President on Pakistan's Ideological Basis, Address by President General Zia-ul-Haq at the inauguration of Shariat Faculty at the Quaid-i-Azam University, Islamabad, 8 October 1979 (Islamabad: Ministry of Information and Broadcasting, n.d.), 2.
2 *Pakistan Times*, July 6, 1977.
3 Ishtiaque, 230–31.
4 General Muhammad Zia-ul-Haq, Interviews to Foreign Media, Vol. 1 (Islamabad: Ministry of Information and Broadcasting, n.d.), 18–21; 69–70; 117–24; 200–5.
5 Mumtaz Ahmad, 382.
6 *Dawn*, October 27, 1982.
7 *Muslim*, June 10, 1980.
8 Mumtaz Ahmad, 384.
9 Ibid.
10 *Nawa-i-Waqat*, Lahore, April 12, 1986; and Hasan Askari Rizvi, 1078.
11 Hasan Askar Rizvi, 1078.
12 *The Frontier Post*, February 26, 1986.

Balochistan and the peace interval (1977–99) 143

13 H. A. Rizvi, "The Civilianization of Military Rule in Pakistan," *Asian Survey* 26, no. 10 (1986).
14 C. G. P. Rakisits, "Centre-Province Relations in Pakistan under General Zia," *Pacific Affairs* (Spring 1988); and Rizvi, ibid.
15 *Monthly Khail Rang*, Lahore, April 1986, 273–88.
16 Bhutto, 270 as quoted by Istiaque, 233.
17 Ishitaque, ibid.
18 Ishtiaque, 281.
19 Ibid., 281–82.
20 Ibid., 282.
21 Ibid., 284.
22 Ibid., 288.
23 Ibid., 292.
24 S. Akbar Zaidi, ed., "Introduction," in *Regional Imbalances and the National Question in Pakistan* (Lahore: Vanguard, 1992), 1.
25 Shahid Javed Burki, "What We Teach and How," *Dawn*, Karachi, May 3, 2005.
26 Shirin Tahirkheli, 24–26.
27 Mehtab Ali Shah, 102.
28 Harrison, 150.
29 Ibid.
30 Dehwar, 410–11.
31 Aziz Bugti, *Baluchistan: Shakseyat ke Ayanee Main* (in Urdu) (Lahore: Fiction House, 1996).
32 Harrison, 153.
33 Ibid., 68.
34 Ibid., 69–70.
35 Ibid., 72.
36 For details, see Rizwan Zeb, "Russia and South Asia," in *Spot Light on Regional Affairs* (Islamabad: Institute of Regional Studies, January 2004).
37 For details, see Zeb, "Russian and South Asia."
38 Mahnaz Ispahani, *Roads and Rivals* (Ithaca: Cornell University Press, 1989), 58.
39 *Weekly Zindagi*, Lahore, November 23–29, 1997, 18.
40 Grant Farr, "The Effect of the Afghan Refugees on Pakistan", in *Zia's Pakistan*, ed. Baxter, 93–110.
41 Wirsing, *Pakistan's Security under Zia*, 52.
42 Harrison, 67.
43 Imitaz Ali, 59.
44 For details about this point, see Isphani, 58–81.
45 Isphani, 76.
46 Ibid.
47 Ibid.
48 Selig Harrison, *In Afghanistan's Shadow: Baloch Nationalism and Soviet Temptations* (Washington, DC: CEIP, 1981).
49 Harrision, 59.
50 Ibid., 60.
51 Bugti; and Harrison, 60–61.
52 Harrison, 45.
53 Ibid., 51.
54 Ibid.
55 Ibid., 51–52.
56 *Dawn*, Karachi, July 2, 1979, Also see Tahir Amin, *Ethno-National Movements in Pakistan, Domestic and International Factors* (Islamabad: Institute of Policy Studies, 1988), 179, 'Baluchistan' (Government of Pakistan, Information Ministry), 5, cited in

144 Centre–Province relations post-independence

Harrison, *In Afghanistan's Shadow*, 169. Lawrence Lifschultz, "Pakistan: A Fundamental Debate," *Far Eastern Economic Review* 111 (1981).
57 Harrison, 64.
58 Ibid.
59 Lifschultz, "Pakistan: A Fundamental Debate"; Lawrence Lifschultz, "Independent Baluchistan: Ataullah Mengal's Declaration of Independence," *Economic and Political Weekly* 18 (1983); and Harrison, 65.
60 Lifschultz, "Pakistan: A Fundamental Debate"; Lifschultz, "Independent Baluchistan"; and Harrison, 65.
61 Harrison, 65.
62 Ibid., 66.
63 Lifschultz, "Pakistan: A Fundamental Debate."
64 Ibid.
65 Ibid.
66 Ibid.
67 Ibid., 743.
68 Ibid.
69 Ibid., 744.
70 Ibid.
71 Ibid.
72 Ibid.
73 Lifschultz, "Independent Baluchistan," 735; Harrison, *In Afghanistan's Shadow*, 153; and Phadnis, *Ethnicity and Nation Building in South Asia*, 189.
74 Harrison, *In Afghanistan's Shadow*, 153; and Phadnis, *Ethnicity and Nation Building in South Asia*, 189.
75 Harrison, 112, 113.
76 Ibid., 117.
77 Bugti, 150.
78 Ibid., 156.
79 Ibid., 157.
80 Ibid., 168.
81 Ibid., 169.
82 Ibid., 172.

6 The return of insurgency in Balochistan

INTRODUCTION

The central questions raised in this chapter are why after a 23-year-long peace interval (absence of militant violence), insurgent violence returned to Balochistan and how and why this contributed to the Baloch nationalist narrative of enduring injustice. These questions are important to understand the Baloch nationalist narrative. As it has been demonstrated in the previous chapters, different developments in Balochistan and centre–province relations contributed in the evolution of this narrative. Had the peace interval continued, the whole Baloch narrative would have fallen apart.

It is important to address these questions for two reasons: *first*, by addressing these questions one can understand the immediate causes for the return of violence, and *second* to understand the overall narrative of enduring injustice faced by the Baloch.

Before October 1999, most Baloch nationalists were part of the mainstream politics, contesting elections and seeking to resolve what they considered the province's grievances through parliamentary means. Nawab Akbar Bugti's JWP was duly represented in the assembly. Khair Bakhsh Marri's sons contested elections – Balach Marri was a member of the Balochistan provincial assembly representing the Baloch Haq Tawar Party. Akhtar Mengal, like Nawab Akbar Bugti, served as the Chief Minister of Balochistan. A group representing the Baloch middle class had its members in the provincial assembly as well as the parliament. Dr. Abdul Hayee Baloch renamed his party as the National Party to underline its all-Pakistan identity.

These positive developments were halted when General Musharraf took over the government and the subsequent developments in and around Pakistan. General Musharraf, soon after assuming power, started taking steps to consolidate his power in the country assisted by a group of like minded political actors. At the same time, he started a number of ambitious developmental projects throughout the country, especially in Balochistan. Prime amongst these projects was the Gwadar Port project. When the Baloch elite opposed these projects, the centre under Musharraf adopted an aggressive policy towards the Baloch and Balochistan.

146 *Centre–Province relations post-independence*

The current insurgency in Balochistan is much more serious than the previous insurgencies in a number of ways. Baloch Insurgents have learned lessons from a number of recent insurgencies around the world. These lessons are discussed in the relevant section of this chapter. In the current insurgency, two new trends have emerged: the targeted killings of settlers, especially ethnic Punjabi and Urdu-speaking settlers and abductions of Baloch nationalists, pro-federation Baloch leaders and activists (the issue of missing persons).

The most plausible explanation for the return of insurgent violence in Balochistan is that the Baloch elite who were till the arrival of General Musharraf enjoying their share in the pie felt totally bypassed and ignored by General Musharraf and his policies towards Balochistan, especially in the mega projects such as the Gwadar Port. This resulted in the use of a narrative of historical injustice against them linking the current situation with the historical injustices towards the Baloch by the centre. This narrative failed to provide an explanation why most of the Baloch elite always sided with the centre or why the Baloch elite were silent on the historical injustices against the Baloch during the Zia regime and the decade of democracy? General Musharraf's regime, in response, used centre's standard narrative in which the Baloch sardars, in particular Nawab Khair Bakhsh Marri and Sardar Attaullah Mengal, were the villains. This time, Nawab Akbar Bugti's name was included in this list as he was asking for a new agreement on gas royalty and increase in land rent rate in the Bugti area. This narrative argued that the Baloch tribal system has always been the biggest impediment to the development of Balochistan. This narrative ignored the fact that other than these two or three so-called trouble-making sardars, more than 90 percent of Baloch sardars always supported the centre. Why had no development work taken place in their areas or why has this not provided the centre enough space to move ahead with their policy of development in Balochistan? Also, why did the centre not develop Balochistan during the peace interval?

As a tribal society, the biggest problem for the Baloch society is that it lacks a single or unified voice. There are a number of tribal feuds in Balochistan: Bugti vs Kalpars, Bugti vs Ahmedans, Bugtis vs Mazaris, Bugtis vs Raisanis, Gazinis vs Bejranis, Marris vs Loonis, Hameedzais vs Ghaibezais, Rind vs Raisani and Suleman Khels vs Lawoons.

At present, a number of insurgent groups are active in Balochistan: the BLA (Baloch Liberation Army), BLF (Baloch Liberation Front), BMDT (Baloch Musalla Defa Tanzeem), BRA (Baloch Republic Army), BLT (Baloch Liberation Tiger), and BSO (Baloch Student Organization). These groups not only differ in their objectives and approach but at times act in cross-purpose. However, Balochistan is facing more than just nationalist violence. Apart from the nationalist violence, Balochistan is also facing different types of violence. Sectarian violence is on the rise in Balochistan. A number of organized criminal groups committing abductions for ransom, carjacking, and attacks on cargo trucks, particularly on the US–NATO cargo destined for Afghanistan, many of whom enjoy political patronage are also present in Balochistan.

MUSHARRAF TAKES OVER AND CONSOLIDATES HIS POWER

On 12 October 1999, the Pakistan Army under the command of the COAS, General Pervez Musharraf, took over the government by arresting Prime Minister Nawaz Sharif on the charge of hijacking the commercial flight on which the COAS was returning from an official visit to Sri Lanka and forbidding it to land in Pakistan. After the military takeover of Pakistan, General Musharraf in his address to the nation on 17 October 1999, said:

> Quite clearly, what Pakistan has experienced in the recent years has been hardly a label of democracy not the essence of it. Our people were never emancipated from the yoke of despotism. I shall not allow the people to be taken back to the era of the sham democracy.

He also announced a seven-point agenda: *rebuild national confidence and morale; strengthen the federation, remove inter-provincial disharmony and restore national cohesion; revive the economy and restore investor confidence; ensure law and order and dispense speedy justice; depoliticize state institutions; devolve of power to the grass roots level and ensure swift and across-the-board accountability.*

Musharraf launched a devolution plan throughout the country that bypassed the provincial assemblies to create local governments entirely dependent on the central government for their survival. Although presented as a form of decentralization, all provinces except Punjab perceived the scheme to be an imposition of a centralized form of government and a negation of provincial autonomy.

For the 2002 elections, General Musharraf revised the eligibility criteria to contest elections. According to the new eligibility criteria, graduation was made compulsory for the candidates. This put a number of leading and experienced Pakistani politicians who have held ministerial positions in the past at a disadvantage. Seasoned politicians like Akbar Bugti who has served as the Defence Minister, Governor and Chief Minister of Balochistan were not eligible to contest elections according to the new eligibility criteria.

This gave the religious parties, especially the recently established Mutahida Majlis-e-Amal (MMA), a huge advantage as the new eligibility criteria accepted the degrees awarded by various religious seminaries as equivalent to a university degree. MMA managed to get maximum seats in the Balochistan and Khyber Pakhtunkhwa provincial assemblies.

In Balochistan, although Jam Yousaf was appointed as the Chief Minister of Balochistan, he was widely believed to be powerless. The Baloch nationalists viewed this as a deliberate attempt to keep them out of the provincial decision making and a tool to be used to legitimize General Musharraf's rule.

148   *Centre–Province relations post-independence*

BALOCHISTAN'S STRATEGIC SIGNIFICANCE AND REGIONAL DEVELOPMENTS

The previous chapter detailed how Balochistan's strategic significance was recognized by Islamabad as well as by the Americans and Pakistan's other Western allies. A number of experts pointed out that the Makran coastal area, especially Gwadar, was ideal for not only a naval base but for a port which would play a very important role in the maritime trade and commercial activity in and around the Indian Ocean. With the independence of the Central Asian states, Pakistan embarked upon projecting itself as an outlet for these states and an energy corridor, but for several reasons, the construction of the Gwadar Port was delayed.

When General Musharraf took over, one of the first decisions he took was to move ahead on the construction of the Gwadar Port. With the Chinese assistance, the construction of Gwadar started. Gwadar and related developmental projects resulted in the influx of Chinese engineers and experts into Balochistan and also of workers and labourers from various parts of the country.

The tragic events of 9/11 and the American response also impacted Balochistan. When General Musharraf decided to side with the Americans in the war against terror, he provided the American forces a number of facilities including the air fields in Pasni and Dalbadin in Balochistan. These developments reinforced the strategic significance of Balochistan and resulted in General Musharraf sending in more troops to ensure the safety and security of the infrastructure as well as of the Chinese engineers and other workers. This also reinforced the Baloch nationalists' view that Pakistan is only interested in exploiting Balochistan's natural wealth.

MUSHARRAF REGIME'S VIEW AND POLICY TOWARDS BALOCHISTAN

General Musharraf's policy towards Balochistan was based on three main points: development, counter-insurgency and collaborating with and facilitating moderate Baloch politicians.

General Musharraf in particular and the centre in general held the view that the tribal culture of the Baloch and their foreign-gained capabilities are the prime reasons for the failure of the Baloch to integrate into Pakistan and that the sardars and their hierarchical tribal structure are a prime reason why the tribes of the Pakistani Baloch have rejected the government of Pakistan. General Musharraf declared the Baloch tribal system, especially the sardari system, as an impediment to the construction of mega projects in particular and to development in Balochistan. The Baloch sardars, especially Khair Bakhsh Marri, Attaullah Mengal and Akbar Bugti, according to General Musharraf, fear that their traditional hold on their areas would be weakened by modernization. Hence, the actual problem in Balochistan was the perseverance of the regressive and archaic sardari or tumandari system.[1] Musharraf believed that apart from these trouble-making sardars, majority of the Baloch people were patriotic Pakistanis who want to see their province progress and prosper.

Return of insurgency in Balochistan 149

Echoing almost every ruler of Pakistan, General Musharraf claimed that the central government has allocated unprecedented funds and resources for projects in Balochistan. He claimed that he allocated these huge resources to eliminate the Baloch sense of deprivation. He rightly claimed that he has worked out a policy to have a greater number of Baloch selected in the Pakistan Army and the civil services of Pakistan.[2] President Musharraf also stated that he does not understand why certain people were opposing the mega projects and what exactly these people want. He also emphasized that his government wanted to end the sense of deprivation in Balochistan.[3] According to Musharraf, his government had increased development funds for Balochistan from 3 to 7 percent and added that works on Gwadar Port, Mirani Dam, Kachhi Canal, Coastal Highway, Subakzai Dam, Greater Quetta Water Scheme, Zhob-Dera Ismail Khan Road and many other projects launched by the federal government were in progress and these projects, once completed, would transform Balochistan.[4]

General Musharraf also decided to disband the levy forces and integrate them into the police. In March 2004, President Musharraf announced a plan to convert the "B" areas in Balochistan into "A" areas. According to the plan, this conversion from B to A area would take five years to complete and every year a select group of towns would be converted. According to media reports,[5] in the first phase, Quetta, Lasbela, Nasirabad, Gwadar, Pishin, and Kila Abdullah; in the second phase, Sibi, Bolan, Zhob, Kila Saifullah, and Kech; in the third phase, Loralai, Musa Khel, Jhal Magsi, Mustung, and Ziarat; in the fourth phase, Awaran, Kalat, Chaghai, Barkhan, and Dera Bugti; and in the fifth and final phase, Khuzdar, Panjgur, Kharan and Kohlu would be converted into A areas.[6]

General Musharraf's government decided to build three new cantonments in Gwadar, Kohlu and Sui mainly to ensure security of the installations and national assets. On the issue of the construction of new military cantonments in Balochistan at Gwadar, Sui and Kholu, the then Director General, Inter-Services Public Relations (ISPR), explained the Musharraf regime's position. He stated that these cantonments were important in ensuring the security of the installations and national assets in these areas. Highlighting the positive impact of the cantonments at Zhob, Khuzdar and Loralai on the lives of common Baloch, he stated that medical and educational facilities in these cantonments have benefited a large number of people in the area.[7] Declaring cantonments, drivers of economic activity, he further added that a cantonment would bring modernization to the area in the shape of road, electricity and modern communication facilities to the area and new economic opportunities for the people of the area.

RETURN OF VIOLENCE IN BALOCHISTAN: FROM BUGTI'S ROYALTY WAR TO FOURTH INSURGENCY IN BALOCHISTAN

This section covers the developments from 2002 when the armed clashes between the Bugtis and Mazaris intensified. During these clashes, a number of rockets targeted

150　*Centre–Province relations post-independence*

gas pipelines in the area. The central and provincial governments claimed that the damage to gas infrastructure was a collateral damage due to the ongoing tribal clash; it soon became clear that it was not. After the lapse of the agreement on the royalty payment between the Sui gas administration and the Bugti tribe and apparent reluctance or delay in renewing it, the pipelines were attacked as a pressure tactic. An attempt to reach a mutually acceptable solution to the problem was initiated, and it seemed that all parties would be able to work out a new agreement when Dr. Shazia, an employee at the Sui hospital, was allegedly raped by an army captain. As the event took place in the Bugti tribal area and the action against the alleged rapist was almost non-existence, the Bugtis felt that their tribal honour was violated. This intensified the violence. Around that time, a number of other violent attacks took place in other areas of Balochistan, and it seemed that the violence in Balochistan was spreading beyond the Bugti area. The complete failure of Prime Minister Zafarullah Khan Jamali, a Baloch sardar's government, in resolving the problem in the beginning also contributed in its expansion. However, the Shujaat–Mushahid committee made significant developments in resolving the problem between the centre and Nawab Akbar Bugti. Despite these developments, the heavy-handed policy of the Musharraf regime resulted in the death of Nawab Akbar Bugti. His death, instead of solving the problem, resulted in him being used as a martyr for the cause of the Baloch. The insurgent violence continued and intensified and, at the time of this writing, is still going on although it has been considerably abated in recent months.

The emergence of the BLA

In 2003 and 2004, the BLA made a series of attacks on provincial infrastructure, targeting military and economic sites, such as military outposts and gas pipelines. The climax of BLA violence came in May 2004 when the group murdered three Chinese engineers working on the Gwardar Port. Since then, the BLA continued its attacks against government convoys, railway tracks, pipelines, and electricity pylons and other government infrastructure.

The Balochistan government registered cases of murder against 12 people including a former chief minister of the province, Sardar Akhtar Mengal, son of Sardar Ataullah Mengal (also a former chief minister), and the secretary general of his Baloch Nationalist Party. The same day, the federal interior minister, Mr Faisal Saleh Hayat, warned that the government would soon launch an operation to get rid of the subversive elements in Balochistan.[8]

Bugti–Mazari clash

The Bugti–Mazari tribal feud started in 1993 between the Mazari and Bugti sub-tribes of Esani and Phank (Mondrani) during the construction of the Kashmore–Rajanpur Indus highway.[9] Since then, both tribes, despite having close family ties between the Bugti and Mazari sardars,[10] were at loggerheads. A fresh wave of tribal violence started when Mazari tribesmen attacked a caravan of Bugti tribesmen passing through their area under FC escort.

Return of insurgency in Balochistan 151

In the subsequent clashes between the Bugtis and Mazaris, the gas pipelines in the Dera Bugti area were targeted.[11] In one of such attacks, the pipeline was damaged and the gas supply was halted.

The Sui Northern Gas Pipeline Limited (SNGPL) stopped supply to all CNG stations and industrial areas in Punjab and the NWFP after two of its four main supply lines on the Punjab–Balochistan border were damaged.[12]

The issue of gas royalty

The situation in Sui turned out to be more than just tit-for-tat clashes between the two rival Baloch tribes on the borders of Punjab and Balochistan.[13] According to media reports, the Bugti camp made it quite clear that it was the royalty and other related matters that were the cause of unrest in the Sui area, and not the Mazari–Bugti clashes. According to one Bugti elder, the royalty of Sui gas was determined on a well-head price of Rs. 9 per 1,000 square feet in the early 1950s. In Sindh it was Rs. 160 and up to Rs. 240 in Punjab. He said that of the total amount received as the well-head price, only 12.5 percent came to Balochistan and the remaining 87.5 percent went to the federal government, PPL and OGDC. He said that jobs for the people of Bugti area in particular and Balochistan in general in gas companies and poverty in the province were issues discussed with the company heads in the presence of the corps commander in 2002.[14]

Akbar Bugti while giving an interview to the BBC stated that there are a number of reasons behind the attacks on the gas pipelines. He also stated that gas is the property of the Baloch which is used by others without their consent or permission. If such things happen for long, people rise up for their right. He emphasized that "There are many reasons of attack on the gas pipelines and the problems further multiply if they are not resolved."[15] Responding to a question about his demands, he said "When someone comes and sits with us, we will discuss the problem with him." However, Akbar Bugti was very clear on the fact that the matter should be resolved through negotiations as he stated in his interview that "the problem can only be solved when talks are held with us." Responding to the question that whether these attacks on the gas pipelines are a method of signalling, Bugti replied, "I cannot say so."[16]

Putting the blame of the delay in working out a new agreement on the issue of royalty on Akbar Bugti, the Ministry of Petroleum and Natural Resources officials were of the view that a new agreement (the previous agreement lapsed on 31 December 2002) could not be reached as Nawab Akbar Bugti wanted the new agreement on his own terms and conditions.[17] According to them, two main issues of difference between the parties are the measurement of land under use and the land rate.[18] For instance, for its Uch field, OGDCL was utilizing 1,100 acres of land, but Nawab Akbar Bugti, according to governmental sources, was demanding rent for 4,300 acres.[19] The ministry sources claimed that the gas companies at the rate of Rs. 12,600 per acre of land as compared to Rs. 10,000 per acre in the Potohar and Hyderabad region were already paying rent for much larger area than they were utilizing, yet now, Akbar Bugti wanted that the rate should be increased

152 *Centre–Province relations post-independence*

to Rs. 17,000 per acre[20] or Rs. 17,600.[21] Some headway was made in the negotiation when the media reported that amidst continuing attacks on the gas pipelines, Sui gas companies and the chief of Bugti tribe Nawab Akbar Khan Bugti have progressed and reached an understanding at Dera Bugti settling various contentious issues concerning Sui and Pirkoh gas fields. Chief Secretary Balochistan, Managing Director PPL and General Manager OGDC took part in the negotiations. According to the agreement, the children of retired and deceased employees of the gas fields would be given jobs.[22] It was also agreed that free gas would be provided to people living in the radius of three kilometres of gas fields. In future, the Bugti tribe would be given jobs at the gas fields according to 70 percent quota fixed for them.[23]

Initial government response

On 4 February 2003, Prime Minister Mir Zafarullah Khan Jamali chaired a high-level meeting on law and order situation in Balochistan with reference to the gas pipelines crisis.[24] This was the first meeting the prime minister presided ever since the eruption of violence in Balochistan. According to the media reports, the participants of the meeting were against the revision of the agreement with the Bugtis that expired on December 31.[25] It was also decided in the meeting that the Bugtis would not be given any big concession and would only be offered to accept the old agreement with the companies.

Petroleum and Natural Resources Minister Chaudhry Nouraiz Shakoor said in a statement that the government was open to negotiate on any unsettled issues rather than allowing damage to oil and gas installations.[26]

It was also decided in the meeting that to ensure the security of the gas field and pipeline, a 500 strong force of Rangers headed by a colonel would be deployed.[27] It was also reported in February 2003 that President General Pervez Musharraf sought a comprehensive report on all kinds of petroleum-related payments made to the Balochistan government and Baloch sardars, including royalties, rentals and illegal gratifications.[28] Sensing the tough attitude of the federal government, the Balochistan government asked the centre not to launch any operation in the troubled areas unless cleared by the provincial government.[29]

The Shujaat–Mushahid committee

The parliamentary committee on Balochistan was set up by Chaudhry Shujaat Hussain in September 2004. It undertook the task of looking into the Baloch grievances. It sent a sub-committee, headed by Mushahid Hussain, to Balochistan to discuss the grievances of the Baloch nationalists.

Baloch nationalist leader Sardar Ataullah Mengal, after his meeting with Chaudhry Shujaat Hussain and Mushahid Hussain Syed, stated that he made it clear to Chaudhry Shujaat Hussain and Syed Mushahid Hussain that the talks cannot be held with the government under "the shadow of gun."[30] Sardar Ataullah Mengal said he told the official delegation that he was not concerned with the Sui

Return of insurgency in Balochistan 153

crisis, but wanted Islamabad to take serious notice of real demands of the Baloch for greater rights. He suggested to Chaudhry Shujaat Hussain to contact Nawab Akbar Bugti if he was only interested in defusing the situation in Sui.[31] While Sardar Attaullah Mengal was right and honest in his view that he could not be of any help in resolving the problem in the Bugti area, this statement in itself is significant for understanding the Baloch tribal and political culture. The problem in the Bugti area was a problem between the Bugti tribe and the government and not a problem of other Baloch tribes. Second, Baloch tribal and political culture does not allow one sardar to interfere in the business of another sardar even when it involves the Baloch honour.

He further stated that he asked the government representatives to improve the situation in Sui and Dera Bugti, adding that he advised the government represent-atives to contact Nawab Akbar Bugti as the situation was deteriorating in Dera Bugti and he might be able to help them.[32] "I proposed them that it is better to first solve the problems which have ignited the prevailing situation and then contact Bugti."

Apparently, in the beginning there was some deadlock on the issue of a meeting between Akbar Bugti and the committee delegation. When asked if he had refused to meet the team till the withdrawal of security forces from Sui, Bugti said: "We have not demanded their withdrawal, but made it clear that talks cannot be held in such a situation." Responding to a question under what circumstances talks would be possible, Bugti said: "It is their task to make the atmosphere free of intimida-tion and fear. It is up to them to do the needful."[33]

Bugti–Mushahid meeting

Senator Mushahid Hussain, a key figure in the senate committee on Balochistan during a meeting with Akbar Bugti told him that for the first time in the his-tory of Pakistan a high-powered committee had been formed to look into the Baloch issue.[34] Nawab Akbar Bugti presented a memorandum to the commit-tee. The memorandum had Akbar Bugti's suggestion about how to resolve the crisis in Balochistan. The memorandum contained Akbar Bugti's views on issues such as the construction of cantonments, Gwadar and other mega projects, the presence of the security and paramilitary forces and provincial autonomy.[35]

Mushahid Hussain and Akbar Bugti met again. This was an indication that both sides were able to break the ice.[36] It was agreed that a three-member committee would be set up to discuss and recommend ways to resolve all matters. It was agreed that one member each would be representing the centre and Akbar Bugti, while the third will be a neutral member agreeable to both sides.[37]

Bugti formula

By the time the parliamentary committee on Balochistan started functioning, another dialogue process was under way with the Baloch nationalists including

154 *Centre–Province relations post-independence*

Akbar Bugti and the Nation Security Advisor to the President of Pakistan, Tariq Aziz, that continued to operate parallel to the parliamentary committee's efforts. It is not clear why the Musharraf regime opted for two separate and uncoordinated channels for talks with Nawab Bugti and the Baloch nationalists instead of focusing their energies on one. Bugti's willingness to talk and interact with both clearly illustrated the fact that Akbar Bugti never shunned from dialogue and was looking for a way out. Akbar Bugti in a media statement stated that he handed over a 15-point formula to Tariq Aziz that could be used to resolve the Balochistan issue. The 15-point formula for the resolution of the Balochistan problem that Akbar Bugti shared with the media was as follows[38]:

1 Provincial autonomy should be granted to the satisfaction of the people.
2 The ownership of the Baloch people of Balochistan's natural resources should be recognized.
3 The reservations of the Baloch regarding the mega projects, including the Gwadar Port and coastal belt, should be redressed.
4 All the revenues generated through all the mega projects should be given to Balochistan, and all employment in the mega projects should be given to the people of Gwadar, Makran and Balochistan.
5 Outsiders should be removed from mega projects and gas fields, and they should be replaced with locals.
6 The right of the Baloch and others to run their own affairs should be recognized.
7 Planned new cantonments should be cancelled, and the land so taken by force should be returned to their owners, and for this purpose, necessary changes should be made in the land revenue record.
8 There are four federating units in Pakistan, with equal representation in the senate. General Zia distorted this by giving Fata and Islamabad seats in the senate, thereby upsetting the whole structure. We want that the original agreed constitutional position be restored.
9 In Marri area, sometime back about 1,000 hostile tribals were raised as a coercive measure by the ISI and the MI as a special Levies Force to suppress and overawe the rest of the Marri tribe and to bring them to heel. But its outcome has been the opposite. This body should be disbanded forthwith and the policy of divide and rule be abandoned.
10 All prisoners kept under various pretexts (political reasons) should be released.
11 All armed force personnel from the interior of Balochistan should be withdrawn.
12 All civil armed forces should be placed under the provinces.
13 All law-making authority for Balochistan be given to the Balochistan assembly.
14 Within the federating units, no federal law should override the provincial laws.
15 Problems with gas companies old (unresolved) and fresh (running) should be resolved.

Bugti's joint Baloch platform proposal

It seemed that Akbar Bugti finally accepted the reality that the biggest impediment to the Baloch was their lack of unity and a unified approach and agenda. This realization led Akbar Bugti to offer to dissolve his party to form a joint political platform for the Baloch people. "If National Party, Baloch Haq Tawar, Balochistan National Party and other groups and personalities dissolve their political and individual entities for the formation of a single joint platform that would be highly appreciated," he stated.[39] Bugti wished that the proposed greater Baloch platform would make concrete planning and adopt a strategy to ensure the identity of the Baloch nation and survival of the homeland besides acquiring their right to rule, protection of coasts and their resources. He said that it is high time to play a historic role by converting deprivations of the Baloch nation into a bright future by putting behind our ego for a greater cause.[40] However, the proposal failed to attract any positive response from other Baloch political leaders and sardars as they were not willing to let go of their hold on their areas of influence.

Recommendations of the senate committee on Balochistan

By the time in 2004, the then Prime Minister Chaudhry Shujaat Hussain announced that a senate committee would be established to study and holistically analyse the Balochistan problem and recommend measures for resolution; the then President of Pakistan General Musharraf's right hand man and national security advisor Tariq Aziz was already negotiating with the Baloch leaders.[41] The committee's final report was indeed a holistic and detailed analysis of the problem and contained workable and acceptable recommendation for resolving the issues between the centre and the province. The committee submitted its report in 2005. The senate committee on Balochistan recommended an increase in the share of gas revenues of Balochistan, an increase in job quota for the Baloch, anda greater role and representation of the provincial government of Balochistan in Gwadar and other mega projects. Another important recommendation was to make Council of Common Interests more effective.[42] It also recommended deletion of 30 items from the concurrent list and bringing the number of items on the concurrent list to 17.[43] Chaudhry Shujaat Hussain informed the house that General Musharraf had already seen the report and had accepted 27 (31 in total) recommendations of the committee.[44]

The reaction of the opposition in the parliament was in line with the political culture of Pakistan: totally ignoring the fact that the committee comprised members from all political parties including the opposition. The opposition insisted that the debates which took place in the committee meetings, especially while finalizing the recommendations, should be repeated in the house.

Baloch nationalist's rejection of the report

The four-party Baloch Alliance rejected the parliamentary committee's recommendations on Balochistan and vowed to continue the struggle for the national rights of Baloch people.[45]

156 *Centre–Province relations post-independence*

Speaking at a joint news conference, Dr. Hayee Baloch read out a four-page statement alleging that the parliamentary committee at the behest of the centre, intelligence agencies, bureaucracy and the anti-Baloch elements had prepared the recommendations.

JWP Senator Amanullah Kasrani and BNP-Mengal's secretary general Habib Jalib Baloch, Opposition Leader in the Balochistan assembly Kachkol Baloch, Senator Sana Baloch, MPAs Saleem Khoso and Akhtar Hussain, Mir Hasil Bizenjo, Sajid Tareen and Malik Wali Kakar were present on the occasion.

Dr. Abdul Hayee stated that the Baloch demands were ignored in the report. According to him, the Baloch wanted that the construction of the Gwadar Port should be stopped. Their other demands were: no more cantonments, end of military operation, release of political prisoners, representation in federal institutions, and recognition of the ownership of the Baloch on its resources.[46]

Despite this press conference and rejection of the report of the committee and its recommendations, the committee, especially Shujaat Hussain and Mushahid Hussain, enjoyed widespread support from all sides. Even Sardar Attaullah Mengal and Nawab Akbar Bugti declared them honest and sincere in their effort. Unfortunately, a golden opportunity was lost. With the passage of time and increased violence in Balochistan, no further progress could be made, and it still remains unclear how much of the committee's recommendations were implemented.

Revival of Shujaat committee and the nationalists reaction

The deteriorating security situation in Balochistan led the then Prime Minister of Pakistan, Shaukat Aziz, to reactivate the dysfunctional parliamentary committee on Balochistan. He called the meeting of the committee on 15 July 2005. The main agenda item of the meeting was to review the progress on recommendations of the parliamentary committee on Balochistan.[47] The meeting also explored ways in which parliamentarians, especially from Balochistan, could play an active and greater role in resolving the crisis in Balochistan.[48]

Baloch nationalists rejected the so-called revival of the parliamentary committee on Balochistan and claimed it to be another political gimmick of the centre. They argued that this step would not satisfy the Baloch who were increasingly getting fed up with such moves. If the centre was sincere and really wanted to resolve the problem of Balochistan, it needed to take solid reconciliatory steps towards the Baloch.

As a first step, Baloch nationalists argued that the Prime Minister Aziz should let the people of Balochistan and Pakistan know how many of the recommendations of the parliamentary committee have been implemented so far. However, one thing which was stated by almost all Baloch nationalist leaders was that if Islamabad was sincere in resolving the Balochistan crisis, it needed to change its approach and policy. Military operation and dialogue for resolution could not go on side by side. Sardar Akhtar Mengal summed up this

Return of insurgency in Balochistan 157

Baloch position when he stated that no self-respecting Baloch leader would talk to Islamabad at gun point.

Dr. Shazia's rape and intensification of violence in the Bugti area

In January 2005, Shazia Khalid, a medical doctor working for Pakistan Petroleum Limited in Sui, was allegedly raped by an army captain. Government's inaction in comprehending the culprits was taken as an insult and violation of the Baloch honour.[49] This resulted in intensification of violence in the Bugti area in which a number of FC personnel lost their lives. In two such attacks which took place between January 7 and 11, almost fifteen FC and Defence Security Guard (DSG) personnel lost their lives. The government responded by registering an FIR against 37 alleged culprits including Nawab Akbar Bugti's son Jamil Bugti and grandson Brahumdagh Bugti.[50]

Attack on General Musharraf and IG FC in Kholu

In the midst of increasing political unrest and violence in Balochistan, General Musharraf visited Kholu. A number of observers thought that this was a highly risky move. Understandably, General Musharraf's government wanted to signal its resolve to the Baloch nationalists that the government's writ would be established and ensured at all cost. Choosing Kholu, the centre of ultra-nationalist Khair Bakhsh Marri's tribal power and widely considered to be the hotbed of insurgent activity for this signalling was an indication of this resolve.[51] Those observers, who considered it a bad move, were of the opinion that at this moment, Balochistan required a reconciliatory touch, not an aggressive posture. General Musharraf and his advisors knew that Khair Bakhsh Marri's son and a sitting member of the Balochistan provincial assembly from the area, Balach Marri would boycott the meeting, but they got much more than they expected. The Baloch militants attempted to assassinate General Musharraf by firing rockets during General Musharraf's speech.[52]

Another event that had significant implications on how Islamabad reacted to the current insurgency was the firing on the helicopter in which Frontier Corps (FC) Balochistan's Inspector-General (IG), Major General Shujaat Zamir Dar, and Deputy Inspector General (DIG) Frontier Force (FC), Brig Saleem Nawaz, were wounded.[53]

Military operation against the Baloch insurgents

In response to these two developments, Pakistan's security forces launched an operation against the Baloch militants involved in the attacks against General Musharraf, Major General Shujaat Zamir Dar and Brigadier Saleem Nawaz.[54] The operation was then expanded into a search-and-destroy-Parari-camps operation. According to security officials, they had reports of the existence of 53 Parari

158 *Centre–Province relations post-independence*

camps. Thirteen camps were in the Marri area, 15 in Bugti area, whereas the remaining were scattered in different areas.

With an influx of forces into the Bugti area, Akbar Bugti questioned the rationale of sending troops to the Bugti area. In a statement, he stated that 15,000 regular army troops, FC, DSG and Rangers were already positioned in the Bugti area.[55] On the official position that these forces were stationed to target the miscreants, Akbar Bugti, in a rare demonstration of emotion retorted that the centre had always declared its opponents miscreants. The Baloch, stated Akbar Bugti, were declared miscreants soon after the independence of Pakistan. Despite the fact that the Baloch are Pakistanis, "the government does not recognize us as Pakistanis and declared us as enemies of the country."[56]

Despite the fact that Nawab Akbar Bugti and the Bugti tribe had nothing to do with the attack on General Musharraf, Akbar Bugti remained the main opponent of the Musharraf regime.

Musharraf regime's steps to weaken Akbar Bugti's hold

General Musharraf was convinced that the three sardars, Nawab Akbar Bugti, Nawab Khair Bakhsh Marri and Sardar Attaullah Mengal, were the main trouble makers in Balochistan. Out of these three, according to General Musharraf, Akbar Bugti was the biggest villain. He followed a step-by-step policy of weakening Akbar Bugti's hold on the Bugti tribe and his position as the sardar of the Bugti tribe.

Return of Masoori and Kalpars to the Bugti area

Musharraf regime decided, encouraged and fully supported the return of the Masoori and Kalpars to the Bugti area.[57] These clans were expelled from the Bugti area after the murder of Salal Bugti. Regardless of who and what was right and wrong, this policy could have resulted in nothing else but disaster. Both the Masoori and Kalpars fully supported the centre's approach towards Balochistan. Leader of the Masooris said that the government should continue the ongoing military operation in Balochistan against the terrorists in order to bring peace and prosperity in the areas.[58]

Speaking at a news conference, Ghulam Qadir Masoori Bugti, responding to a question about who was supporting the terrorists, said that Akbar Bugti was providing every kind of support to these anti-Pakistani people.[59] He claimed that a number of political leaders including Makdoom Amin Fahim, Chairman PPP, Maulana Fazal-ur-Rahman and Qazi Hussain Ahmad had information about the real situation, yet they were opposing the ongoing operation.[60]

Echoing General Musharraf's stated position on the Balochistan issue, Tariq Masoori Bugti in an interview on Geo TV claimed that only two to three sardars were vitiating the atmosphere of Balochistan. He further claimed that the Baloch want to free themselves from the clutches of these so-called sardars.[61] Claiming that Akbar Bugti annually received Rs. 370 million as gas royalty, he questioned

Return of insurgency in Balochistan 159

that how much of this amount was spent for the development of the Bugti tribe. He said that even as the governor and Chief Minister of Balochistan, Akbar Bugti did nothing for the development of his home constituency and the welfare of its people.

As part of a well-worked-out plan, more than 4,000 Kalpars and Masooris were brought back to the Bugti tribal area under the protection of security forces. According to media reports, despite the military escort, the returning tribesmen were "armed to the teeth"[62] to avoid any mishap or clash.[63]

This further complicated the situation for Akbar Bugti. He realized that he was left with no other option but to leave his fiefdom which he ruled as an authoritative and almost tyrannical ruler and go to the mountains and take up arms. According to a few media reports, about 200 Baloch militants belonging to the Marri tribe came to Dera Bugti and escorted him out of the area.

The surrender game

In the next phase, government claimed that a number of Bugti militant leaders have surrendered their arms and requested pardon. According to details, four top commanders of Brahumdagh Bugti, the second-in-command of armed Bugti tribesmen, surrendered to the government on 13 July 2006 along with 40 armed men.[64] Prime Minister Shaukat Aziz said that the government would not consider any proposal to accord general amnesty to those involved in subversion, insurgency or any other criminal activities in Balochistan.[65]

The Balochistan government claimed that after the Bugti militiamen, miscreants from the Marri tribe had begun surrendering to the government. According to government officials, 38 guerrillas led by Wadera Jumma Khan, a prominent elder from the Marri tribe, had surrendered to the Kohlu administration and surrendered a large number of weapons including rocket launchers, Kalashnikovs and ammunition.[66]

This development resulted in Balochistan governor's declaration of victory against militant tribesmen, saying that the revolt led by Nawab Akbar Khan Bugti had been quelled. According to the government, with more and more Bugti and Marri tribesmen laying down their arms and surrendering to the government forces in the troubled tribal belt of Dera Bugti and Kohlu, the problem was heading towards a resolution.[67]

Anti-Akbar Bugti Jirga

A pro-Musharraf and anti-Akbar Bugti Jirga of the Bugti tribe was held on 24 August 2006 in which tribal elders of sub-clans of the Bugti tribe participated.[68] Wadera Jalalur Rahman, Wadera Ali Mohammad Masoori, Wadera Mewa Khan Notkani, Wadera Mir Ahmadan, Wadera Mohammad Hussain Mundrani, Sardar Sobdar Kiazai and Wadera Nabi Bakhsh Perozani attended the jirga.[69] The jirga adopted 15 resolutions. The jirga participants pledged their loyalty to Pakistan and announced that from this day onwards, the laws of the state of Pakistan would be

160 *Centre–Province relations post-independence*

implemented and followed in the Bugti area. The jirga demanded that the Marris should hand Akbar Bugti over to them so that he could be tried according to the Baloch tradition. The jirga also called for the confiscation of Akbar Bugti and his family's assets and property and its distribution to the victims of his tyranny.[70]

Akbar Bugti's death

Despite all these developments, neither the violence in Balochistan stopped nor did Akbar Bugti become an insignificant threat or irritant in Musharraf regime's eye.[71] The security forces continued their operation against the Baloch militants. On 26 August 2006, Akbar Bugti was killed in a military operation. The accounts of how exactly this happened vary. According to initial media reports, security forces faced stiff resistance from a location when they were conducting routine search-and-destroy operations against the Parari camps on August 24 and 25. In keeping with the intense resistance the security forces faced, it was presumed that there is a high-value target in the area. Security forces called for reinforcement. During the heavy exchange of fire, the cave collapsed, killing all the militants inside the cave. It was assumed, and later confirmed, that Akbar Bugti was among the dead.[72]

Bugti's death and the way he was buried resulted in a strong wave of anguish throughout Balochistan. The death of a prominent sardar and his burial under tight security net was taken as a huge dishonour to all Baloch. Violent protests started soon after the news of Bugti's death broke. A question which was repeatedly asked by ultra-Baloch nationalists was that if Islamabad was capable of doing this to one of its long-term ally and supporter, what would it do to others? Akbar Bugti's death was condemned by almost all political parties in Pakistan.[73] Musharraf regime projected Akbar Bugti as an anti-Pakistan Baloch sardar. It was argued that Akbar Bugti was an extremely stubborn, uncompromising, tyrannical and ruthless Baloch sardar.

Was Akbar Bugti anti-Pakistan or was just struggling for what he believed was the right of the Bugtis? The views are extremely divided on this, but the fact of the matter is that despite adopting a tough posture, Nawab Bugti was open to any possibility of a respectable solution of the problem. About the possibility of his meeting with President Pervez Musharraf, publically, he stated he would not beg for a meeting as he (Bugti) was not weak.[74]

Publically, he maintained a tough posture and stated that he would not set any conditions or demands to resolve the crisis and that demands or conditions are like making requests, and that they do not make requests. Yet, he not only agreed to meet General Musharraf but also to travel to Islamabad for this meeting. Had the meeting between the two taken place, the situation might have been different today. According to a media report, a private aircraft was sent to fly Bugti from Sui to Islamabad. However, at the last moment, according to an Express Tribune report, "some hawkish elements within the military establishment apparently scuttled the entire scheme by delaying the aircraft on the pretext of a technical failure."[75] After waiting for two hours for the repair to finish, Akbar Bugti decided

Return of insurgency in Balochistan 161

to go back to Dera Bugti. He would still be in the vicinity of the Sui airport when the airplane took off.[76]

Akbar Bugti's death in a military operation made him a martyr for the Baloch nationalists,[77] despite the fact that Akbar Bugti was never in the forefront of Baloch nationalism, when compared to other Baloch leaders like Khair Bakhsh Marri or Attaullah Mengal. He remained primarily a Bugti, fighting for his own tribe and in particular his sub-tribe. Even during the ongoing insurgency, the Bugtis fought primarily for their own rights, and not for any pan-Baloch cause. More jobs and increased royalties for the Sui gas to the Bugtis were his main demands. As late as three years before his death, the Bugtis were fighting the other tribes in Balochistan.

His death, however, changed the position of Akbar Bugti. Attaullah Mengal made an important observation: Bugti's death had drawn a line between Balochistan and Pakistan.

Baloch insurgency: Post-Bugti death

Bugti's death might have divided and weakened the Bugti tribe's armed resistance, but the problem of insurgent violence in other areas not only continued but has over the years intensified.

In November 2006, Akhtar Mengal was arrested and tried in the Karachi Anti-Terrorism Court for treason, a charge many believed was politically motivated. Another important development was the death of Balach Marri. Nawabzada Balach Marri, the top leader of the BLA, was killed on November 21 in Afghanistan reportedly in a drone strike.

A BLA spokesman told The News on Sunday that Balach Marri was killed by security forces but refused to disclose the location where the killing had taken place. "Balach Marri was killed inside Afghanistan...," said Balochistan Governor, Owais Ahmed Ghani. A fresh wave of violence erupted in Quetta and some other Baloch-dominated areas of Balochistan following the killing of Balach Marri. Railway tracks were blown up at various places, including tracks in main Sibi and Quetta.

2008 NATIONAL ELECTIONS IN PAKISTAN

Although initially Baloch political leadership started planning on how to conduct their election campaigns and win maximum seats in provincial assembly and national assembly, yet the situation on the ground was increasingly getting unfavourable for such a political activity. Militant groups such as the BLA considered participating in elections as a betrayal of the Baloch. A significant number of Baloch youth influenced by this view considered parliamentary politics as insufficient to address Baloch grievances and hence a waste of time.[78] The political actors and parties in Balochistan were also divided and lack coherence. Khair Bakhsh Marri declared that he would not be participating in the elections. His sons were facing a number of cases and hence could not have participated in the elections anyways. The only exception was his son Jangez Marri who was with PML (Q).

162 *Centre–Province relations post-independence*

The Balochistan National Party (Mengal) decided that it would participate in the elections. Attaullah Mengal argued that although he is convinced that the Baloch would never get their rights through the parliament, yet he would not proscribe the elections and give Islamabad the opportunity to get its own agents elected.

Akbar Bugti's Jamhoori Wattan Party (JWP) was a significant political party of Balochistan and could have, following the political culture of Pakistan, capitalized on Akbar Bugti's death to win a considerable number of seats from Balochistan. But a number of factors made it impossible: After the death of Akbar Bugti, his family developed bitter differences on the question of who would replace him as the sardar of the Bugti tribe. The JWP was also splintered into two groups: one led by the grandson of Akbar Bugti, Brahumdagh Bugti. Brahumdagh Bugti was also leading a militant group. He rejected the idea of participation in the elections. The other faction was led by Akbar Bugti's son Talal Bugti. Talal faction believed in political struggle within the constitutional framework of Pakistan and declared that it would participate in the elections. However, the arrival of the Kalpars, Masooris and other anti-Akbar Bugti sub-tribes in Dera Bugti and the large scale migration of the Bugti tribesmen from Dera Bugti, made it almost impossible for JWP-Talal to win from Dera Bugti. The Baloch militant groups also started an active campaign against the elections in Balochistan.[79] Baloch militant groups cautioned the Baloch from visiting polling stations on February 18.

Talking to the BBC, Baloch Republican Army spokesman Sarbaz Baloch said that people had been directed not to participate in the polls as it was not offering any solution to their issues. Due to all these factors, Baloch nationalist political parties decided to boycott the elections. This decision resulted in PML-Q's candidates winning most of the seats. Other parties that managed to reach the Balochistan provincial assembly were the PPP, JUI-F and a number of independent candidates. The decision to boycott the elections turned out to be an error of judgment on the part of the Baloch nationalists as it served no purpose for them in their struggle and made others who these nationalists blamed for their troubles, the decision-makers in Balochistan for the next five years.[80]

PPP GOVERNMENT

The Pakistan Peoples Party once again emerged as the majority party in Pakistan in the 2008 elections except in Balochistan. The signals coming from the top leadership of the party including its new President Asif Ali Zardari indicated that the coming PPP government would follow a policy of reconciliation and accommodation. This took an unprecedented shape when Asif Ali Zardari apologized to the Baloch people for the injustices against them. During a meeting of the parliamentary committee of the PPP, a resolution was passed that read: "The PPP, on behalf of the people of Pakistan, apologizes to the people of the province of Balochistan for the atrocities and injustices committed against them and pledges to embark on a new highway of healing and mutual respect."[81]

Most observers of Pakistani politics viewed this apology as an intelligent move to win hearts and minds in Balochistan where the PPP was numerically struggling in the Balochistan assembly. The general view was that the apology was a right move and would have positive implications for Pakistan.[82] The response of the Baloch nationalist leadership on the apology was mixed. Attaullah Mengal considered it a positive yet an insufficient step. Attaullah Mengal also claimed that the PPP would not be able to achieve much as the country was run by a military–bureaucratic nexus and not by the politicians.[83]

After some traditional political wrangling, the centre appointed a Baloch political heavyweight Nawab Zulfiqar Ali Magsi as the governor of Balochistan. This move indicated that the centre intended to initiate a reconciliation process to pacify the disenchanted people of the province.[84]

The PPP nominated Nawab Muhammad Aslam Raisani as the chief minister. The new government in Balochistan offered dialogue to the Baloch militants. The Baloch insurgents rejected the offer. BLA spokesman Beebarg Baloch said: "We regard the government's offer for talks as its defeat because previously it was not ready even to recognize the existence of the BLA."[85] The BLA also issued a hit-list.[86] The hit-list included former Balochistan governors Amir-ul-Mulk Mengal and Owais Ahmed Ghani, former Balochistan chief minister Jam Muhammad Yousaf and former federal minister Sardar Yar Muhammad Rind.

Brahumdagh Bugti also rejected the offer. Brahumdagh Bugti said the Baloch resistance movement was aimed at protecting the land and resources of the Baloch people.[87] Brahumdagh Bugti said: "We are owners of our land and resources and there is no need to talk with others on our resources. Talks will be held only with those who accept our right on Balochistan's resources."

PPP GOVERNMENT'S ALL-PARTY CONFERENCE ON BALOCHISTAN

As a next step, the Pakistan Peoples Party co-chairman Asif Ali Zardari set up a committee to convene an all-party conference (APC) on Balochistan for addressing the grievances of its people and bringing them into the national mainstream.[88] The committee, headed by Mr Zardari, comprised PPP secretary general Jehangir Badar, PPP's Balochistan chapter president Mir Lashkari Raisani, MNA Ijaz Jhakrani, Senator Dr Babar Awan and deputy general secretary of the PPP Balochistan, Saadullah.

The committee was tasked to contact leaders of all political parties and other groups and people concerned to attend the conference to launch a concerted effort for bringing normality to the province.[89]

AGHAZ-E-HUQOOQ-E-BALOCHISTAN PACKAGE, THE NFC AWARD AND THE 18TH AMENDMENT

On 24 November 2009, the PPP government presented its Aghaz-e-Haqooq-e-Balochistan package to a special joint session of the parliament.[90] This was

164   *Centre–Province relations post-independence*

considered an historic document by government members of the parliament. This document had 39 recommendations, and most of these had the echoes of the parliamentary committee on Balochistan's report. The package[91] recommended the deletion of the concurrent list, Police order 2002 and Balochistan local government act. It recommended the restructuring of the NFC award criteria, effective implementation of article 153 of the constitution, withdrawal of army from Sui, postponement of the construction of cantonments at Sui and Kohlu, creation of a judicial commission on the issue of missing persons, revision of the royalty formula and greater representation in the mega projects.

A positive development which took place during the PPP government was the signing of the 7th National Finance Commission Award in December 2009.[92] In the award, Balochistan's share was increased in the divisible pool from 5.11% to 9.09%. It was decided that Balochistan will also receive Rs. 120 billion over a period of 12 years on account of Gas Development Surcharge (GDS) arrears. An additional amount of Rs. 10 billion will also be released by the federal government on account of equalization of well-head price with effect from 2002.[93] According to Zafarullah Khan,

> The 7th NFC award finalized at Gwadar on December 31, 2009 could be described as a step forward for Pakistani federalism. It redefined the Federal-Provincial share 44:56 respectively and opted for a multi-indicator formula for horizontal distribution i.e. population 82 percent, poverty/ backwardness 10.30 percent, revenue collecting/ generation 5 percent and inverse population density 2.70 percent. The provinces were also allowed to levy and collect general sales tax on services.[94]

Another important development was the passing of the 18th amendment to the constitution of Pakistan on 8 April 2010. The President of Pakistan approved it on 19 April 2010. The 18th amendment changed about 100 articles of the constitution. According to a report:

> Part V and VI of the Constitution especially articles 141-174 specifically deal with relations between federation and provinces. Out of these thirty four (34) articles, seventeen (17) were amended in April 2010… The major amendments included; redefining legislative competence of the parliament and provincial assemblies after the abolition of the concurrent list, inclusion of a provincial legislative ratification clause if the provincial government entrusted any function to the federation. It also included reforms in the Council of Common Interests, National Economic Council, National Finance Commission and a constitutional obligation to submit annual/bi-annual performance reports to both houses. Mandatory consultation with the concerned provincial government prior to a decision to conduct hydro-electric power stations, protection to current provincial share and possibilities of increase only in future awards of the National Finance Commission, and provincial power to raise domestic or international loans and a fifty percent share in natural resources.[95]

2013 ELECTIONS AND THE APPOINTMENT OF DR. MALIK BALOCH AS THE CHIEF MINISTER OF BALOCHISTAN

Just before the 2013 elections, Akhtar Mengal agreed to come back to Pakistan. During his brief stay in Islamabad in September 2012, Balochistan National Party President Akhtar Mengal met the leaders of two mainstream parties, Nawaz Sharif of PML-N and Imran Khan of the Tehreek-e-Insaf. This indicated that Mengal was ready for a political dialogue. It was reported that the PML-N offered to propose his name as the caretaker prime minister, which he declined. On the military side, the then Chief of Army Staff, General Ashfaq Parvez Kayani responded to that proposal by stating that the army would extend its support "to a political solution to the Balochistan problem provided that the solution be in accordance with the constitution of Pakistan" adding that "any steps taken in violation of the constitution would be unacceptable."[96]

Mengal's six points

Mengal also presented his six-point solution to the problem of Balochistan. Sardar Mengal's six points were:

1 All overt and covert military operations against the Baloch should end.
2 All missing persons should be produced before the court of Law.
3 All proxy death squads created by the ISI and MI should be disbanded.
4 Baloch nationalist parties should be allowed free political play without interference from ISI and MI.
5 Those responsible for the killings and disappearances should be brought to the book.
6 Thousands of Baloch displaced by the conflict should be rehabilitated.

In 2013 elections, Nawaz Sharif-led Pakistan Muslim League (PML-N) emerged as the majority party in the centre as well as in the province of the Punjab. It also managed to gather enough seats to form a government in the province of Balochistan. However, in an unprecedented move, Nawaz Sharif decided to appoint Dr. Malik Baloch, a moderate Baloch leader from Hazil Bizenjo's party as the Chief Minister of Balochistan. Incidentally, Dr. Malik was the first CM of Balochistan who was not a tribal sardar and represented the Baloch middle class. The decision to appoint him as the CM was widely hailed as a positive and mature political gesture towards the Baloch and Balochistan.

However, by the end of 2013, it became clear that Dr. Abdul Malik's government could not perform according to the expectation of the Baloch nationalists. This fact was acknowledged by Hazil Bizenjo, the party chairman. According to Mr. Bizenjo, the provincial government has no powers when it comes to issues regarding Balochistan. Mailk Siraj Akbar, a Baloch journalist and editor of online Baloch Hal, commented:

166 *Centre–Province relations post-independence*

> While Mr. Bizenjo's ultimatum to quit the provincial government seems like a mere political gimmick, the cost of failure for Dr. Malik's government to recover the missing persons will, however, be very high. Balochistan will once again be plunged into a deep crisis if the government fails to change the policies of those whom Mr. Bizenjo described as the "bosses of the bosses."[97]

An important development that took place during this period was the induction of 10,082 Baloch youth into the Pakistan Army. This brought the number of Baloch to 18,700 (700 officers and 18,000 soldiers). This was part of the plan to induct Baloch youth in the army by then army Chief General Ashfaq Parvez Kayani. As part of this plan, a number of educational institutes were established: a college in Sui, Balochistan Public School in Sui, Quetta Institute of Medical Sciences (QIMS), GIT (Gwadar Institute of Technology), Chamalang Beneficiary Education Programme (CBEP), BITE (Balochistan Institute of Technical Education) and Army Institute of Mineralogy (AIM). According to media reports, 400 cadets were studying at the Sui Military College. Army is also providing free-of-cost education and boarding/lodging to 4,300 local children in Army Public Schools/Colleges across the country. A medical college has also been established in Quetta by the army where 100 local students are undergoing training.[98] Pakistan Navy also established a recruiting centre at Gwadar. Navy also introduced an N-cadet scheme in Balochistan. According to this scheme, youth from Balochistan would be selected and educated at cadet colleges for five years. After this, they would be given a choice to join Pakistan Navy. According to media reports, "officers from the province will be inducted into the Short Service Commission without undergoing ISSB tests and they will be given special relaxation in the standard academic and age criteria."

HOW THE CURRENT INSURGENCY IS DIFFERENT FROM THE PREVIOUS INSURGENCIES?

The current violence/insurgency in Balochistan is quite different from the earlier insurgent violence which took place in Balochistan in the past. This time, the movement has a new leadership which has *no interest* or exposure in the politics of Pakistan. Unlike the previous insurgencies in which the Brahuis (Mengals and Marris) were involved, this time the Bugti tribe is also actively involved in the insurgency. As it has been demonstrated in this book, Bugtis were never a part of the Baloch nationalist movement and were only interested in safeguarding their own rights. The inclusion of the Bugti tribe in the insurgency has added a new element to the situation.

As compared to the previous insurgencies, this time the insurgents have latest weapons and equipment. Another important aspect of the enhanced capabilities of the insurgents is the use of media. Apart from print and electronic media, the Baloch nationalists are actively using the social media to send their message across.

Another important aspect of current insurgency that differentiates it from the previous one is the presence of comparatively free news media in Pakistan which regularly reports developments in Balochistan to the people of Pakistan. This has resulted in greater awareness among the people of other three provinces about the situation in Balochistan.

Targeted killings and missing persons

One of the most unique features of the ongoing crisis in Balochistan is the targeted killings of Punjabi settlers in Baluchistan.[99] Associated with the targeted killings is another phenomenon of atrocities committed against the Baloch people that pertains to the abduction and dumping of dead bodies by the unidentified perpetrators.[100] The data available on these crimes are not highly reliable, and most of them begin from 2010 onwards. Coupled with this is the lack of reliable sources from where authentic data can be obtained on the issue.

On 25 October 2009, the Minister for Education Shafiq Ahmed Khan was killed in an incident of targeted killing. Three days later, the secretary of education was killed. Previously, in April 2009, pro-vice chancellor of the University of Baluchistan was shot dead in front of the university. Although the resentment against the Punjabi settlers has always been there in certain quarters. In the past, they have often been equated with Islamabad and declared establishment's supporters and agents of the rulers. There have been demands for their expulsion from the province in the past,[101] yet mostly they were able to live in peace. During the current insurgency, the Baloch insurgents started targeting university teachers, doctors, government officers, labourers and barbers. There are cases in which a person was killed only because his identity card had a residential address in Punjab. Several teachers have asked the education department to transfer them from the Baloch-majority areas of the province to Quetta or the Pashtun-populated areas. Shafiq Ahmed Khan, the provincial minister for education, who later himself became a victim of targeted killing, told the media that 14 college lecturers and 22 school teachers have been transferred from the Baloch-majority areas to other parts of the province. In fact, a BLA spokesman, who had claimed responsibility for the killing of a senior teacher in Kalat, maintained that the slain teacher was not allowing Baloch students to sing the Baloch national anthem in the Government High School in Kalat.

The targeted killings of the Punjabi settlers began with the day labourers, barbers and tailors who the BLA and other such groups accused of spying for the security forces, then came the more well-off Punjabi businessmen, and then they started targeting teachers.[102] As a result, the property rates in Punjabi-dominated localities of Quetta have fallen remarkably as Punjabis hastily sell their homes to try and escape the insurgency-hit province. As per the records, in 2009 alone, 83 Punjabis and Sindhis were killed in Balochistan.[103] BLA accepted responsibility for most of these killings. Brahumdagh Bugti, in an interview, has justified these and such killings.[104] According to details, the Baloch Republican Party (BRP) chief said he agreed with a recent article he had read that encouraged the Baloch to conduct more targeted killings. He said the same article had also advocated extending the practice into Punjab. To questions on the killing of 20 Baloch policemen in Naseerabad district and the targeted killing of Punjabi teachers,

168 *Centre–Province relations post-independence*

the BRP chief said he supported the actions of the separatists.[105] Azad Baloch, a spokesman of BLA, has accepted the responsibility for the killings of Punjabis and said that they were spying for the intelligence agencies against the ongoing Baloch struggle and that was why they were attacked. Around 100,000 settlers in Balochistan from other parts of Pakistan have left the troubled province so far because of violence involving Baloch separatist militants, the then Interior Minister Rahman Malik told the Senate. In 2010 alone, at least 250 people from other provinces who had settled in Balochistan had been killed in attacks, Malik said.[106] According to Najam Sethi, the targeted killing of the settlers in Balochistan is part of a well-thought-of strategy by the separatists. It did not exist in any of the earlier movements for independence, not even in the 1970s when state repression was at its height. This is the first time that Baloch insurgents have tried to eliminate Punjabis from Balochistan as part of a political framework.

Nothing explains the resentment against the Punjabis and Punjab more than what Nawab Marri once opined: "I can co-exist with a pig but not with a Punjabi."[107]

Missing persons

Majority of the missing persons belong to the local tribes while a few are coal miners, professors, traders, and security officials. A majority of them were allegedly kidnapped by the security forces and the Baloch nationalists. The data from HRCP confirms that the incidents of "missing and dead persons" had been occurring since 2000 though the number was very minimal. It is not known how many people have gone missing. The Baloch nationalists claim several thousands are missing, but have only identified several hundreds. The Human Rights Watch stated that soldiers, police and intelligence agencies in Pakistan torture and kill abducted activists in a campaign to quash the separatist movement in Balochistan, and hundreds of so-called "enforced disappearances" have been committed since 2005. Brad Adams (Asia Director HRW) said, "Pakistan's security forces are engaging in an abusive free-for-all in Balochistan as Baloch nationalists and suspected militants 'disappear,' and in many cases are executed."[108] Human rights groups and Baloch nationalist political parties had claimed that 13,000 people are missing in the province, while the provincial government acknowledges that fewer than 1,000 Baloch have been taken into custody. Government and the security forces also deny any role in targeted killings. Former COAS, General Ashfaq Kayani, for instance, made it clear that the army had no role in the murders of political activists. The independent Lahore-based Human Rights Commission of Pakistan (HRCP) reports: "In some cases it is not known where they are being detained, and furthermore the government has also not disclosed the identities of persons arrested during these operations." The HRCP also noted that the government gave contradictory accounts of the number of persons arrested in Balochistan. While no official statistics are available, human rights groups have attempted to document cases of missing persons. But reliable data are difficult to compile, and the range of estimates is very wide. The HRCP, in its report for 2006, says that of the total 99 abductions that took place in the country, 73 were from Balochistan. The former Pakistani interior minister Aftab Ahmed Khan Sherpao stated in December 2005 in the National Assembly that over 4,000 persons had been detained in Balochistan since 2002. Of this number, Sherpao stated less than 200 people have been presented before the courts.

The exact number of enforced disappearances perpetrated in Balochistan is unknown. Baloch nationalists claim "thousands" of cases. In 2008, the then Interior Minister Rehman Malik mentioned at least 1,100 victims, but in January 2011, Balochistan Home Minister Zafrullah Zehri said that only 55 persons were missing.[109] An editorial dated 11 September 2012, in the *Express Tribune*, indicated that the bodies of 57 missing persons had been found since January 2012. However, other papers mention figures over 100 during the same period. In its August 2012 report, the Human Rights Commission of Pakistan indicates that it has verified 198 cases of enforced disappearances in Balochistan between January 2000 and 12 May 2012, and that 57 bodies of missing persons had been found in Balochistan in 2012 alone.[110] The Pakistani press, as well as international and Pakistani non-governmental organizations, have documented a number of cases. According to the Human Rights Watch and Human Commission of Pakistan, most of these disappearances have been allegedly perpetrated by Pakistan's "intelligence agencies and the Frontier Corps, often acting in conjunction with the local police."[111] It is further alleged that in most of such cases, the perpetrators acted openly in broad daylight.[112] A claim that is very strongly contested by these organizations.

External hand

Islamabad is of the view that the Baloch sardars and militants are supported by external actors who want to destroy Pakistan and make Balochistan an independent country to achieve their objectives. This view considers the insurgency in Balochistan as a part of a larger conspiracy against the very existence of the state of Pakistan. Those who hold this view consider India, Afghanistan, USA, Russia, Gulf States, and Iran a party to this conspiracy in one way or the other because all of these states would be adversely affected if the true potential of Balochistan is realized. For instance, Gwadar Port would be a serious challenger to the monopoly of the Gulf States in the maritime sector. Iran would be perturbed because it wanted its Chabahar Port to be the outlet for the central Asian energy-rich states.

Those who hold this view question the source of the latest weapons and equipment used by the Baloch insurgents. What is often ignored in this line of reasoning is that Balochistan is also a significant corridor for drug and small arms smuggling. One of the routes for the arms and heroine from Afghanistan to the outside world is via Balochistan. Haji Juma Khan, based at Baramcha in Chagai, was a well-known member of this smuggling net.[113]

Islamabad claims that it has ample proof of Indian involvement in Balochistan and its support for the Baloch insurgents. Khalid Khokar described the Indian consulates in Afghanistan as "centers of terrorism" and the primary conduits by which the Indians are "planning, commissioning and preparing acts of terrorism in Balochistan." Pakistani Senator Mushahid Hussain Sayed asserted that these

170 Centre–Province relations post-independence

consulates "serve as launching pads for undertaking covert operations against Pakistan from the Afghan soil."[114] In February 2006, it was reported that President Musharraf presented Afghan President Hamid Karzai with evidence that India was using bases within Afghanistan to create problem in Balochistan. Pakistani Senator Mushahid Hussain in an interview with the Pakistani paper *The News* accused India's Research and Analysis Wing (R&AW) of establishing training camps near the Pakistan–Afghanistan border in order to train Baloch dissidents in the use of explosives and sophisticated weapons. At the conference of nonaligned states in Egypt, both Prime Ministers Gilani of Pakistan and Manmohan Singh of India agreed to look at the Baloch issue.[115] Georgetown University Professor and expert of South Asian affairs, C. Christine Fair indirectly implied that the Indian consulates are a supporter of Baloch separatists there. She later clarified that her statement was misunderstood.

Most of the outside world disagrees with Pakistan's view on Indian involvement in Balochistan. Former U.S. Secretary of State Hillary Clinton asserted that there is no evidence of India's involvement in Balochistan despite Pakistani allegations.[116] One of the leading analysts of Pakistan, Dr. Farrukh Saleem discussing external hand in the Baloch insurgency wrote:

> Which foreign hand has an interest in destabilizing Balochistan? Is Iran arming Baloch insurgents?... Will Iran prop up Baloch nationalism in Pakistan at the risk of encouraging nationalist fervour in Iranian Balochistan? … Is Afghanistan arming Baloch insurgents? The US has the Bagram Air Base (Parvan, Charikar), Kandahar Air Base, Khost Airbase (Paktia) and Mazar-e-Sharif Airbase. … Can the state of Afghanistan arm Baloch separatists without the explicit authorisation of the USA? … Is America arming Baloch insurgents? Right now, a stable Pakistan is in America's best strategic interest. Is India arming Baloch insurgents? The only way that India can arm Baloch insurgents is either through Iran or through Afghanistan. Clearly, India cannot support Baloch insurgents through Iran without the explicit permission of the supreme leader Sayyid Ali Khamenei. Again, India cannot arm Baloch insurgents through Afghanistan without the explicit permission of the Americans. Additionally, an instable Balochistan jeopardises India's pipeline dreams and is not in India's long-term economic interests. There is little doubt that arms are flowing into Pakistan's Balochistan both through Iran and Afghanistan. That, however, in no way means that the states of Iran or Afghanistan are directly involved.[117]

However, the view that India is playing a role in Balochistan cannot be totally ruled out. According to WikiLeaks, a number of diplomatic dispatches from Western embassies in Islamabad to their capitals expressed such concerns. According to media reports, a former chief of the Indian army, V.K. Singh, sanctioned the Tactical Support Division (TSD), an Indian army unit raised after Mumbai attacks on the directives of the Defence Minister and National Security Adviser Shivshankar Menon to conduct clandestine operations on both sides of the contentious Line of Control (LOC) between Pakistan and India.[118] According to a report published in influential Indian weekly, the *India Today*, between October and November 2011, TSD had claimed money "to try enrolling the secessionist chief in the province of a neighbouring country" and "Rs. 1.27 crore (Indian currency) to prevent transportation of weapons between neighbouring countries". In early 2011, TSD claimed an unspecified amount for carrying out "eight low-intensity bomb blasts in a neighboring country."[119] According to the news report published in the News, quoting Indian sources,

> India's Director General of Military Operations (DGMO) Lt Gen Vinod Bhatia, who headed a Board of Officers' inquiry under the direct orders of Gen Bikram Singh, Indian army chief, to review the functioning of the TSD submitted the report in March this year to the Indian government. While report is not being publicised, however, TSD was closed in December 2012.[120]

Chuck Hagel also pointed to New Delhi's support and finance to terrorist elements to create problems for Pakistan.[121]

Since Prime Minister Modi took over the helm of affairs in New Delhi, India's support to Baloch insurgents and Tehreek-e-Taliban Pakistan (TTP) has intensified. He acknowledged this in his speech on Indian Independence Day pledging to raise the issue of "Pakistani atrocities in Balochistan" in international forums.

According to media reports, India also decided to grant Brahumdagh Bugti and his aides citizenship of India. This would enable him to travel around the world freely. This arrangement according to New Delhi would be just like Dalai Lama who uses Indian passport for his travel and international engagements. Brahumdagh's spokesperson confirmed that after long negotiation, India has decided to provide Indian citizenship and travel documents to him and his aides:

> We will use Indian papers to travel around the world to campaign against Pakistan and to highlight our case. We have openly thanked Narendra Modi for his support and we are no more hiding anything. We have no other option. We don't care what our opponents think of our support for Modi and his support for us.

Indian National Security Advisor (Principle Secretary to the Prime minister) Ajit Doval was quite open when he stated "you do another 26/11, you lose Balochistan."[122]

CONCLUSION

Balochistan is burning once again. The issues that have resulted in this resurgence of violence are not new. However, a number of new factors have been introduced and have further complicated the issue.

It started when the centre chose to ignore the Baloch leadership and went ahead with a number of projects in Balochistan. The Baloch elite felt ignored

172 *Centre–Province relations post-independence*

and side-lined. This led to another phase of centre–province clash which turned violent. The problem in Dera Bugti area and between Akbar Bugti and the oil and gas companies as well as the government could have been settled locally, had better sense prevailed and if the decision makers in Islamabad had a better understanding of the Baloch political culture and negotiating style. Akbar Bugti was only struggling for what he believed was his and his tribe's birth right. One could not ignore the manipulative aspect of pressure tactics that he was using in terms of asking for more money, yet what Islamabad failed to understand is that this is not an end itself but a means to an end. When Islamabad failed to respond according to his wishes, he started using the standard narrative of actual and/or perceived historical and enduring injustice in Balochistan conveniently forgetting that in this so-called enduring injustice suffered by the Baloch, he sided most of the time with the perpetrators of this alleged enduring injustice.

The Baloch insurgency became stronger with the death of Akbar Bugti. Akbar Bugti, who was never in the forefront of the Baloch nationalist politics, overnight became the martyr for the Baloch cause.[123] In the 1970s, he was equated with Tikka Khan and Bhutto. The wall chalking in Quetta and elsewhere read: amriat key teen nihsan, Bhutto, Tikka aur Akbar Khan (Bhutto, General Tikka Khan and Akbar Bugti are three symbols of dictatorship).

General Musharraf's takeover was not supported by the Baloch political leadership in general as they were comfortably settled in the previous system of governance. The steps that General Musharraf took to consolidate his power and hold in Pakistan as well as his vision for developing Pakistan had no role for the Baloch political elites. This side-lined the Baloch elite. Post-9/11 developments in Afghanistan, just like during the 1980s, resulted in an increase of Pakistan Armed Forces movement in Balochistan and influx of investors and workers from outside (other parts of Pakistan) in Gwadar and elsewhere. All these factors reinforced the historical Baloch fear that they would become a minority in Balochistan and that Balochistan was colonized by the Punjabi colonizers.

The Baloch insurgents once again claimed that the current crisis in Balochistan is a violent reaction to the neglect of the Baloch populace and the exploitation of their natural resources by the Punjabi "colonialists" from Islamabad. Much like the Baloch revolts of the past, one of the central issues of dispute in today's crisis in Balochistan is the allocation of natural resources. The Sui gas field located in Balochistan was the largest natural gas field in Pakistan.[124] In total, the province of Balochistan provides the nation with between 36 and 45 percent of the national demand for natural gas. Despite this, many districts in Balochistan are still without gas transmission facilities. This includes areas immediately surrounding the Sui gas field.[125] Only four of the twenty-six Balochistan districts receive natural gas.

The province remains the poorest province of Pakistan. The Baloch leadership is of the view that Balochistan is poor not because of lack of resources and wealth but due to the neglect of the centre as it is not interested in developing Balochistan and provide basic human needs to the Baloch people. Instead, it treats Balochistan

Return of insurgency in Balochistan 173

as a colony and plunders its resources for its own use, depriving the Baloch of their right.

Another important aspect of the problem is that whenever the centre offered Balochistan, be it economic aid or packages such as Aghaz-e-Haqooq-e-Balochistan, the political leadership in Islamabad projects it as an out of the way favour to the Baloch that the Baloch must acknowledge. The Baloch consider it as an overdue step that needed to be substantiated with action. Zafarullah Khan has aptly pointed that

> the federal government emphasizes its contributions in quantitative terms, whereas the Baloch hope for impact on the ground in qualitative terms. The qualitative improvements in reality will require a well thought out strategy to bring elected and non-elected (who boycotted elections-2008) political leaders into a dialogue and initiate a meaningful discussion with those annoyed forces that are moving towards militancy.[126]

The PPP government also failed to engage the provincial leadership and the provincial assembly in the process. The elected provincial leadership was neither included nor provided a role in the decision making regarding the package, its implementation and accountability.

The centre in the past presented two such packages or recommendations, the senate committee on Balochistan, which was widely respected and acknowledged even by top Baloch nationalists, and Aghaz-e-Haqooq-e-Balochistan package offered by the PPP government. The committee's recommendation could have been the beginning of a solid start towards reconciliation and integration of Balochistan with Pakistan, yet the implementation was halted due to the lack of interest or enthusiasm of the Shakuat Aziz government. The PPP government opted to reinvent the wheel and, after taking a long time to prepare its package, presented its package in the joint session of the parliament. The package was never truly implemented. A lot of money was provided to the Baloch politicians and members of assembly, but due to the lack of prioritization, accountability and focus, it failed to have any desired impact.

The complicated divisions within the Baloch leadership further complicate the prospects of a resolution of the Baloch problem. The Baloch nationalists believe that the state of Pakistan is only interested in its energy and mineral wealth and it does not care about the Baloch people. Baloch anger is directed towards the Army and the province of Punjab because they believe that the country is run by them and that they have never allowed the Baloch to have their rights within the state of Pakistan as they either still donot consider the Baloch true Pakistanis as the Baloch do not follow their policies or at least consider them third-rate or lower-level Pakistanis who cannot have equal rights. These are the issues and grievances that need to be addressed and resolved. Unless this is done, offering packages, incentives and/or appointing a nationalist Baloch leader would not solve the problem.

This chapter demonstrated that during this phase the Baloch elite including Akbar Bugti, Attaullah Mengal and Khair Bakhsh Marri started to link the

174   *Centre–Province relations post-independence*

developments that were taking place in the province with the developments that took place in the past and established a link between the two.

The Baloch nationalist narrative that was developed and used claimed that General Musharraf's regime's treatment of the Baloch and policy towards Balochistan is nothing new. This has happened in the past. Linking present with the past, this narrative argued that the centre has always treated the Baloch this way: from Kalat's forcible accession to brutal military action against the Baloch and deprivation of its resources and mineral wealth. In this narrative, the Baloch elite conveniently ignored the role played by the fellow Baloch elite (sardars) and the developments that took place during the almost 23-year-long peace interval. The timing and selective use of the historical memory is important in understanding the Baloch narrative.

The developments that took place during this phase and the use of a narrative based on a selective historical memory by the elite clearly indicates that for the employment of a narrative to politicize an ethnicity and mobilize the masses, there has to be a sparking event or an injustice happening at the time when the elite would use it to politicize and mobilize the ethnic group.

Notes

1   For details, see Robert Wirsing, *Baloch Nationalism and the Geopolitics of Energy Resources: The Changing Context of Separatism in Pakistan* (April 2008).
2   "Pakistan President Warns 'Miscreants' Will be Dealt with 'Iron Hand,'" *Global News Wire – Asia Africa Intelligence Wire*, December 14, 2005; and "Pakistan's Musharraf Speaks to Nation on Baluchistan, Dams," *Islamabad PTV World*, January 17, 2006.
3   Saleem Shahid, "Talks Under Way on Balochistan Issue: Musharraf – Demand for Provincial Autonomy Backed," *Dawn*, September 11, 2004.
4   Ibid.
5   Ihtashamul Haque, "New Force to Replace Levies in Balochistan," *Dawn*, November 5, 2004, "Work on Cantonments Not Yet Begun: ISPR," *Dawn*, November 5, 2004.
6   Haque, "New Force to Replace Levies in Balochistan, " "Work on Cantonments Not Yet Begun: ISPR."
7   "New Garrisons in Balochistan to Ensure Safety of Key Installations: ISPR," *The News*, September 26, 2004.
8   "Careful in Balochistan!" *Daily Times*, August 5, 2004.
9   "Tribesmen Attack Radar Station Near Rojhan," *The News*, May 14, 2003; and Zulfiqar Shah, "Lawlessness Rule of the Unruly," *The News*, May 18, 2003.
10   "Bugti, Mazari Tribes Clash Again in Rajanpur," *The News*, January 31, 2003.
11   "Rockets Fired at Gas Pipeline," *The Nation*, December 6, 2002.
12   Ahmad Faraz Khan, "Supply to Industries Stopped: Rocket Attack on Gas Pipelines," *Dawn*, January 22, 2003.
13   Nadeem Saeed, "Another Gas Pipeline Attacked," *Dawn*, January 23, 2003.
14   "Gas Crisis to Help Bring Royalty Issue into Focus," *Dawn*, January 24, 2003.
15   "Many Reasons Behind Attack, says Bugti Many Reasons Behind Attack, says Bugti," *The Nation*, January 23, 2003.
16   Ibid.
17   Khalid Mustafa, "New Gas Agreement Stalled Over Bugti's Inflexibility," *Daily Times*, January 28, 2003.
18   Ibid.
19   Syed Irfan Raza, "Talks Being Held with Bugtis for Cops Release," *Dawn*, January 29, 2003; Tariq Saeed Birmani, "Anarchy in Rojhan Mazari," *Dawn*, January 29,

Return of insurgency in Balochistan 175

2003; and "Officials Offer Talks to Bugtis Over Gas Issue," *The News*, January 29, 2003.

20 Mustafa, "New Gas Agreement Stalled Over Bugti's Inflexibility."

21 Munawar Hasan, "Who Is Behind Attacks," *The Nation*, January 28, 2003.

22 "Gas Companies, Bugti Reach Agreement," *The Nation*, March 13, 2003.

23 Ibid.

24 Ihtasham ul Haque, "Jamali for Resolving Issue as per Accords: Army Not to Guard Installations," *Dawn*, February 4, 2003.

25 Rauf Klasra, "PM Orders Crackdown on Bugtis, Mazaris, Jamali Chairs High-Level Meeting to Discuss Gas Pipeline Security; Agreement with Bugtis Will Not be Revised," *The News*, February 4, 2003.

26 Syed Irfan Raza, "Forces Sent to Guard Gas Installations," *Dawn*, January 28, 2003.

27 "500 Rangers to Patrol Gas Pipeline," *The News*, January 30, 2003.

28 Khaleeq Kiani, "Report on Oil Rentals, Royalties Sought: President's Move on Gas Crisis," *Dawn*, January 31, 2003.

29 Klasra, "PM Orders Crackdown on Bugtis, Mazaris, Jamali Chairs High-Level Meeting."

30 "No Talks Under Shadow of Gun, says Mengal," *The Nation*, January 26, 2005.

31 Ibid.

32 Ibid.

33 Muhammad Ejaz Khan, "Army Sets Up Garrison in Sui Bugti says Time Will Tell How We React," *The News*, January 27, 2005; "Cantonment to be Built in Sui: Army," *Dawn*, January 27, 2005; "The Shujaat Mission," *The Nation*, January 27, 2005; Ahmed Hasan, "Musharraf Firm on Protecting Key Installations," *Dawn*, January 28, 2005; Syed Irfan Raza, "No Demand Conveyed by Bugti: Sherpao," *Dawn*, January 28, 2005; S. Raza Hasan, "Atmosphere Not Ripe for Talks, says Bugti," *Dawn*, January 28, 2005; By; "Train Track Blown Up in Balochistan," *Dawn*, January 28, 2005.

34 "Mushahid Optimistic About Outcome of Talks with Baloch Nationalists," *The News*, November 7, 2004; and Saleem Shahid, "Committee Meeting with Bugti 'Fruitful'," *Dawn*, November 8, 2004.

35 Four federal ministers: Minister for Ports and Shipping Babar Khan Ghauri, Minister for Safron Sardar Yar Muhammad Rind, Minister for Social Welfare and Special Education Zobaida Jalal and Minister of State for Petroleum and Natural Resources Naseer Mengal-as well as senators Prof Khursheed Ahmed, Maulana Muhmmad Khan Sherani, Sanaullah Baloch, Dilawar Abbas, Saeed Hashmi, Ismail Buledi, Aslam Buledi, Raza Muhammad Raza, Mohim Khan Baloch and MNA Abdul Rauf Mengal also accompanied Senator Mushahid.

36 "A Good Beginning on Balochistan," *Daily Times*, March 29, 2005; Muhammad Ejaz Khan, "Talking Time It Is Too Early to Put Weight Behind the Mushahid-Shujaat Thrust for Normalcy in Balochistan," *The News*, April 3, 2005; Mubasher Bukhari, "Govt Unlikely to Agree to Bugti's Demands," *Daily Times*, April 4, 2005; "Committee Formed to Implement Govt-Bugti Pact," *The News*, April 5, 2005; Ahmed Hassan and Salim Shahid, "Monitoring Team Takes Shape: 3rd Round of Talks with Bugti," *Dawn*, April 5, 2005; Saleem Shahid, "Struggle for Rights to Continue, says Bugti," *Dawn*, April 6, 2005; and "Four Rockets Hit Kohlu," *Daily Times*, April 7, 2005.

37 "No Compromise on Baloch Rights: Bugti Nawab Akbar Bugti," *Daily Times*, April 7, 2005.

38 "Bugti Proposes 15-Point Formula to Resolve Balochistan Issue," *The News*, September 23, 2004; and "15-Point Demand Given to Tariq Aziz, says Bugti," *Dawn*, September 23, 2004.

39 Muhammad Ejaz Khan, "Bugti for Joint Baloch Platform," *The News*, May 16, 2005.

40 "Bugti Seeks Broader Baloch Platform," *Dawn*, May 16, 2005.

176   *Centre–Province relations post-independence*

41 "What Will Balochistan Committee Discuss?," *Daily Times*, August 26, 2004.
42 Shakil Shaikh, "Deletion of 30 Items from Concurrent List Proposed CCI to be Made Effective to Ensure Autonomy; Subcommittee Report Presented to PM," *The News*, May 4, 2005.
43 The meeting was attended besides Shujaat Hussain and Wasim Sajjad by Senators Maulana Samiul Haq, Saeed Ahmed Hashmi, Mushahid Hussain, Raza Muhammad Raza, Muhammad Sarwar Khan Kakar, Mir Wali Muhammad Badini, Mrs Kalsoom Parveen, Ms Agha Pari Gul, Dr Muhammad Ismail Buledi, Muhammad Ishaq Dar, Prof Khursheed Ahmed, Rehmatullah Kakar, Muhammad Ali Durrani, Syed Dilawar Abbas, MNAs Maulana Muhammad Khan Sherani, Al-Syed Abdul Qadir Jamaluddin Al-Gillani, Dr Noor Jehan Panezai, Sardar Yar Muhammad Rind, Ms Bilqis Saif and Sardar Muhammad Yaqoob Khan Nasir. Chief Minister Balochistan Jam Muhammad Yousaf and Senators Mrs Roshan Khursheed Bharucha, Dr Khalid Ranjha, S. M. Zafar attended the meeting on special invitation.
44 Muhammad Najeeb, "Politics Heading Nowhere," *The News*, May 15, 2005.
45 "Baloch Alliance Rejects Committee's Proposals," *Dawn*, July 4, 2005.
46 Ibid.
47 "23 Killed in Dera Bugti Offensive Seven Farari Camps Destroyed; 30 Surrender," *The News*, July 10, 2006; Saleem Shahid, "23 Killed in Dera Bugti Operation," *Dawn*, July 10, 2006; Amanullah Kasi, "Mengal Alleges Bid to Kill Baloch Leaders," *Dawn*, July 10, 2006; Saleem Shahid, "FC Soldier Among Six Injured," *Dawn*, July 11, 2006; Tariq Butt, "PM to Review Mushahid Committee Recommendations," *The News*, July 12, 2006.
48 "Shujaat-Led Body on Balochistan Revived," *Daily Times*, July 9, 2006.
49 Akbar S. Ahmed, *The Thistle and the Drone*, 136.
50 Rashed Rahman, "The Fifth Balochistan War," *Daily Times*, January 25, 2005.
51 Sarfaraz Ahmed, "Musharraf's Kohlu Visit Not a Wise Move," *Daily Times*, December 20, 2005.
52 Ibid.
53 Muhammad Ejaz Khan, "Rockets Fired at FC Camp Prior to President's Visit; BLA Claims Responsibility for Attack Saboteurs Cannot Hamper Progress: Musharraf Announces Rs. 1.5bn Package for Kohlu," *The News*, December 15, 2005; Muhammad Ejaz Khan, "FC IG Hurt as Chopper Fired upon in Kohlu," *The News*, December 16, 2005; Saleem Shahid, "FC Chief, Deputy Injured in Firing," *Dawn*, December 16, 2005; Latif Baloch, "Mengal Condemns Agencies for Victimization," *Dawn*, December 16, 2005; By "The Message from Balochistan," *Daily Times*, December 17, 2005.
54 Shahzada Zulfiqar, "Operation Launched in Kohlu Agency," *The Nation*, December 18, 2005; Muhammad Ejaz Khan, "Crackdown on Militants Launched in Kohlu," *The News*, December 19, 2005; By Saleem Shahid, "Troops Move Against Marris in Kohlu," *Dawn*, December 19, 2005.
55 "Army Deployed for Mass Killing of Bugti Tribe: Nawab Bugti," *The News*, December 20, 2005.
56 "The Action in Kohlu," *The News*, December 20, 2005; Saleem Shahid and Amanullah Kasi, "Paramilitary Action in Kohlu Continues: Over 50 Killed, say Tribesmen," *Dawn*, December 20, 2005; Shahzada Zulfiqar, "Kohlu Action Geared Up," *The Nation*, December 20, 2005.
57 "Return of the Native: Kalpars Jubilant on Being Back in Hometown," *The News*, February 2, 2006.
58 "Masoori Tribe Chief Supports Operation in Balochistan," *The Nation*, January 10, 2006.
59 Ibid.
60 Ibid.

Return of insurgency in Balochistan 177

61 "Some Sardars Vitiating Atmosphere, says Baloch Leader," *The News*, January 17, 2006.

62 "Risky Tactics," *The Post*, March 26, 2006.

63 Ibid.

64 "Four More Bugti Commanders Surrender: Govt," *Daily Times*, July 13, 2006.

65 Muhammad Saleh Zaafir, "No General Amnesty in Balochistan: PM," *The News*, July 14, 2006; "Three Bugti Clan Chiefs Surrender with 630 Tribals," *The News*, July 16, 2006; Zubeida Mustafa, "What Next in Balochistan?" *Dawn*, July 19, 2006; "Arms, Ammunition Seized," *The News*, July 20, 2006, *The News*, July 21, 2006; "10 SAMs Seized in Dera Bugti," *Dawn*, July 21, 2006; "Three More Bugti Men Surrender," *The Post*, July 21, 2006; "41 Militants Killed in Swoop on Ferrari Camps Shahid Bugti, Humayun Marri Put Under House Arrest," *Daily Times*, July 21, 2006; "Six Commanders, 500 Men Surrender: Govt," *Dawn*, July 22, 2006; "Over 4,000 Baloch Youth in Illegal Detention," *Daily Times*, July 25, 2006; and "Three Bugti Commanders Surrender," *Daily Times*, July 25, 2006.

66 Malik Siraj Akbar, "38 Marri Loyalists Surrender," *Daily Times*, August 3, 2006.

67 "98pc of Bugti Tribesmen Surrendered," *The Post*, August 3, 2006.

68 "Bugti Jirga to Announce End of Sardari System on 24th," *The News*, August 23, 2006.

69 "Bugti jirga Scraps Sardari System," *The Nation*, August 25, 2006. Kalpar, Masoori, Firozani, Shambhani, Mandrani, Raheja, and Marhata sub-tribes, known in the past for nursing feuds with Nawab Akbar Bugti.

70 "Bugti Jirga to Announce End of Sardari System on 24th," *The News*, August 23, 2006.

71 "Gas Pipeline Blown Up Near Sui," *The News*, August 9, 2006; "All Is Not Well in Balochistan," *The News*, August 9, 2006; "Attack on Pipeline Hits Gas Supply," *Dawn*, August 9, 2006; "Kalpars Vow to Work for Country's Development," *The News*, August 11, 2006; "Blast Damages Bridge," *Dawn*, August 11, 2006; Shahzada Zulfiqar, "Bridge Bombed in Balochistan," *The Nation*, August 11, 2006; Saleem Shahid, "Eight Die in Balochistan Explosions, Clashes," *Dawn*, August 16, 2006; "Balochistan's Law and Order Has Improved, says Governor," *Daily Times*, August 19, 2006; "Seizes Weapon Caches in Noshki, Dera Bugti," *Daily Times*, August 20, 2006; "Bugti says BLA, BLF Getting Popular Support," *Dawn*, February 9, 2005; "Attacks in Balochistan: Musharraf Rules Out Military Action," *Daily Times*, February 10, 2005; Mir Mohammad Ali Talpur, "The Real Challenge in Balochistan," *Daily Times*, February 23, 2005–; "Parliamentary Body on Balochistan Fails to Meet," *Dawn*, March 18, 2005; "Fierce Clashes in Dera Bugti: Conflicting Reports About Casualties," *Dawn*, March 18, 2005; "Benazir, Imran Concerned Over Balochistan Issue," *Dawn*, March 18, 2005; "MQM Condemns Killings," *Dawn*, March 18, 2005; "Attack on Dera Bugti Criticized," *Dawn*, March 18, 2005; "Baloch Alliance Holds Protest," *Dawn*, March 18, 2005; "Gunbattle in Dera Bugti," *The Nation*, March 18, 2005; "Dera Bugti Tense After Clashes," *The News*, March 19, 2005; "Fighting at Dera Bugti," *The News*, March 19, 2005; Saleem Shahid, "Dera Bugti Calm but Tense," *Dawn*, March 19, 2005; "Dera Bugti Action Condemned," *Dawn*, March 19, 2005; and Syed Mohibullah Shah, "Balochistan: A 'Jewel in the Crown' of Pakistan," *Dawn*, March 19, 2005.

72 "Akbar Bugti Killed in Major Operation," *The News*, August 27, 2006.

73 Muhammad Ejaz Khan, "Body Politic Is Political Outrage Over Bugti's Killing an Opportunistic Venting of Anti-Government Ire?" *The News*, September 3, 2006.

74 "Opposition Can Resolve Crisis: Bugti Refuses to Talk to Govt Representatives; FC Commander Warns of Brewing Danger," *The News*, March 23, 2005; and Muhammad Ejaz Khan, "Dera Bugti Tense as Tribesmen Besiege FC Compound," *The News*, March 21, 2005.

178   *Centre–Province relations post-independence*

75 Umer Nangiana, "CRSS Report: Hawks Prevented a Planned Bugti-Musharraf Rendezvous," *Express Tribune*, May 28, 2011.
76 Ibid.
77 Ahmed, *Thistle and the Drone*, 136.
78 Jamil Ahmed, "Baloch Nationalists' Dilemma," *Dawn*, October 29, 2007.
79 "Explosions Near Poll Offices of PPP, PML-Q," *Dawn*, February 15, 2008; and "Pamphlets Warn People to Stay Away from Polls," *The Nation*, February 15, 2008.
80 Jawad Hussain Qureshi, "Balochistan Neglected," *The News*, February 26, 2008.
81 Latif Baloch, "Baloch Leaders Unimpressed by PPP Apology," *Dawn*, February 27, 2008.
82 "Apologising to Balochistan," *Dawn*, February 26, 2008; and "A Welcome Gesture," *The Post*, February 26, 2008.
83 Baloch, "Baloch Leaders Unimpressed."
84 "Move for Conciliation in Balochistan Likely: Magsi's Appointment Made with PPP's Consent," *Dawn*, February 28, 2008.
85 "BLA Rejects Govt's Offer for Talks," *Dawn*, April 10, 2008.
86 "The Way Forward," *The Nation*, April 11, 2008; "Two Killed in Mine Blast," *Dawn*, April 13, 2008; "Govt Claims of Talks 'Pack of Lies,'" *Daily Times*, April 17, 2008.
87 Amanullah Kasi, "Bramdagh Refuses to Hold Talks with Govt," *Dawn*, May 31, 2008.
88 Inamullah Khattak, "Move for APC on Balochistan," *Dawn*, April 21, 2008.
89 *The News*, May 4, 2008.
90 Zafarullah Khan, *Solace for Balochistan?* (Islamabad: SPO National Centre, 2012), 4.
91 *Daily Times*, November 25, 2009.
92 Khan, *Solace for Balochistan?* 4.
93 *What Does NFC Award Holds for Baluchistan*, November 25, 2009, www.balochistan.gov.pk/images/NFC_points%20for_GoB_Web%20Portal.pdf.
94 Ibid., 5.
95 Ibid., 7.
96 Frédéric Grare, *Pakistan: The Resurgence of Baluch Nationalism* (Washington, DC: CEIP, 2006), 80.
97 Malik Siraj Akbar, "Bizenjo's Ultimatum," *The Baloch Hal*, December 10, 2013. http://thebalochhal.com/2013/12/11/bizenjos-ultimatum/.
98 http://balouchistantimes.blogspot.com.au/search?q=Baloch+in+Pakistan+army.
99 "Punjabi Settlers Biggest Victims of Bugti Aftermath, Civil Society in Balochistan Has Remained Silent Over Killings Due to Fear of Nationalist Backlash," *Daily Times*, July 9, 2009, www.dailytimes.com.pk /default.asp?page=2009%5C07%5C09%5Cstory_9-7-2009_pg7_13, www.dailytimes.com.pk/default.asp?page=200979\story_9-7-2009_pg7_13, www.thefreelibrary.com/83+Punjabi+and+Sindhis+killed+in+Balochistan+during+last+year-a0219107597; Malik Siraj Akbar, "Bramdagh Justifies Civilians Target killings in Balochistan," www.dailytimes.com.pk/default.asp...009_pg7_40, "The Massacre in Balochistan," www.friendskorner.com/forum/f137/news-massacre-balochistan-145557/, "100,000 Settlers Have Migrated from Balochistan," *The News*, July 28, 2010.
100 Ahmed, *Thistle and the Drone*, 136–37.
101 Zahid Chuadhray, *Balochistan, Pakistan ki Sayassi Tahreek* (in urdu) (Lahore: Taqleqaat, 1994).
102 Malik Siraj Akbar, "Punjabi Settlers Biggest Victims of Bugti Aftermath," www.dailytimes.com.pk/default.asp?page=2009%5C07%5C09%5C-story_9-7-2009_pg7_13.

103 www.thefreelibrary.com/83+Punjabi+and+Sindhis+killed+in+Balochistan+during+last+year-a0219107597.

104 Akbar, "Bramdagh Justifies Civilians Target killings in Balochistan," www.dailytimes.com.pk/default.asp?page=2009826story_26-8-2009_pg7_40

105 Ibid.

106 "100,000 Settlers Have Migrated from Balochistan," *The News*, July 28, 2010; and "Violence Drives Settlers Out of Province," *Gulf News*, July 28, 2010.

107 "Time for Solutions in Balochistan," *Daily Times*, June 10, 2008; and "Marri Ready to Negotiate on Behalf of BLA Only Says Punjabis Must Vacate Balochistan as Primary Condition," *Daily Times*, June 14, 2008.

108 "Pakistan Accused Over Separatists Who Disappear," http://tribune.com.pk/story/219317/pakistan-accused-over-separatists-who-disappear/.

109 Grare, *Pakistan: The Resurgence of Baluch Nationalism.*

110 Ibid.

111 Ibid.

112 Ibid.

113 Kamal Hyder, "Iran to Wall Off Baluchistan Border," *AlJazeera*, June 11, 2007.

114 Khalid Khokhar, "India Feasts on a Volatile Situation in Balochistan," *Pakistan Ka Khuda Hafez*, April 25, 2009, http://pakistankakhudahafiz.wordpress.com/2009/04/25/india-feasts-onvolatile-situation-in-balochistan/; Embassy of India, Kabul, Afghanistan, *Embassy of India, Kabul, Afghanistan*, http://meakabul.nic.in/; and Mariana Babaar, "How India Is Fomenting Trouble in Pakistan via Afghanistan," *The News*, April 15, 2006.

115 Reuters, "India, Pakistan Prime Ministers' Joint Statement," *Reuters India*, July 16, 2009.

116 "No Proof of Indian Involvement in Balochistan: Hillary to Pak," *The Economic Times*, November 2, 2009.

117 Dr. Farrukh Saleem, "Foreign Hand in Balochistan?" *The News*, January 8, 2006.

118 Umar Cheema, "Ex-Indian Army Chief Admits Sponsoring Terrorism in Balochistan," *The News*, October 21, 2013, www.thenews.com.pk/Todays-News-2-209274-Ex-Indian-Army-chief-admits-sponsoring-terrorism-in-Balochistan.

119 Ibid.

120 Ibid.

121 For a YouTube clip see; www.youtube.com/watch?V=J5f87LF-YY.

122 Hein G. Kiessling, *Faith Unity Discipline The ISI of Pakistan* (London: Hurst, 2016), 250.

123 Ahmed, *The Thistle and the Drone*, 136.

124 Harrison, *In Afghanistan's Shadow*, 7; Pakistan Petroleum Limited, "Rahman Visits Sui Gas Field," *Pakistan Petroleum Limited*, November 23, 2008, www.ppl.com.pk/media/Lists/Press%20releases/PressReleaseDispForm.aspx?List=09342a8a-823a-4104-9845-d2506f00835c&ID=24, accessed February 3, 2010; Fazl-e-Haider, "Higher Poverty in Balochistan," *Dawn*, February 6, 2006; Grare, "Pakistan," 5; Niazi, "Democracy, Development and Terrorism," 286; and Wirsing, *Baloch Nationalism and the Geopolitics of Energy Resources*, 4.

125 Fazl-e-Haider, "Higher Poverty in Balochistan," *Dawn*, February 6, 2006; Harrison, *In Afghanistan's Shadow*, 7; Grare, "Pakistan," 5; Niazi, "Democracy, Development and Terrorism," 286; and Wirsing, *Baloch Nationalism and the Geopolitics of Energy Resources*, 4.

126 Khan, *Solace for Balochistan*, 5.

Conclusion

The ongoing insurgency in Balochistan is different from previous insurgencies in a number of ways: *firstly*, the current leadership of the insurgency, unlike the past leadership has no stake in the constitutionalism and politics in Pakistan; *secondly*, the issue of missing persons; *thirdly*, the targeted killing of the settlers mostly Punjabis as a strategic tool by the insurgents; *fourthly*, the level of training, sophistication of attacks and better weaponry and equipment; and *fifthly*, use of media, especially social media, by the Baloch insurgents.

A closer look at the current insurgency clearly proves the point that for an ethnic conflict to get violent, certain contributing factors are required such as a regime or government in transition; this could be a transition in the type of the regime, from democratic to authoritative and/or transiting from one policy to another. The timing of the beginning of the Baloch insurgency coincides with General Musharraf's consolidating its position and hold on power in Pakistan and also changing its Afghanistan policy. The changed geostrategic landscape in the region, especially in Afghanistan, Musharraf's pushing for the construction of mega projects in Balochistan, construction of new cantonments mainly to address the changing situation in Afghanistan and Balochistan, side-lining of the Baloch leadership as they did not share Musharraf's view on Pakistani politics contributed to the increase in the political unrest in Balochistan.

Geography also played an important role in the instigation of the insurgency and its sustenance. This happened in two ways: one, Balochistan was right next to Afghanistan where since 2002, a war was going on and the American troops were using the Pakistani air bases to conduct air raids and military operations in Afghanistan. This made Balochistan strategically and militarily significant. Second, once the insurgency began, it soon became obvious that the Baloch insurgent were at advantage due to the topography of the area and their knowledge of the terrain.

The policy followed by General Musharraf in Balochistan was taken as an insult to the Baloch honour by most of the Baloch elite. The Baloch, under the tribal code, believed that they were duty bound to take every possible step to restore the Baloch honour, hence the beginning of the insurgent violence in different parts of Balochistan.

Contrary to almost all of the observers of the insurgency in Balochistan, this book argued that Nawab Akbar Bugti was never and was not part of the current insurgent violence in Balochistan. Nawab Akbar Bugti was pure and plain Bugti. He never went beyond his tribal demands. He was fighting for what he believed was his and Bugti tribe's right. The attacks on gas pipelines were a part of the pressure tactics to push the government to accept the demands. He was struggling for the Bugtis. He lived a Bugti and died a Bugti.

Nothing illustrates the fact that tribal divisions still are the key to understanding the Baloch politics than Ataullah Mengal's advise to Mushahid Hussain and Chaudhry Shujahat Hussain that if they want to solve the problem in Sui, they need to discuss it with Nawab Akbar Bugti as it is the Bugti area. In other words, he signalled his inability to do anything as it was not his tribal jurisdiction. The death of Nawab Akbar Bugti has been beneficial to a number of actors in Baloch politics for two main reasons: first, the biggest, egoistic and perhaps the most towering Baloch politician was dead which opened up the way for a number of other people; second, although loved by many and hated by many, a dead Nawab Bugti was much more beneficial for Baloch nationalists and insurgents as he became the rallying point for any one claiming to be struggling for the Baloch rights. He became the symbol of the Baloch resistance. In other words, a martyr that would make the insurgency even more popular and wide spread.

The side-lining of the Baloch political leadership, construction of mega projects, death of Nawab Akbar Bugti and the centre's inability to come up with a solid plan to address the Baloch problem are the factors or the triggers of the current insurgency. These factors or triggers are linked with the historical narrative of constant injustices aimed at the Baloch to deny them their rights.

The Baloch narrative begins with the arrival of the British. According to this narrative, Balochistan (not just Kalat) was an independent state before the British occupied it. This book argued that this is factually incorrect. Balochistan was neither a state nor independent before the arrival of the British. The British occupy such a position in this Baloch narrative because for the first time in history, the Baloch had to deal with an invader, who was not crossing through their land but wanted to stay and establish military posts and camps.

This book argued that the only reason the British got involved and eventually occupied Balochistan was the geostrategic competition in the region, especially the threat of a possible Russian invasion of India via central Asia and Afghanistan and through Balochistan. British policy makers were divided on the issue of Balochistan. Throughout their engagement in Balochistan, the British officials remained confused and never were able to work out a clear policy towards Balochistan.

British hold on Balochistan solidified with the emergence of Robert Sandeman on the scene. However, as the British involvement in Balochistan was purely for geostrategic reasons, they made no attempt to inculcate any administrative and social development program in Balochistan. This is the only reason why almost all of British construction and the development of railway and other such projects were aimed at consolidating their military position and not the improvement of

182 *Conclusion*

the Baloch masses per se. This, according to the British officials in India, was one of the main reasons why Balochistan was not incorporated into the British India. According to the British, Kalat and the larger Balochistan were economically and socially backward and geographically too huge with minimal population; hence, it was financially and administratively not viable to incorporate Kalat into British India. However, British officials made it clear to Ahmed Yar Khan, the last Khan of Kalat more than once that the British consider Kalat a normal princely state of India.

The Baloch narrative, however, claims that the British treated Kalat as an independent, non-Indian state. They claim that the British treatment of Kalat was similar to its treatment of Nepal. British policy and position, however, is different. British policy makers in India considered Kalat as an Indian state, yet could not incorporate it into the British India due to administrative and political reasons. A number of British documents and statements point to this paradox in the British policy. This failure in bringing clarity to its position on Balochistan created problems for Pakistan after 1947.

The last Khan of Kalat, Mir Ahmad Yar Khan after becoming the Khan, tried hard to convince the British to accept the independent status of the Kalat state and him as the undisputed ruler of Balochistan. Now with the British decision to leave the Indian subcontinent in 1947 and grant India and Pakistan independence, the Khan of Kalat made one last attempt to achieve his goal.

He got partial success when Quaid-e-Azam Muhammad Ali Jinnah agreed to accept Kalat's status as different from the rest of the princely states of the subcontinent during the negotiation between him and the Khan for a possible merger of Kalat with Pakistan. Quaid-e-Azam Muhammad Ali Jinnah as his policy and statements regarding princely states that would join Pakistan indicated, was more than willing to provide Kalat maximum autonomy, with Pakistan taking responsibility of defence, foreign and economic affairs only. In keeping with his personal relations with Ahmed Yar Khan, Quaid-e-Azam Muhammad Ali Jinnah hoped that he would accede Kalat to Pakistan. Quaid-e-Azam Muhammad Ali Jinnah underestimated Ahmed Yar Khan's intentions, who dreamed of becoming the ruler of an independent country. He gave different and totally contradictory signals to Pakistan, especially Quaid-e-Azam Muhammad Ali Jinnah and the Baloch sardars and people of Kalat and Balochistan.

On the one hand, he kept ensuring Quaid-e-Azam Muhammad Ali Jinnah and the Pakistani government that everything would be sorted out which would be mutually acceptable; on the other hand, with Baloch sardars and so-called elected representatives, he discussed Kalat's historical place and destiny. His decision to not take the decision to accede to Pakistan alone and ask his rather hastily and dubiously *elected* House of Lords and Commons was nothing but delaying tactics.

However, despite all this, Ahmad Yar Khan had to sign Kalat's accession agreement with Pakistan, although seeds of discontent and misperception between Pakistan and the Baloch were sown deep by then.

The use of different narratives and tone by him in his communication with Quaid-e-Azam Muhammad Ali Jinnah and with Baloch sardars not only resulted

Conclusion 183

in confusion between the Baloch opinion makers and the centre, but also developed the perception that Pakistan wanted to occupy Kalat. It was this role played by Mir Ahmad Yar Khan that resulted in Prince Karim's localized armed struggle against Pakistan. The letter which he wrote to Ahmad Yar Khan is a clear indication of the fact that Baloch perception about Quaid-e-Azam Muhammad Ali Jinnah and Pakistan became extremely negative as early as 1948. Once Pakistan managed to get the accession of Kalat and British Balochistan voting in its favour, it started working on administrated reforms in the province. Pakistani policy makers failed in moving beyond the British model and policy of ruling Balochistan.

A number of steps and measures were taken with mixed results. The One Unit policy, the ill-conceived arrest of Ahmed Yar Khan in 1958 on dubious charges, the mishandling and disrespectful treatment of Nauroz Khan added to Baloch grievances towards the centre which, according to Baloch nationalist narrative, was strongly anti-Baloch and consisted of the Punjabi ruling elites.

For the first decade of Pakistan's history, the centre's main focus or concern was how to address the Bengali problem. This one-point agenda and the policies which were made due to this created further problems for the centre and its relations with the smaller provinces and ethnic groups of Pakistan. Pakistan's policy makers pursued the same policy towards Balochistan which was followed by the British and the policy debates about how to or not introduce reforms in Balochistan which took place among the Pakistani policy circles were not very different from how the British administration viewed this issue. British policy makers viewed Balochistan's tiny population, huge geography and lack of education as few of the reasons why it is not financially viable to introduce large scale reforms in the area. Same arguments were made by Pakistani policy makers in the deliberations of the reform committee on Balochistan.

In the 1970s, when the Baloch leadership got the opportunity to establish their government and run the provincial administration of Balochistan, they could not perform. This book argued that the lack of political acumen of the Baloch leadership, Bugti and Mengal–Marri rivalry, tribal feuds in Balochistan, Bhutto's unwillingness to share power and accept the existence and the mandate of the NAP, state's security perception in the wake of the 1971 war and separation of East Pakistan were the main reasons for the political instability in Balochistan during the 1970s.

In the Baloch narrative, this decade (1970s) is the decade of bloodshed and the centre's or Islamabad's so-called brutal military action against Baloch masses and whatever they held dear. The fact of the matter is that this was also the decade where the Baloch leadership failed to perform. The Baloch nationalist narrative claims that the NAP or Baloch elected leadership was not successful because the Punjabi establishment, the Pakistan Army and the federal government created problems for them. In this narrative, there is no mention of the infighting, tribal feuds, miscalculated and impractical decisions made by the Baloch/NAP leadership.

The differences between Ataullah Mengal and Akbar Bugti and how Bugti sided with Bhutto against his own fellow Baloch sardars played an important role in the

184   *Conclusion*

events which followed. The tribal feuds and the clashes between the Jamotes and Mengals, the role of the Zehri brothers and the tribal way Mengal as CM reacted to all these problems by mobilizing a Mengal lashkar against them are cases in point.

There is no denying the fact that Bhutto also contributed to the problems NAP-Balochistan faced. He wanted the PPP to be the single political power in the country and Pakistan to be a single-party country; however, most of his partners in all what he did were Baloch sardars: Raisani, Akbar Bugti and none other than the Khan of Kalat Ahmed Yar Khan.

General Zia, a strong believer in making Pakistan an Islamic state and a strong opponent of a multiethnic and multicultural Pakistan, followed a policy of reconciliation in Balochistan even prior to the Soviet invasion of Afghanistan in 1979. He withdrew the army from various parts of Balochistan, dissolved the Hyderabad tribunal, declared amnesty for Baloch insurgents and provided them compensation money. However, after the Soviet invasion of Afghanistan and the emergence of an American–Pakistani–Saudi–Chinese alliance to support the Afghan resistance, Balochistan gained a strategic position for the Pakistani and American decision-makers as it was Balochistan which provided the USSR its shortest and most viable outlet to the warm waters of the Indian Ocean. Zia poured in a lot of money to build roads, airports, gas supply and other developmental projects which, other than being visible development projects, were also strategically important in case of a Soviet invasion of the area. General Zia-ul-Haq channelled in a lot of money into Balochistan in the shape of developmental projects, yet his main concern was strategic as he could not afford any trouble in Balochistan in the wake of the Soviet presence in Afghanistan.

During the peace interval in Balochistan (1977–99), hardly anything changed for the common Baloch and the province of Balochistan, yet it remained peaceful. There are a number of reasons for this: divisions in the political and militant leadership of the Baloch nationalist movement, two of the three Baloch nationalist leaders left Balochistan and settled in London, the Soviet invasion of Afghanistan and the Afghan war as a result of which the Pakistan Army concentrated more on Balochistan. Balochistan was considered a possible target of the Red Army. During the second phase of the peace interval, Pakistan went through its decade of democracy (1988–99). Baloch leaders participated in the political activities in the country, and a number of Baloch sardars and politicians such as Akbar Bugti, Bizenjo and Zafarullah Khan Jamali emerged as national-level politicians and played significant roles in Pakistani politics.

During the decade of democracy, Balochistan was never a major issue for the central government and/or for the Balochistan provincial governments which continued to conduct business as usual. During this phase, a number of elections took place in which the Baloch leaders fully participated. Nationalist leaders and their sons actively participated and supported their candidates in the elections and became chief minister of the province (Akhtar Mengal is a case in point). A number of Baloch politicians for the first time in Pakistani history participated in the politics at the national level. This all happened without any

Conclusion 185

major change in the lives of the Baloch people, and they continued to follow the same system of governance. The only reason which explains the absence of violence and Baloch participation in politics is that during this period the centre decided not to follow a policy of confrontation and pursued a policy of engagement. As a result of this policy of engagement, there was no sparking or triggering event using which the Baloch leaders could continue or start a new wave of violent conflict. Another factor which proves this point is that a number of projects and developments which later became contributing reasons for the return of insurgency in Balochistan actually started during this period, but no major violence took place.

During the decade of democracy, Baloch politicians participated in Pakistani politics. Akbar Bugti, Zafar Jamali and Bizenjo played important roles in national politics. Akbar Bugti was projecting his Jamhoori Wattan Party as the third political force in the country. A new generation of Baloch politicians emerged and actively participated in politics. This group included people like Akhtar Mengal, Abdul Hayee Baloch, Abdul Malik and a number of others.

Throughout this period, it became clear that Baloch politics is still conducted on tribal lines and that the sardars play the key role in the Baloch politics. This was despite the emergence of a number of political parties in Balochistan as every Baloch political party sought the patronage of a sardar. Baloch National Movement which is led by Dr. Abdul Haye Baloch, representing the Baloch middle class, only became a significant political player in Baloch politics when it got the support of Akbar Bugti and Ataullah Mengal. These were positive signs for Balochistan, Pakistan and centre–province relations. This, however, changed and insurgent violence returned to Balochistan in early 2000s.

Since the return of violence in Balochistan a number of attempts have been made to address the Baloch grievances. However, an important point in this regard is that the centre, whenever it presents a special package or program for Balochistan projects it as a out-of-the-way gesture and as a special favour for the Baloch people, whereas the Baloch nationalist leadership takes it as an insult due to the fact that it considers such packages or programs, even if they reject it, as an acknowledgement of their long overdue right.

In the ongoing phase of violence/insurgency of Balochistan, the centre presented two special packages to Balochistan: Recommendations of the Senate sub-committee on Balochistan led by Senator Mushahid Hussain which had national-level support including in Balochistan (Bugti accepted it, and even Sardar Mengal considered it a sincere effort). However, it is not clear how much of its recommendations were ever implemented. When the PPP took over the helm of affairs at the centre, instead of trying to implement the committee's recommendation, it tried to reinvent the wheel and prepared and presented its own Aghaz-e-Huqooq-Balochistan package. It was claimed that it is a historical step towards national reconciliation. This book argued that the main reason that it failed was: *first*, there was hardly anything new in it for the Baloch leadership; they had heard all that before; and *second*, it lacked a clear focus, priority and strategy for implementation.

186 *Conclusion*

Professor Akbar S. Ahmed has pointed that Pakistan must address the concern of the people living in the periphery (Balochistan). According to Professor Ahmed, "Right now we are in a state of civil war in Pakistan," ... "People in the periphery think they have been neglected, humiliated and culturally looked down upon by the Centre. This is absolutely the same thing we did with the Bengalis. Pakistan is in a very fragile condition. Both civil and military leadership must urgently show wisdom and vision to come out of this situation."[1] According to him, Balochistan is the key to the survival of Pakistan. He argued, "We can't afford to make the Baloch feel like second class citizens. Their demands are valid and some of these demands have been overlooked for several decades. Islamabad should make urgent accommodation with the Baloch. You can't fool around with them. One day you offer them talks and the next day you kill their leaders. They should be treated as equal partners in the federation."[2]

Notes

1 Malik Siraj Akbar, "We Don't Have Much Time Left: Dr Akbar Ahmed," *Dawn*, December 17, 2011, www.dawn.com/news/681200/we-dont-have-much-time-left-dr-akbar-ahmed.
2 Ibid.

Epilogue

Balochistan, Gwadar, CPEC and the Future of Pakistan

Although Balochistan is considered to be the most neglected and overlooked province of Pakistan, a closer look at Pakistan's history points that it always remained central to political and strategic developments taking place inside and around Pakistan. At present, Pakistan is at crossroads and its political stability and economic and financial viability depend on Balochistan. The strategic significance of Gwadar[1] was realized even before Pakistan was created in 1947. It was the realization of its geostrategic significance that Pakistan bought it back from Oman. The Bhutto government considered developing it, but the idea could not materialize. During the Afghan jihad in 1980s, not only Makran and Gwadar were identified as one of the points that the Red Army was eying for as an outlet to the warm waters of the Indian Ocean, a number of American and Western strategists identified them as ideal locations for a naval base.[2] After the disintegration of the USSR and independence of the Central Asian Republics (CARs), the *stans*, Pakistan envisaged itself as a doorway for the CARs through Balochistan (Gwadar). However, domestic, regional and international developments stopped this from materializing. When General Musharraf took over, construction of the Gwadar Port was one of his top priorities.

Pak–China friendship is described as higher than mountains, deeper than the oceans, and, of late, sweeter than honey. It is a unique case in the international system.[3] China and Pakistan are involved in several joint projects. Therefore, it came as no surprise for Pakistan-watchers when China got actively involved in the construction of the Gwadar Port.

Gwadar Port

China was involved in the project from the very beginning and was its main financer. It also provided major technical assistance during various stages of its construction. The project is of immense strategic importance as Gwadar is strategically located. The port is just 180 nautical miles from the Strait of Hormuz, through which 40 percent of all globally traded oil is shipped. Gwadar provides China access to the Persian Gulf and an opportunity to diversify and secure its crude oil import routes through the Arabian Sea, especially for its Xingjian region.

188 *Epilogue*

Gwadar Port complex, inaugurated in January 2007[4] and now fully operational, provides a deep-sea port, warehouses, and industrial facilities for more than twenty countries.

Since the beginning of this century, Islamabad is working hard to project and make Pakistan an energy and trade corridor for the region. It has taken a number of steps in this regard. Both countries agreed to cooperate in achieving this objective. A memorandum was signed between China and Pakistan, where both countries agreed to step up co-operation in the energy sector, promising to give China access to the gas and oil resources of Central and Western Asia. Islamabad pointed that China should build direct pipelines to Karachi or Gwadar, where this would then be the shortest route for ensuring a stable and fast supply of oil to China.[5] "We particularly look forward to materializing cooperation in the energy sector where establishment of oil refineries, oil storage facilities and gas pipelines stand out," said then President of Pakistan General Musharraf, adding "When the Karakoram Highway was built, the world called it the eighth wonder, we can create the ninth and tenth wonders by establishing energy pipelines and railway linkages between the two fast growing economies."

After ensuing legal battle, the Port of Singapore Authority (PSA) that was initially entrusted to administer the Gwadar Port cancelled its contract; Islamabad, which accused the PSA of failing to fulfil its commitments, handed over the Gwadar Port to the China Overseas Port Holdings Company.[6]

Several ambitious projects have been identified in Gwadar. These include an international airport, Pak–China Friendship Hospital, technical and vocation education and training institute, a university and a fresh water treatment and distribution plant.[7] Chairman of Gwadar Port Authority stated that an industrial zone with manufacturing zones will be established in Gwadar in which a number of industries would be invited to participate.

According to Dostain Khan Jamaldini, Chairman of Gwadar Port Authority, by 2055, Gwadar is destined to become a modern port city divided into two parts: eastern and western Gwadar. The western Gwadar will have several tourist facilities, whereas the eastern Gwadar would be an industrial city that would include steel mills, terminals for liquefied natural gas, oil refineries and other facilities.

At present, the biggest problem that Gwadar is facing is a lack of electricity and potable water. Its current requirement is 4.6 million gallons of water that is likely to increase manifold with developmental works. Currently, Gwadar is dependent on rain water and is supplied through Akra Kaur Dam that could only supply 2.5 million gallons of water. 200,00 gallons is supplied through the Karwat desalination plant.[8] Gwadar is also facing shortage of electricity and load shedding problem.[9]

One Belt One Road

One Belt One Road (OBOR), a modern-day silk road, was launched in 2013. This ambitious plan aims to link the ancient silk road with Europe. According to several reports, China is spending approximately $150 billion per year in the

Epilogue 189

68 countries that are currently involved in OBOR and its different related projects.[10] According to reports, China has already spent above a trillion dollar and is likely to spend several more in the coming years.[11] This project is mostly likely to change the geostrategic map of the world and shift the global balance of power in favour of China.

China Pakistan Economic Corridor (CPEC)

Two months after the administration of the Gwadar Port was handed over to the Chinese, in May 2013, during his visit to Pakistan, the Chinese Primer hinted on an idea that would later materialize into China–Pakistan Economic Corridor (CPEC). In fact, it was General Musharraf who first came up with the idea of Pakistan as a corridor for Chinese goods. Andrew Small believes that "plans for an economic corridor running from China through Pakistan to the Middle East and beyond are not new. As long ago as the 1960s, Zhou Enlai had discussed using Karachi as an outlet for rediscovering an 'ancient trade route ... lost to modern times, not only for trade but for strategic purposes as well.'"[12]

Next came Nawaz Sharif's visit to China in November 2014. During this visit, among the many things discussed was the construction of a 2,000-kilometre road and rail link connecting Kashgar with Gwadar.

However, it was the visit of the Chinese President Xi Jinping to Pakistan in April 2015 that played the significant role in this regard. During this visit, China pledged US$ 46 billion investment in Pakistan.

According to the Chinese, the purpose of the China–Pakistan Economic Corridor is to transform the social and economic structure of Pakistan and that it is designed to wean the populace {of Pakistan} from fundamentalism.[13]

China–Pakistan Economic Corridor (CPEC) is the flagship project of the One Road One Belt (OBOR) as it is likely to serve as a link between the continental Eurasian Silk Road Economic Belt and a Southeast Asian Maritime Silk Road.[14] US $ 46 billion has been invested into CPEC. According to media reports, so far 59 projects have been initiated under CPEC.

According to the details of the plan, along CPEC, a total of nine special economic zones will be established. Pakistan will pay back the principle plus interest in over 30 years.

CPEC and the Asian geostrategic fault lines

OBOR and especially CPEC have challenged the existing geostrategic order and balance in the region and have the potential to alter the geostrategic fault lines in Asia. Many believe that through OBOR, China is attempting to declare its arrival on the global stage and proclaim to be the dominant global player and super power. CPEC provides China an alternative to its dependence on the South China Sea.

USA, India, Australia, and Japan have already voiced their concerns about OBOR. India has formally protested about a few projects within CPEC as New Delhi claims that these pass through Kashmir and the Gilgit-Baltistan region. New

190 *Epilogue*

Delhi for some time now is working to bypass Pakistan by establishing an alternative route for Afghanistan and Central Asian states through Chabahar Port in Iran. It has recently opened Afghanistan–India air corridor through which it can bypass and reach Afghanistan and Central Asian states. It has already dispatched its first flight carrying material worth $5 million.

According to several media reports, USA, Australia, Japan and India are in negotiation to identify ways to counter increasing Chinese influence and develop a rival project to Chinese One Belt One Road.[15]

CPEC and Baloch nationalists

The Baloch nationalists consider the Gwadar Port and CPEC as a threat to their very survival. According to them, it will change the demographics of the province and would have an influx of the outsiders that will make the Baloch a minority in their own province. They also fear that these projects will result in a deployment of a greater number of Pakistan Army creating further problems for them. Baloch nationalists argue that the benefits of these projects will be taken away from them. The moderates within the Baloch political leadership are also sceptical of these projects. They believe that the Baloch and Balochistan would not get their due share from the benefits and dividends of these projects.

This is why the Baloch insurgents have attacked the Gwadar Port and the Chinese engineers and workers have been targeted by them since 2004 when the Baloch Liberation Army (BLA) killed three and injured nine Chinese engineers using a car bomb. Since then, Baloch insurgents have targeted the Gwadar airport, Chinese workers, and the infrastructure related to these projects.[16] According to Baloch journalist Malik Siraj Akbar:

> The Baloch nationalists have repeatedly warned China to stay away from Gwadar or to at least directly negotiate with them about Balochistan's coastal and mineral resources instead of going through Islamabad. In a nutshell, the nationalists' posture toward China is based on these key messages: Stay out of Balochistan. Don't usurp the province's resources. Don't become a party in the Baloch-Islamabad conflict.[17]

Baloch nationalists claim that Baloch are not given employment at the Gwadar Port and that there is no opportunity for vocational training for the locals. They claim that the Chinese are not hiring locals and are bringing in their countrymen as labourers. A leading politic economist of Pakistan and former advisor to the Chief Minister of Balochistan, Kaiser Bengali stated that "employment for locals is a serious issue and ... has found people from other areas of Pakistan brought here for jobs. "Almost all the staff of the biggest hotel in Gwadar belongs to Karachi."[18]

This perception and view is not limited to Baloch nationalists alone. The Chief Minister of Balochistan Mir Abdul Quddus Bizenjo speaking at the Meet the Press program at the National Press Club claimed that "...his province was being neglected by the federal government in the China-Pakistan Economic Corridor

Epilogue 191

(CPEC) project." Adding "More than Rs. 5,000 billion is being spent on the CPEC, but Balochistan is not receiving even one percent of it," and that "… the people of the province were ignored in development activities being made under the project. We have to see what benefit the people of Balochistan will get from the CPEC."[19]

CPEC, Balochistan and the future of Pakistan

The significance of Balochistan in the future stability of Pakistan cannot be over-emphasized. It's geostrategic location, hard-working and brave people, vast resources and critical projects such as the Gwadar Port and China–Pakistan Economic corridor (CPEC) are too vital for Pakistan. Due to these factors, Balochistan has become a centre of attention of regional and global players. While this might provide the Baloch insurgents more reasons to fight the state of Pakistan, yet for exactly these factors Islamabad is unlikely to let its guard down. However, it would make sense if Islamabad considers its policy options regarding Balochistan. One way of doing this is working out an arrangement like the Alaska Permanent Fund for Balochistan.

Although it is too soon to objectively analyse the prospects and pitfalls of CPEC, especially when the available data are limited, one can easily infer from what is publicly available that once CPEC is fully operational, it has the potential to transfer Pakistan from just a South Asian state to a West-Central and South Asian state. This would also provide India and Pakistan ample options and choices to revisit their hostile relationship.

Notes

1 Gwadar is a Balochi word meaning door of wind.
2 For details on these points, see Mahnaz Ispahani, "Roads and Rivals" (Ithaca: Cornell University Press, 1989); Nadir Mir, "Gwadar on the Global Chessboard Pakistan's Identity, History Culture" (Lahore: Ferozsons, 2010); Maqsudul Hasan Nuri, Azhar Ahmad, and Farhat Akram, "Balochistan: Rationalisation of Centre-Province Relations" (Islamabad: Islamabad Policy Research Institute, 2010).
3 "Pakistan and China: Sweet as Can Be?" *The Economist*, May 12, 2011, at www.economist.com/node/18682839.
4 Andrew Small, "The China Pakistan Axis Asia's New Geopolitics" (Haryana: Vintage, 2015),101.
5 Tarique Niazi, "Gwadar: China's Naval Outpost on the Indian Ocean," *The Jamestown Foundation*, vol. 28 February 2005, at www.jamestown.org/single/?no_cache=1&tx_ttnews%5Btt_news%5D=3718.
6 Small, "The China Pakistan Axis Asia's New Geopolitics," 101.
7 Shahzada Irfan Ahmed, "The Port in Question," *The News*, May 28, 2017, http://tns.thenews.com.pk/port-question/#.Ws7JFExuLIU.
8 Dr. Farrukh Saleem, "Gwadar," *The News*, www.thenews.com.pk/print/149434-Gwadar.
9 Ibid.
10 "What is China's Belt and Road Initiative? The Many Motivations Behind Xi Jinping's Key Foreign Policy," *The Economist*, May 15, 2017, www.economist.com/blogs/economist-explains/2017/05/economist-explains-11?fsrc=scn/tw/te/bl/ed/.

192   *Epilogue*

11 Zahid Hussain, "China's New World Order," *Dawn*, May 17, 2017, www.dawn.com/news/1333603.
12 Muhammad Mumtaz Kalid, History of the Karakaoram Highway, Vol. II, Rawalpindi: Hamza, 2009, p. 5; Small, "The China Pakistan Axis Asia's New Geopolitics," 188.
13 Small, "The China Pakistan Axis Asia's New Geopolitics," 191.
14 Hussain, "China's New World Order," *Dawn*, May 17, 2017, www.dawn.com/news/1333603.
15 Australia, US, India and Japan attempt to counter China's OBOR, February 20, 2018, www.globalvillagespace.com/australia-us-india-and-japan-attempt-to-counter-chinas-obor/.
16 "Chinese, Pakistanis back at Work in Gwadar," *Reuters*, May 7, 2004; "6 Rockets Fired Near Gwadar Airport," *Dawn*, May 22, 2005; "Rockets fired on PC Hotel Gwadar," *Daily Times*, July 7, 2010 as quoted in Andrew Small, 102.
17 Malik Siraj Akbar, "Beijing to Balochistan," *The News*, March 4, 2018.
18 Ahmed, "The Port in Question," *The News*, May 28, 2017, http://tns.thenews.com.pk/port-question/#.Ws7JFExuLIU.
19 "Balochistan being Neglected in CPEC, says Bizenjo," *Dawn*, April 12, 2018, www.dawn.com/news/1401117/.

Bibliography

Abbasi, Ansar. "What Balochistan Deserves." *The News International*, Islamabad, September 7, 2006.

Adeney, Katharine. *Federalism and Ethnic Conflict Resolution in India and Pakistan*. New York, NY: Palgrave, 2007.

Afzal, M. Rafique. *Political Parties in Pakistan*. Islamabad: National Commission on Historical Research, 1976.

Ahmad, Syed Faruq. *Tarikh Pakistan-wa-Balochistan* [The History of Pakistan and Balochistan]. Karachi: NP, 1977.

Ahmad, Manzooruddin, ed. *Contemporary Pakistan: Politics, Economy and Society*. Karachi: Oxford University Press, 1982.

Ahmed, Akbar S. *Pakistan Society: Islam, Ethnicity and Leadership in South Asia*. Karachi: Oxford University Press, ND.

Ahmed, Feroz, ed. *Focus on Baluchistan and Pushtoon Question*. Lahore: People's Publishing House, 1975.

Ahmed, Feroz, ed. *Ethnicity and Politics in Pakistan*. Karachi: Oxford University Press, 1998.

Ahmed, Feroz. "Ethnicity and Politics: The Rise of Muhajir Separatism." *South Asia Bulletin*, no. 8 (1988).

Ahmed, Ishtiaq. *State, Nation and Ethnicity in Contemporary South Asia*. London: NP, 1996.

Aitchinson, C. V., ed. *A Collection of Treaties, Engagements and Sanads*. Calcutta: Government of India Central Publication Branch, 1931.

Akhund, Iqbal. *Trial and Error: The Advent and Eclipse of Benazir Bhutto*. Karachi: Oxford University Press, 2000.

Alavi, Hamza. "Nationhood and the Nationalities in Pakistan." In *Economy and Culture in Pakistan: Migrants and Cities in a Muslim Society*, edited by Hastings Donnan and Pnina Werbner. London: Macmillan, 1991.

Alavi, Hamza. "Nationhood and Communal Violence in Pakistan." *Journal of Contemporary Asia* 21, no. 2 (1991): 152–78.

Alavi, Hamza and F. Halliday, eds. *State and Ideology in the Middles East and Pakistan*. Lahore: Macmillan, 1977.

Ali, S. Mahmud. *The Fearful State: Power, People and Internal War in South Asia*. London, 1993.

Ali, Tariq. *Can Pakistan Survive? The Death of a State*. London: Penguin, 1983.

194   Bibliography

Amin, Tahir. *Ethno-National Movements of Pakistan: Domestic and International Factors.* Islamabad: Institute of Policy Studies, 1988.

Amin, Tahir. "Pakistan in 1993: Some Dramatic Changes." *Asian Survey* 34, 2 February, 1994.

Amin, Tahir. "Pakistan in 1994: The Politics of Confrontation." *Asian Survey* 35, 2 February, 1995.

Arif, K. M. *Working with Zia: Pakistan's Power Politics 1977–1988.* Karachi: Oxford University Press, 1995.

Amin, Tahir. *Khaki Shadows, The Pakistan Army, 1947–1997.* Karachi: Oxford University Press, 2000.

Awan, A. B. *Baluchistan: Historical and Political Processes.* London: New Century Publishers, 1985.

Axmann, Martin. *Back to the Future: The Khanate of Kalat and the Genesis of Baloch Nationalism, 1915–1955.* Karachi: Oxford University Press, 2008.

Ayres, Alyssa. 2009. *Speaking Like a State: Language and Nationalism in Pakistan.* Cambridge: Cambridge University Press.

Aziz, Sartaj. *Between Dreams and Realities: Some Milestones in Pakistan's History.* Karachi: Oxford University Press, 2009.

Azam, Jean-Paul. "Looting and Conflict between Ethnoregional Groups. Lessons for State Formation in Africa." *Journal of Conflict Resolution* 46, no. 1 (2002): 131–53.

Azam, Jean-Paul. "On Thugs and Heroes: Why Warlords Victimize Their Own Civilians." *Economics of Governance* 7, no. 1 (2006): 53–73.

Azam, Jean-Paul and Anke Hoeffler. "Violence Against Civilians in Civil Wars: Looting or Terror?" *Journal of Peace Research* 39, no. 4 (2002): 461–85.

Baloch, Inayatullah. *The Problem of Greater Baluchistan: A Study of Baluch Nationalism.* Stuttgart: Steiner Verlag Wiesbaden GMBH, 1987.

Baloch, M. Sardar Khan. *History of Baluch Race and Baluchistan.* Karachi: Process Pakistan, 1958.

Baloch, Manzoor Ahmed. *Balochistan and Political Parties.* Quetta: Kalat Press, ND.

Baloch, Mir Khuda Bakhsh Bijrani Marri. *A Judge May Speak.* Lahore: Feorz Sons, 1990.

Baloch, Mir Khuda Bakhsh Bijrani Marri. *Searchlights on Baloches and Balochistan.* Karachi: Royal Book Company, ND.

Baluch, Mir Ahmad Yar Khan. *Inside Baluchistan.* Karachi: Royal Book Company, 1975.

Baluch, Muhammad Sardar Khan. *The Great Baluch: The Life and Times of Ameer Chakar Rind 1454–1551 A.D.* Quetta: PNNG, 1965.

Baluch, Muhammad Sardar Khan. *A Literary History of the Baluchis.* Quetta: PNNG, 1977.

Baluch, Muhammad Sardar Khan. *History of Baluch Race and Baluchistan.* Quetta: Khair-un-Nisa Traders, 1984.

Barlas, Asma. *Democracy, Nationalism and Communalism; The Colonial Legacy in South Asia.* Boulder, CO: PUBLISHER, 1995.

Baxter, Craig. *Pakistan on the Brink: Politic, Economics and Society.* Karachi: Oxford University Press, ND.

Baxter, Craig, ed. *Zia's Pakistan: Politics and Society in a Frontline State.* Boulder, CO: PUBLISHER, 1985.

Baxter, Craig, ed. *Mohammad Ayub Khan Diaries, 1966–72.* Karachi: Oxford University Press, 2007.

Benson, Michelle and Jacek Kugler. "Power Parity, Democracy, and the Severity of Internal Violence." *Journal of Conflict Resolution* 42, no. 2 (1998): 196–209.

Bibliography 195

Best, Geoffrey. *Humanity in Warfare: The Modern History of the International Law of Armed Conflicts.* . London: Methuen & Co., Ltd, 1983.

Breseeg, Taj Mohammed. *Baloch Nationalism: Its Origin and Development.* Karachi: Royal Book Company, 2004.

Bueno de Mesquita, Ethan. "Conciliation, Counterterrorism, and Patterns of Terrorist Violence." *International Organization* 59, no. 1 (2005): 145–76.

Burki, Shahid Javed. *Pakistan: Fifty Years of Nationhood.* Lahore: Vanguard, 2004.

Burki, Shahid Javed and Craig Baxter. *Pakistan Under the Military.* Boulder, CO: Westview Press, 1991.

Burki, Shahid Javed, et al. *Government and Politics in South Asia.* Boulder, CO, 1993.

Burki, Shahid Javed. *Pakistan Under Bhutto, 1971–1977.* London: NP, 1977.

Burki, Shahid Javed. "Pakistan Under Zia 1977–88." *Asian Survey* 28, 10 October, 1988.

Burki, Shahid Javed and Craig Baxter. "Socio-Economic Indicators of the People's Party Vote in the Punjab: A Study at the Tehsil level." *Journal of Asian Studies* 34, no. 4, August (1975): 913–30.

Carina Jahani, ed. *Language in Society: Eight Sociolinguistic Essays on Balochi.* Uppsala: Uppsala University, Year.

Caroe, Sir Olaf. *The Pathans.* Oxford: Oxford University Press, 2006.

Cheema, P. I. "The Afghan Crisis and Pakistan's Security Dilemma." *Asian Survey* 23, no. 3, March (1983): 227–43.

Cheema, P. I. *The Armed Forces of Pakistan.* Karachi: Oxford University Press, 2002.

Chishti, F. A. *Betrayals of Another Kind: Islam, Democracy and the Army in Pakistan.* London: NP, 1989.

Clifford, James and George E. Marcus, eds. *Writing Vulture: The Politics of Ethnography.* Berkeley: University of California Press, 1986.

Cloughley, Brian. *War, Coups and Terror: Pakistan's Army in Years of Turmoil.* Barnsley: Pen and Sword Books, 2008.

Cohen, Stephen Philip. *The Pakistan Army.* Karachi: Oxford University Press, 1999.

Cohen, Stephen Philip. *The Idea of Pakistan.* Washington, DC: Brookings Institution Press, 2004.

Coll, Steve. *Ghost Wars: The Secret History of the CIA, Afghanistan and Bin Laden.* London: Penguin, 2005.

Christer, Ahlström and Kjell-Åke Nordquist. *Casualties of Conflict, Report for the World Campaign for the Protection of Victims of War.* Uppsala: Department of Peace and Conflict Research, Uppsala University, 1991.

Dames, M. Longworth. *Popular Poetry of the Baloches.* London: Royal Asiatic Society, 1907.

Dames, M. Longworth. *The Baloch Race: A Historical and Ethnological Sketch.* London: Royal Asiatic Society, 1904.

Dani, Ahmad Hassan. *Peshawar: Historic City of the Frontier.* Lahore: Sang-e-Meel, 2002.

de Figueiredo Jr, Ru and Barry R. Weingast. "The Rationality of Fear: Political Opportunism and Ethnic Conflict." In *Civil Wars, Insecurity, and Intervention,* edited by Barbara F. Walter and Jack Snyder. New York: Columbia University Press, 1999.

Dewey, Clive. "The Rural Roots of Pakistan Militarism." In *The Political Inheritance of Pakistan,* edited by D. A. Low, 255–84. Basingstoke, PUBLISHER, 1991.

Downes, Alexander B. "Desperate Times, Desperate Measures: The Causes of Civilian Victimization in War." *International Security* 30, no. 4 (2006): 152–95.

Drake, C. J. M. *Terrorists' Target Selection.* Basingstoke: Macmillan Press, 1998.

196 *Bibliography*

Dunne, Justin S. *Crisis in Balochistan: A Historical Analysis of the Baluch Nationalist Movement in Pakistan.* Monterey: Naval Postgraduate School (Master's), 2006.

Embree, Ainslee T., ed. *Pakistan's Western Borderlands.* Durham: DUP, 1977.

Eubank, William and Leonard Weinberg. "Terrorism and Democracy: Perpetrators and Victims." *Terrorism and Political Violence* 13, no. 1 (2001): 155–64.

Eubank, William Lee and Leonard Weinberg. "Does Democracy Encourage Terrorism?" *Terrorism and Political Violence* 6, no. 4 (1994): 417–43.

Faruqui, Ahmed. *Rethinking the National Security of Pakistan.* Aldershot: Ashgate, 2003.

Fearon, James D. "Rationalist Explanations for War." *International Organization* 49, no. 3 (1995): 379–414.

Feldman, Herbert. *The End and the Beginning: Pakistan, 1969–71.* Karachi: Oxford University Press, 1976.

Gilmartin, D. *Empire and Islam: Punjab and the Making of Pakistan.* Berkeley: University of California Press, 1988.

Gandhi, Leela. *Postcolonial Theory: A Critical Introduction.* New York: Columbia University Press, 1998.

Garare, Frederic. *Pakistan: A Resurgence of Baloch Nationalism.* Washington, DC: CEIP, 2006.

Garare, Frederic. "Pakistan: The Resurgence of Baluch Nationalism." *Carnegie Papers* (2006): 1–14.

Garare, Frederic. *Rethinking Western Strategies towards Pakistan: An Action Agenda for the United States and Europe.* Washington, DC: CEIP, 2007.

Gauhar, Altaf. *Ayub Khan: Pakistan's First Military Ruler.* Lahore: Sang-e-Meel Publications, 1993.

Gurr. *Peoples versus States: Ethnopolitical Conflict and Accommodation at the End of the 20th Century.* Washington, DC: USIP Press, 2000.

Gurr, John L. Davies, and Ted Robert Gurr, eds. *Preventive Measures: Building Risk Assessment and Crisis Early Warning Systems.* Lanham, ML: Rowman & Littlefield Publishers Inc., 1998.

Gurr and Barbara Harff. *Ethnic Conflict in World Politics.* Boulder, CO: West View, 1994.

Gottlieb, Gidon. *Nation Against State: A New Approach to Ethnic Conflicts and the Decline of Sovereignty.* New York: Council on Foreign relations, 1993.

Hardin, Russell. *One for All: The Logic of Group Conflict.* Princeton: PUP, 1995.

Harrison, Selig. "Baluch Nationalism and Superpower Rivalry." *International Security* 5, no. 3 (1980–81): 152–63.

Harrison, Selig. *In Afghanistan's Shadow: Baloch Nationalism and Soviet Temptations.* Washington, DC: Carnegie Endowment for International Peace, 1981.

Harrison, Selig. "Baluch Nationalism and Superpower Rivalry." *International Security* (Winter 1980–81): 152–63.

Harrison, Selig. "Pakistan's Baluch Insurgency." *Le Monde Diplomatique – English Edition*, October, 2006. http://mondediplo.com/2006/10/05baluchistan.

Harrison, Selig. "Nightmare in Baluchistan." *Foreign Policy* 32 (Fall 1978): 136–60.

Hasan, Muhammad Usman. *Baluchistan in Retrospect.* Karachi: Royal Book Company, 2002

Hoodbhoy, Pervez and Abdul Hameed Nayyer. "Rewriting the History of Pakistan." In *Islam, Politics, and the State: The Pakistan Experience*, edited by Asghar Khan, 164–77. London: Zed Books, 1985.

Horowitz, D. *Ethnic Groups in Conflict.* Berkeley: University of California Press, 1985.

Bibliography 197

Horowitz, D. "Ethnic and Nationalist Conflict." In *World Security: Challenges for a New Century*, edited by Michael T. Kalre and Daniel C. Thomas. New York: St. Martin's, 1999.

Hussain, Haqqani. *Pakistan: Between Mosque and Military*. Lahore: Vanguard, 2005.

Hussain, Zahid. *Frontline Pakistan: The Struggle with Militant Islam*. London: I.B. Tauris, 2007.

Ibbetson, Sir Denzil. *Panjab Castes*. Lahore: Sang-e-Meel, 2001.

Iqbal, Khuram. *Counter-Insurgency in Balochistan: Pakistan's Strategy, Outcome and Future Implications*. Islamabad: Pakistan Institute for Peace Studies, July 2008.

Ispahani, M. Z. *Roads and Rivals: The Political Uses of Access in the Borderlands of Asia*. Ithaca: CUP, 1989.

Jaffrelot, Christophe, ed. *A History of Pakistan and Its Origins*. London: Anthem Press, 2004.

Jahan, Rounaq. *Pakistan: Failure in National Integration*. New York: Columbia University Press, 1972.

Jalal, Ayesha. *The Sole Spokesman, Quaid-e-Azam Muhammad Ali Jinnah, the Muslim League and the Demand for Pakistan*. Cambridge: Cambridge University Press, 1985.

Jalal, Ayesha. *The State of Martial Rule*. Cambridge: Cambridge University Press, 1990.

Jalal, Ayesha. *Democracy and Authoritarianism in South Asia: A Comparative and Historical Perspective*. Cambridge: CUP, 1995.

James, William E. and Subroto Roy, eds. *Foundation of Pakistan's Political Economy: Towards an Agenda for the 1990s*. New Delhi: NN, 1992.

Jānmahmad. *Essays on Bloch National Struggle in Pakistan*. Quetta: Gosha-e-Adab, 1988.

Jones, Owen Bennett. *Pakistan: Eye of the Storm*. London: Yale University Press, 2009.

Karim, W., "The Nativised Self and the Native." In *Gendered Fields: Women, Men and Ethnography*, edited by D. P. C. Bell and E. J. Karim, 248–51. London: Routledge, 1993.

Kaufman, Stuart. *Modern Hatreds: The Symbolic Politics of Ethnic War*. Ithaca: Cornell University Press, 2001.

Kennedy, Charles H. "The Politics of Ethnicity in Sindh." *Asian Survey* 31, no. 10 (1991).

Kennedy, Charles H., Kathleen McNeill, Carl Ernst, and David Gilmartin, eds. *Pakistan at the Millennium*. Karachi: Oxford University Press, 2003.

Khan, Adeel. *Politics of Identity: Ethnic Nationalism and the State in Pakistan*. London: Sage, 2005.

Khan, Ahmad Yar. *Inside Baluchistan: A Political Autobiography of His Highness Baiglar Baigi*. Karachi: Royal Book Company, 1975.

Khan, Asghar. *We've Learnt Nothing from History: Pakistan-Politics and Military Power*. Karachi: Oxford University Press, 2005.

Khan, Gul Hasan. *Memoirs of Lt. General Gul Hasan Khan*. Karachi: Oxford University Press, 1993.

Khan, Roedad. *Pakistan: A Dream Gone Soar*. Karachi: Oxford University Press, 1997.

Khan, Yasmin. *The Great Partition: The Making of India and Pakistan*. Yale: Yale University Press, 2007.

Kundi, Mansoor Akbar. "Tribalism in Balochistan: A Comparative Study." In *Tribal Areas of Pakistan: Challenges and Responses*. Islamabad: Islamabad Policy Research Institute and Hanns Seidel Foundation, 2005.

Kux, Dennis. *Pakistan: Flawed Not Failed State. Foreign Policy Association Headline Series*. no. 332, Summer 2001.

Laqueur, Walter. *Guerrilla Warfare*. New Brunswick: Transaction, 1997.

198   *Bibliography*

Lyon, Stephen M. *An Anthropological Analysis of Local Politics and Patronage in a Pakistani Village*. Lewiston, NY: Edwin Mellen, 2004.

Malik, Iftikhar H. "Ethno-Nationalism in Pakistan: A Commentary on the Muhajir Qaumi Mahaz (MQM) in Sindh." *South Asia Bulletin* 18, no. 2 (1995).

Malik, I. H. *State and Civil Society in Pakistan: Politics of Authority, Ideology and Ethnicity*. Basingstoke: NN, 1997.

Mascrenhas, Anthony. *The Rape of Bangladesh*. New Delhi: Vikas, 1972.

Matheson, Sylvia. *The Tigers of Balochistan*. Karachi: Oxford University Press, 1967.

Mazari, Sherbaz Khan. *A Journey to Disillusionment*. Karachi: Oxford University Press, 2000

Milam, William B. *Bangladesh and Pakistan: Flirting with Failure in South Asia*. London: Hurst, 2009.

Mujahid, Sharif al. *The Ideology of Pakistan*. Islamabad: Islamic Research Institute, 2001.

Mumtaz, Soofia, Jean-Luc Racine, and Imran Anwar, eds. *Pakistan: The Contours of State and Society*. Karachi: Oxford University Press, 2002.

Musharraf, Pervez. *In the Line of Fire: A Memoir*. New York, NY: Free Press, 2006.

Naipaul, V. S. *Among the Believers: An Islamic Journey*. London: Picador, 2003.

Nadeem, Azhar Hassan. *Pakistan: The Political Economy of Lawlessness*. Karachi: Oxford University Press, 2002.

Nawaz, Shuja. *Crossed Swords: Pakistan, Its Army and the War Within*. Karachi: Oxford University Press, 2008.

Niazi, Zamir. *Press in Chains*. Karachi: Maktaba Aaj, 1986.

Niazi, Tarique. "Democracy, Development and Terrorism; The Case of Baluchistan (Pakistan)." *International Journal of Contemporary Sociology* 42, no. 2 (2005): 267–93.

Niazi, Tarique. "Gwadar: China's Naval Outpost on the Indian Ocean." *The Jamestown Foundation: China Brief* 5, no. 4 (February 2005).

Noman, Omer. *The Political Economy of Pakistan, 1947–85*. London: Kegan Paul, 1985.

Pande, Sivita. *Politics of Ethnic and Religious Minorities in Pakistan*. New Delhi: NNG, 2005.

Pandey, Gyanendra and Samad Yunas. *Fault Lines of Nationhood*. New Delhi, 2007.

Pehrson, Robert N. *The Social Organization of the Marri Baloch*. Chicago, IL: Wenner-Gren Foundation, 1966.

Qaddus, Syed Abdul. *The Tribal Baluchistan*. Lahore: Feroz Sons, 1990.

Rashid, Ahmed. *Descent into Chaos*. New York, NY: Penguin, 2008.

Rizvi, Hasan-Askari. *Military, State and Society in Pakistan*. Lahore: Sang-e-Meel, 2003.

Sayeed, K. B. *Pakistan: The Formative Phase, 1857–1948*. London: NN, 1968.

Sayeed, K. B. *Politics in Pakistan: The Nature and Direction of Change*. New York, NY: NN, 1980.

Schmidle, Nicholas. *To Live or To Perish Forever: Two Tumultuous Years in Pakistan*. New York: Henry Holt and Company, LLC, 2009.

Shah, Abid Hussain. *The Volatile Situation of Balochistan – Options to Bring It into Streamline*. Monterey: Naval Postgraduate School (Master's), 2007.

Shaikh, Farzana. *Making Sense of Pakistan*. London: Hurst, 2009.

Siber, Ivan. "Psychological Approaches to Ethnic Conflict." In *Ethnic Conflict Management: The Care of Yugoslavia*, edited by Dusan Janjic. Ravenna: Longo Editore, 1997.

Siddiqi, Akhtar Husain. *Baluchistan (Pakistan): Its Society, Resources and Development*. Lanham: University Press of America, 1991.

Siddiqa, Ayesha. *Military Inc. Inside Pakistan's Military Economy*. Karachi: Oxford University Press, 2007.

Bibliography 199

Singh, Gurharpal and Ian Talbot. *Punjabi Identity: Continuity and Change.* New Delhi: Manohar Publishers, 1996.

Smith, Anthony. *The Ethnic Origins of Nations.* New York: Blackwell, 1986.

Spivak, Gayatri Chakravorty. *Critique of Postcolonial Reason: Toward a History of the Vanishing Present.* Cambridge: Harvard University Press, 1999.

Syed, Anwar H. *Pakistan: Islam, Politics and National Solidarity.* New York: NN, 1982.

Talbot, Ian and Shinder Thandi. *People on the Move: Punjabi Colonial and Post-Colonial Migration.* Oxford: Oxford University Press, 2004.

Talbot, Ian. *Pakistan: A Modern History.* London: Hurst, 2005.

Talbot, Ian. *Provincial Politics and the Pakistan Movement: The Growth of the Muslim League in Northwest and Northeast India, 1937–1947.* Oxford: Oxford University Press, 1988.

Talbot, Ian, ed. *The Deadly Embrace: Religion, Politics and Violence in India and Pakistan, 1947–2001.* Karachi: Oxford University Press, 2007.

Titus, Paul, ed. *Marginality and Modernity: Ethnicity and Change in Post-Colonial Balochistan.* Karachi: Oxford University Press, 1996.

Titus, Paul. "Honor the Baloch, Buy the Pashtun: Stereotypes, Social Organization, and History in Western Pakistan." *Modern Asian Studies* (July 1998): 657–87.

Titus, Paul and Nina Swidler. "Knights, Not Pawns: Ethno-Nationalism and Regional Dynamics in Post-Colonial Balochistan." *International Journal of Middle East Studies* 32, no. 1 (February 2000): 47–69.

Verkaaik, Oskar. "A People of Migrants: Ethnicity, State and Religion in Karachi." *Comparative Asian Studies* 15. Amsterdam: VU University Press, 1994.

Waseem, M. *Politics and the State in Pakistan.* Lahore: Vanguard, 1989.

Weiss, A. M. *Culture, Class and Development in Pakistan: The Emergence of an Industrial Bourgeoisie in Punjab.* Boulder, 1991.

Wilcox, W. *Pakistan: The Consolidation of a Nation.* New York, 1963.

Wirsing, R. G. *Pakistan's Security Under Zia, 1977–1988: The Policy Imperatives of a Peripheral Asian State.* Basingstoke, 1991.

Wirsing, R. G. *The Baluchis and Pathans.* London: NN, 1987.

Wirsing, R. G. *Baloch Nationalism and the Geopolitics of Energy Resources: The Changing Context of Separatism in Pakistan.* Carlisle, PA: Strategic Studies Institute, U.S. Army War College, 2008.

Wolpert, Stanley. *Zulfi Bhutto of Pakistan: His Life and Times.* London: Oxford University Press, 1993.

Yong, Tan Tai. *The Garrison State: Military, Government and Society in Colonial Punjab, 1849–1947.* Lahore: Vanguard Books, 2005.

Zaidi, Akbar. *Regional Imbalances and the National Question in Pakistan.* Lahore: Vanguard Books, 1992.

Ziring, Lawrence. *Pakistan in the Twentieth Century: A Political History.* Karachi: Oxford University Press, 1997.

Ziring, Lawrence. *Pakistan in the Twentieth Century: A Political History.* New York: Oxford University Press, 2000.

Ziring, Lawrence. *Pakistan: The Enigma of Political Development.* Boulder: NN, 1980.

Reports

Balochistan: Conflicts and Players. Islamabad: Pakistan Institute for Peace Studies, 2008.

Christer, Ahlström and Kjell-Åke Nordquist. *Casualties of Conflict, Report for the World Campaign for the Protection of Victims of War.* Department of Peace and Conflict Research, Uppsala University, 1991.

200   *Bibliography*

International Crisis Group. "Pakistan: The Forgotten Conflict in Balochistan." *International Crisis Group* Asia Briefing No. 69 (October 2007).

Parliamentary Committee on Balochistan. *Report of the Parliamentary Committee on Balochistan*. Report, Government of the Islamic Republic of Pakistan, Islamabad: Government of Pakistan, 2005.

Journals and Newspapers

Asian Survey
Economics of Governance
Foreign Affairs
International Affairs
International Security
International Organization
IPRI Journal
Journal of Conflict Resolution
Journal of Peace Research
Modern Asian Studies
Peace and Conflict Studies
Terrorism and Political Violence
South Asia Journal
South Asian Survey
Strategic Studies
Survival
African and Asian Studies
Asian Affairs
Asian Ethnicity
Christian Science Minotor
Assaap, Quetta
Azadi Quetta
Bakhabar, Quetta
Business Recorder
Daily Times
Dawn
Express
Friday Times
Frontier Post
Islam
Jang
Quaid-e-Azam Muhammad Ali Jinnah
Khabren
Nawa-e-Waqt
Newsline
Weekly Nida-e-Millat
Pulse

Salarmonthly
Weekly Takbeer
The Herald
Ummat
Baluchistan Express
Balochistan Post
Daily Independent
Le Monde Diplomatique – English
The News
The New York Times
The Washington Post

Internet Websites

Balochistan: Political Landscape, www.balochvoice.com/
Balochistan History. www.baloch2000.org/history/baloch.htm
Trade across Frontiers in Balochistan www.balochunity.org/index.php/facts
www.baloch2000.org
www.balochfront.org
www.balichistan.gov.pk
www.balochistan.org.pk
www.balochistaninfo.com
www.balochistanvoice.com
www.balochmedia.net
www.balochonline.com
www.balochunity.org
www.balochvoice.com
www.balochwarna.com
www.san-pips.com

Index

Page numbers followed by 'n' refer to notes.

abadkars (settlers) 83, 100; resentment against 83, 167–8; targeted killings of 146, 166–7

Abdul Hayee Baloch 95, 139, 142, 145, 185

Abdul Karim, Prince 78–9, 90n71

Abdul Rehman Brahui 68, 89n20

Abdul Samad Achakzai 67

Abdul Waheed Kakar, General 127

Adams, Brad 168

Afghan war 50, 121, 184

Afghanistan x, xii, 13, 19n59, 28–30, 35–6, 39, 41–2, 45, 47, 49–50, 57, 68–9, 71–2, 74–6, 79–80, 84, 90n73, 93, 108, 113–14, 118n64–22, 131–3, 135, 140–1, 143n48–4n73, 146, 161, 169–70, 172, 179n114–81, 184, 190; Soviet invasion of 121, 130, 132–3, 140–1, 184

Afridi, Lt. General K.K. xi

Afzal Bangesh 125

agencies xi, 49, 116, 134, 155, 167–9, 176n53

Agent to Governor General (AGG) 69, 81

Agha Abdul Karim, Prince 79

Agha Daud Jan 85

Agha Nasir Khan 70

Aghaz-e-Huqooq-e-Balochistan package: NFC award and 18th amendment 163–4, 178n93

Ahmad Yar Khan 8–9, 14–15, 40, 52–6, 58–59n36, 63–4, 67–9, 71–86, 88–90n38, 103, 182–3; appointment as Khan of Kalat 40, 52–3; arrest of 64, 104, 111, 115, 183; BSU and 81; contact with India 75; declaration of independence and reforms 69; Jinnah and 14, 63–4, 71–4, 80, 182–3; Mirza

and 83; Nauroz Khan's armed resistance against Pakistan Army, 8, 85, following arrest of 85–6; negotiation between Pakistan and 182; Pakistan Army took action against 85; planning to secede from Pakistan 106; protesting against One Unit 97; referendum in British Balochistan 67; signing Kalat's accession agreement with Pakistan 63, 182; standstill agreement 68–9; warned Soviets interest in Gwadar 132

Ahmadzai Brahuis 25

Ahmadzais, rise of 28

Ahmed, Akbar S. 35, 38n66, 78, 90n67, 191n1

Ahmed, Ishtiaq 84, 89n1, 96, 117n10

Ahmed Khan 28, 37n56, 130, 167–8

Ahmed Nawaz Bugti 87

Ahmed Rashid 19n56, 105

Ahmed Shah Abadali 29

Ajit Doval 171

Akbar Bugti xi, 9, 11–12, 15, 25, 29–30, 36n11–7n43, 83, 87–8, 93–4, 101–2, 108, 110–13, 116, 121, 128, 138–40, 142, 145–8, 150–4, 156–62, 171–3, 175n37, 177n69, 181, 183–5; BBC interview 151; BNYM support 139; Bugti–Mazari tribal feud 150; Bugti–NAP differences 112; commenting on Nasir Khan and Kalat 29; confiscation of 159; death 30–1, 35, 39, 42, 48, 50, 52, 72, 86, 126, 150, 159–62, 165, 172, 181; 15-point formula for resolution of Balochistan problem 154; governorship 99, 102–3, 113; and his tribal demands 181; issue of gas royalty 151; issue of no-confidence motion 139; Jamhoori

Wattan Party (JWP) 11, 140, 142, 161, 185; establishment of 28, 35, 81, 83, 86, 109, 136, 140, 188; joint Baloch platform proposal 154; and Mushahid meeting 153; and Musharraf regime 148–50, 153, 158–60; participation in political activities 11, 121, 142, 184; political career 11, 85, 94, 112, 135; post-Bugti death 161; protesting against One Unit 83; rivalry between Bizenjo and 111; weakening his hold on Bugti tribe 158–60
Akbar Musti Khan 135
Akhtar Hussain 156
Akhtar Mengal see Sardar Akhtar Mengal
Alaska Permanent Fund for Balochistan xii, 191
Alexander the Great 27
Ali Muhammad Mengal 104
All India Congress 51, 65, 71, 77
All India Muslim League 65
All India Radio report: about Khan's contact with India 75
all-party conference (APC) 163
Amanullah Kasrani 156
Amir-ul-Mulk Mengal 163
Anglo-Afghan War 53
animus dominandi 99
Anjuman Itahaad-e-Balochan group 51
Anosheervan 26
anti-Akbar Bugti Jirga 159
Arbab Sikander 98
Ardeshir (King) 26
armed Parari movement 88
Army Institute of Mineralogy (AIM) 166
Army of Indus 41–2
Article 3, of Treaty of 1876 56
Article 58 (2-B) of constitution 127
Asad Rehman 105
Asghar Khan 123, 125
Ashfaq Parvez Kayani, General 165–6
Asian geostrategic fault lines, CPEC and 189
Aslam Beg 126–7
Aslam Khan 64, 72, 74
Aslam Khattak 101
Ataullah Mengal, Sardar see Sardar Ataullah Mengal
Attlee, Clement 64
Awami League 93–5, 97, 101
Awan, A.B. 81, 83, 85, 89n23–91n85, 105–6, 118n41–19n109
Axmann, M. 35, 37n38, 53, 55, 58n2, 70

Ayub Khan 84–8, 94, 112, 124
Azad, Abdus Samad 102
Azad Baloch 168

Babar Awan 163
Bahadur Gul Muhammad Khan 52
bajar tax 34
Balach Marri 145, 157, 161
Balkrishna Sharma 77
Baloch: dishonouring of 85; insurgency xi–xii, 12–13, 15–16, 79, 89, 93, 96, 103–5, 108, 114, 122, 129, 146, 149, 157, 159–61, 166–7, 169–70, 172, 180–1, 185; narrative x, xiii, 1–3, 5–12, 14–15, 17n26–18n34, 35–6, 39, 46, 58, 64, 80, 87–8, 93, 104, 106, 109–11, 115–16, 121, 141, 145–6, 172–4, 181–3
Baloch Haq Tawar Party 145
Baloch, Inayatullah 70–1, 75, 79, 89n33–90n38
Baloch leadership: Bhutto factor 113; Bugti–NAP differences 112; failed to perform, reasons for 115, 183; NAP leadership's lack of political acumen 112; tribal feuds 25, 93, 107, 112, 116, 131, 146, 183–4
Baloch nationalist movement: decline of 137; during peace interval (1988–99) 121
Baloch Peoples Liberation Front (BPLF) 116
Baloch Students Organization (BSO) 95, 116, 137
Baloch tribes x, 23–5, 32, 34, 39, 42, 44–7, 50, 57–8, 79, 85, 112–13, 151, 153; and Afghanistan x, xii, 13, 19n59, 28–30, 35–6, 39, 41–2, 45, 47, 49–50, 57, 68–9, 71–2, 74–6, 79–80, 84, 90n73, 93, 108, 113–14, 118n64–22, 131–3, 135, 140–1, 143n48–4n73, 146, 161, 169–70, 172, 179n114–81, 184, 190; and centrality of sardars 32–5; culture xiii, 33–4, 47, 80, 122, 127, 148, 152–3, 155, 161, 171, 191n3; justice system 34; master narrative 7–8; origin and development 25, 36n19, 118n73; Sandeman dealing with 43–9; structure of xii, 32, 38n61, 43, 106, 189; tribal system 24, 32, 34–5, 47–8, 146, 148
Baloch–Afghan commission (1895) 49
Balochistan Dehi Muhafiz (BDM) 100, 106
Balochistan National Alliance (BNA) 138

204   *Index*

Balochistan National Movement (BNM) 139

Balochistan National Party (Mengal) 154, 161, 164

Balochistan National Youth Movement (BNYM) 139

Balochistan Reserved Police 109

Balochistan States Union (BSU) 80, 94

Balochistan viii–xiv, 8–16, 19n60, 23–30, 33–53, 55–9n22, 63–4, 66–7, 69–71, 77–8, 80–4, 86–103, 105–19n87, 121–5, 128–42, 145–87, 190–2; and 1970 elections 93–5, 97, 101, 113, 137; and Afghanistan, demarcation of border between 49; under Akbar Bugti's governorship 102; Basic Democracies system in 86–7; British involvement in 40, 57–8, 181; during British rule in India 39; Bugti–Mazari tribal feud 150; Bugti's royalty war to fourth insurgency in 149; cantonments in 87, 149, 153–4, 156, 163, 174n5, 180; centre's economic and development policy towards 133; CPEC and xii–xiii, 14, 16, 189–92n20; current insurgency in 12, 146, 157, 166–7, 180–1; declaration of independence, issuance of (1983) 69, 77, 136, 138, 143n59; declaring amnesty to insurgents 125; development for 15, 93; division of 48, 65; educational institutes, establishment of 166; emergence of BLA 150; ethno-political conflict in 2, 8–9, 14; facing violence 141; 15-point formula, to resolving issue 153–4, 175n38; finding other allies in 131; gas royalty, issue of 12, 146, 151, 158; geography 12, 24, 88, 180, 183; geostrategic concerns of British and 40; government of Pakistan's white paper on 108; induction of Baloch youth into Pakistan Army 166; insurgent groups in 146; involvement and role of Iran in 114; Iran and xii, 23, 26, 32, 41, 69, 71–2, 113–14, 170; Jamhoori Wattan Party (JWP) 11, 140, 142, 161, 185; joint political platform 154; Mengal's six points solution 165; military operation against Baloch insurgents 157; Musharraf regime's view and policy towards 148; Muslim Central Asian Republics (CARs) 140; N-cadet scheme in 166; NAP government and leadership in 100–1, 103, 108, 110–11, 113, 116; nationalist movement xiii, 121, 134, 137–8, 166, 184; Nauroz Khan's armed resistance in 84–5; new political parties in 138–9; One Unit and 14, 64, 81–6, 88, 94, 115, 124, 129, 136, 183; ongoing crisis in 166; Pakistan and USSR's invasion of Afghanistan 131; Pakistan's view on Indian involvement in 170; parliamentary committee on 152–3, 155–6, 162–3; participation in politics 122, 185; during peace interval (1988–99) 129; policy confusion of British about 51, 55; political activities during decade of democracy 138; political awakening in 51; political developments in 15, 51, 73, 87, 93, 107, 116, 122; PPP government's all-party conference on 163; regional developments 147; rejection of committee's recommendations on 155–6; releasing Baloch prisoners 130; return of violence in 16, 145, 149, 185; revival meeting (2005) 156; rise in resentment against abadkars (settlers) in 83, 100; Sandeman system in 40, 48, 51, 55; Sandeman's mission to 45; Sandeman's policy towards 46; senate committee recommendations on 153, 155, 173, 185; and separation of India 66; Shazia's rape and intensification of violence 156; strategic significance 49, 56, 84, 130, 133, 141, 147–8, 187; Sui gas field in 172, 179n124; targeted killings and missing persons 166; in wake of Soviet invasion of Afghanistan 121, 132–3, 140–1, 184; Zia's approach and policy towards 129; see also centre–Balochistan relations

Balochistani Gandhi 67

Baluch, M.S.K. 58

Banerjee, Sashanka 101, 118n45

Bangladesh 13, 96–7, 101–2, 116n2, 118n45

Basic Democracies system, in Balochistan 86–7

Batay Khan 86

Battle of Kosovo 4

Battle of Plassey 41

Beebarg Baloch 163

Beglar Begi (Chief of Chiefs) 31

Belusis 25

Benazir Bhutto 126–7, 139–40

Berlin Wall, fall of 140

Index   205

Bhutto, Zulfikar Ali 96, 117n32–19n78; factor xii, xiv, 2–3, 9, 12–13, 15, 40–1, 46, 53, 76, 93, 111, 113, 124, 137, 185; and London plan 100–1; Mengal and Marri's attitude towards 113; role in downfall of NAP government 113; against sardari system 34, 103, 106, 110, 115, 148, 177n68; and Shah relationship 114; visiting Balochistan (1976) 103; and Zia 15–16, 111, 116, 120n124, 122–6, 128–38, 140–1, 143n41, 146, 154, 184

Bikram Singh 171

BITE (Balochistan Institute of Technical Education) 166

Bizenjo, Ghaus Bakhsh see Ghaus Bakhsh Bizenjo

Bizenjo sardar 31, 111, 130

BLA (Baloch Liberation Army) 146, 190; emergence of 2, 25, 39, 50–1, 89n12–90n56, 117n28, 124, 140–2, 150, 181, 184–5

BLF (Baloch Liberation Front) 146

BLT (Baloch Liberation Tiger) 146

BMDT (Baloch Musalla Defa Tanzeem) 146

bolaks (groups) 32

Bosnia–Herzegovina, ethnic conflicts in 1

boundary stories 5

BRA (Baloch Republic Army) 146

Brahui group 24

Brahumdagh Bugti 157, 159, 162–3, 167, 171

Brig Saleem Nawaz 157

British Balochistan 34, 40, 49, 63, 66–7, 69, 183; referendum in 67

British government: involvement in Balochistan 40, 57–8, 169–70, 179n116, 181; transferring of power to Indian leadership 64

Brzezinski, Zbigniew 133

BSO (Baloch Student Organization) 131, 146

Bugti, Aziz 36n11–8n62, 119n107, 135, 143n31

Bugti, Nawab Akbar see Akbar Bugti

Bulliet, Richard 10

Bush, George 1, 16n4

Cabinet Mission plan 65

Caroe, Olaf 56

Central Asian Republics (CARs) 140, 142, 187

centre versus Baloch narrative 106

centre–Balochistan relations (1969–77); Akbar Bugti's governorship 102; Baloch insurgency x, 12–13, 16, 79, 89, 104, 108, 114, 161, 170, 172, 180; developments in 14–15, 51, 73, 93, 96, 107, 114, 116, 122, 145, 150, 166, 172; London Group 105; London plan 100–1; major events during NAP government 99

centre's economic and development policy: towards Balochistan 46, 57, 88, 129–31, 133, 146, 148, 158, 173, 181, 183

Chakar the Great 26, 28

Chamalang, battle at 104, 114

Chamalang Beneficiary Education Programme (CBEP) 166

Chaudhry Muhammad Ali 81

Chaudhry Nouraiz Shakoor 152

Chaudhry Shujaat Hussain 152, 155

Cheddadi, Abdesselam 10

China 13, 187–92n11

China–Pakistan Economic Corridor (CPEC) xii, 14, 189, 191; and Asian geostrategic fault lines 189; and Baloch nationalists 9, 15, 28, 30, 58, 80–2, 86–7, 103, 111–12, 115, 132, 145–8, 152–3, 156–7, 160, 162, 165–6, 168, 173, 175n34, 177n78, 181, 190; Balochistan and future of Pakistan 16, 191

Choudhury, G.W. 94, 117n3

Chretien, Jean-Pierre 6, 17n24

Chuck Hagel 171

civil war 28, 30, 39, 93, 110, 114, 141, 186

Clinton, Hillary 170

Clive, Robert 41

closed border policy school 57

Cold War 1, 5, 84, 131, 140; end of x, 1, 5, 16n3, 46, 50, 64, 132, 134–5, 140–1, 156, 165, 168n177

collective memory: of ethnic group 2–6, 10; role in narrative creation 7

conflict narratives 7

conflict-supportive narratives 8–10; ethnic elite and 2–5, 10–13

constitution of 1973 xiii, 65, 70, 85, 98–9, 117n26, 119n98, 123, 125, 127, 129, 164–5

Council Muslim League (CML) 98

Council of Common Interests 155, 164

Dahwar, Saeed 81

Dalip Johny Das 105

206   Index

Daptar Shaar (Chronicle of Genealogies) 25

Dar-ul-Awam (House of Commons) 69, 72–3

Dar-ul-Umra (House of Lords) xiii, 63, 69, 72, 182

Dasta Jhalawan (regiment of Jhalawan) 31

Dasta Khas (special regiment) 31

Dasta Sarawan (regiment of Sarawan) 31

Daultana Muslim League 94

decade of democracy (1988–99) 121–2, 126–8, 138, 141–2, 146, 184–5; emerging trends of political culture of Pakistan during 127; political activities in Balochistan during 51, 138; return of democratic practices 127

Dehawars 28

delegitimization 8

Dera Bugti xi, 11, 140, 149–51, 153, 159–60, 162, 171, 176n47–7n65

Dera Ghazi Khan 83

devolution plan, launching 147

Doda Khan Zarakzai 110, 112–13, 138

Dostain Khan Jamaldini 188

Dundas, Sir Ambrose 78

Durand, Henry Mortimer 49

Dyer, Brigadier 50

East Pakistan: separation and 1970 national elections 95

Eastern Baloch 24

economic and development policy, in Balochistan 133

Economic Cooperation Organization (ECO) 140

Edwina Mountbatten 65

18th amendment, passing to Pakistan constitution 164

elections: in 1970 15, 93–5, 97, 101, 111, 113, 137; in 1988 126–7, 138–9; in 2002 147; in 2008 162; in 2013 164–5

enforced disappearances 168–9

Enlai, Zhou 189

ethnic conflicts 1–3, 5–6, 11; in Bosnia and Rwanda 6; in Yugoslavia 4–5, 16n7–18n40

ethnic elite: and conflict-supportive narratives 8–10; fear of other group, creating 10, 76, 100, 190; in politicization of ethnicity 2–5, 12, 15; role of 2–3, 9, 33–4, 40, 43–4, 47, 87, 94, 97, 108, 113–14, 116, 124, 184

ethnicity, politicization of 2–5, 12, 15

ethno-political conflicts 2, 8–9; narratives role in 7

event-specific narratives 8

Evera, Van 6

external actors 169

Fair, C. Christine 170

Faisal Saleh Hayat 150

Faiz Ali Chishti, General 122

Farooq Leghari 127

Farrukh Saleem 170, 179n117, 192n9

The Father's Bow (Redaelli) 36, 54

Fell, Douglas 64, 71–2, 80

Feroz Khan Noon 84

15-point formula: for resolution of Balochistan problem 154

Fill, Douglas 71

financial aids, for projects in Balochistan 134, 148, 171, 180

Firdosi (poet) 26

Forward policy school 57

France and England, rivalry between 39–40

Franz Ferdinand, Archduke, murder of 1, 16n1

Fukuyama, Francis 1, 16n3

gas royalty, issue of 151

Geertz, Clifford 65

General Abdul Waheed Kakar 127

General Ashfaq Parvez Kayani 165–6

General Faiz Ali Chishti 122

General Mirza Aslam Beg 126

General Pervez Musharraf 15, 147, 152; announced seven-point agenda 147; attack on 43, 104, 151, 157–8, 174n12, 177n71; policy of weakening Bugti's hold 158; regime's view and policy towards Balochistan 148; takes over and consolidates his power 147

General Sherof see Sher Muhammad Marri

General Yahya Khan 15, 93–4

geostrategic fault lines, in Asia 189

Ghaus Bakhsh Bizenjo xi, 15–16, 67, 72, 77, 79, 94, 98–9, 104, 107–8, 110, 112, 128–30, 134

Ghous Bakhsh Raisani 83, 109, 112

Ghulam Ishaq Khan 126–7

Ghulam Mustafa Khar 9

Ghulam Qadir Masoori Bugti 158

GIT (Gwadar Institute of Technology) 166

Government of India Act 1935 56, 73

Great War (World War I) 49, 51

Green, Henry 43

group identities, crystallization of 4
guerrillas 86–7, 104–5, 114, 135, 159
Gul Khan Naseer 24–5, 36n4–7n29, 58n1–
9n22, 76, 86
Gwadar xi, xiii, 13, 30, 37n47, 84, 132–4,
140–2, 145–6, 148–9, 153–6, 164,
166, 169, 172, 187–92n9, Gwadar Port
xii, 141, 145–6, 148–9, 154, 156, 169,
187–91

Habib Jalib Baloch 156
Habibullah Khan 74
Hafeez Pirzada 125
Hajaj bin Yusaf 27
Haji Juma Khan 169
Hamid Karzai 169
Harrison, Captain 44
Harrison, Selig 36, 80, 86, 90, 104, 114,
129, 135
Hatu Ram, Rai Bahadur 26, 36n5
Hayat Mohammed Sherpao 117n14
Hayee Baloch 95, 139, 142, 145, 155, 185
Hazil Bizenjo 165
Hirschon, Renee 6
historical narratives 10, 17n28
Human Rights Commission of Pakistan
(HRCP) 168–9
Human Rights Watch 168–9
Huntington, Samuel P. 85, 91n106
Hutu–Tutsi conflict 4

Ichthyophagi group 27
Ijaz Jhakrani 163
Independence Act 1947 73
India: British colonization of 40; joined
TAP pipeline project 141; Kalat and
24, 28–9, 31, 36, 39–40, 42–5, 47–51,
53–8, 63–4, 67–9, 71, 73–4, 76, 85, 88,
90n62, 115, 182–3; Khan's contact with
75; Pakistan's view on involvement
in Baloch issue 170; separation of 66,
94–6, 111, 117n9, 183
Indian federation, issue of Kalat joining 56
Indian subcontinent, partition of viii, 64
Indonesia, ethnic conflicts in 1
insurgency: Baloch 79–80, 104–6, 161;
return of xii, 16, 28, 53, 69, 82, 84,
86, 88, 97, 122, 135, 145–6, 149, 158,
176n57, 185
interim constitution 98, 117n26
Iran x, xii, 13, 23, 26–7, 32, 41, 69, 71–2,
84, 111, 113–14, 169–70, 179n113, 190
Islam 27, 38n66, 97–9, 123–4, 129, 138
Islamabad xii, xiii, 8, 14–16, 19n57,

36n3, 74, 90n50, 99, 101, 112, 114–15,
118n58–19n78, 131–2, 136, 141–3n36,
147, 152, 154, 156–7, 160–1, 164, 167,
169–72, 174n2, 178n90, 183, 186, 188,
190–1
Islamic Jamhoori Ittehad (IJI) 126
Islamization of Pakistan 123
Isphani, Mahnaz 134

Jam Ghulam Qadir 110, 113
Jam Ghulam Shah 30
Jam Muhammad Yousaf 163, 176n43
Jamhoori Wattan Party (JWP) 11, 140,
142, 161, 185
Jamiat-e-Ulema-e-Islam (JUI) 97, 128
Jamiat-e-Ulema-e-Pakistan (JUP) 98
Jangez Marri 161
Jehangir Badar 163
Jhalawan Brahui group 24
Jinnah see Quaid-e-Azam Muhammad Ali
Jinnah
jirgas 34, 70
joint jirgas 34
Junajo 138

Kachkol Baloch 156
Kai Khusru (Cyrus the Great) 27
Kaiser Bengali 190
Kalat State National Party (KSNP) 52, 70,
77, 88; creation on 1937 66
Karakoram Highway 188
Kasehkoran/Kasmakoran 26
Kenya 3
Khair Bakhsh Marri see Nawab Khair
Bakhsh Marri
Khair Jan Bizenjo 104
Khalid Bin Sayeed 99, 116n1
Khalid Khokar 169
Khan Abdul Ghaffar Khan 66
Khan Abdul Wali Khan 97, 101, 125, 132;
Khan Khudadad Khan 56
Khan sahib 83
Khanate of Kalat: British position and
debates about status of 40; during
British rule in India 49–50; chequered
relationship with tribal sardars 31;
declaration of independence and
reforms 69, 77; establishment of 27,
35, 81; forcible accession of 9, 78, 174;
growing administrative quandary 50;
and India viii, xii–xiii, 1, 13–14, 19n58,
27, 35–7n38, 39–46, 48–59n9, 63–9,
71–9, 89n11–90n48, 96, 98, 101–2,
105, 118n45, 123, 131–4, 141, 148,

208   Index

169–71, 179n114, 181–2, 189–92; issue of accession 67, 69, 72–3; and Pakistan xii–xiii, 63–5, 67–9, 74, 76, 89n11, 116, 122–3, 128, 134–5, 140, 147, 156, 161, 169, 182–4, 187–8, 191
Kharan 30, 49, 55–6, 66–7, 74–6, 78–82, 149
Khilafat Movement 50–1
Kholu 149, 157
Khun Bha (blood feuds) 33
Khyber Pakhtunkhwa see NWFP
King Ardeshir 26
Kissinger, Henry x
Kurds 26
Kurosawa, Akira 1
Kuwait Fund for Arab Economic Development (KFAED) 134

Lahore Resolution (1940) 125
Laitin, David 3
land reforms 107
Las Bela 9, 42, 48–50, 55–6, 67, 74–6, 78–82, 110, 134
Lasbela incident 110
Lauang Khan 104
leased areas 40, 67–9, 82, 88
Lemarchand, Rene 4
Liaquat Ali Khan 66, 80
Lifschultz, Lawrence 136, 143n56
local jirgas 34, 70
London Group 105
London plan 100–1; Bhutto regime and 101, 104, 106, 113, 118n58, 123, 125
loose federation, establishing 134
Lord Louis Mountbatten 65
Lord Lytton 45
Lord Northbrook 45

Maharaja Ranjit Singh 41
Mahi Khoran (fish eaters) 26
Major General Shujaat Zamir Dar 157
Makdoom Amin Fahim 158
Makran Baloch 24
Makran x–xi, 24, 26–7, 30, 41, 50, 74–5, 78–9, 100, 108, 132–4, 141, 187; Arabs in 27; Chagatai invaded 27
Malik, Abdul 142, 165, 185
Malik, Hafeez ix, 117n28, 131
Malik, Rahman 167
Malik Baloch 164–5
Malik Faiz Muhammad Yusafzai 52
Malik Siraj Akbar 117n66, 178n97, 186n1, 190, 192n18
Malik Wali Kakar 151

maliya, collection of 34
Marri and Bugti tribes 46, 49
Marri, Khair Bakhsh see Nawab Khair Bakhsh Marri
martial laws, in Pakistan 84
Masoori and Kalpars, return of 158
Masson, Charles 31, 37n53
master conflict-supportive narrative 8
master narratives 7
Mastung Settlement 45
Masud, M. 67
Maulana Abul Kalam Azad 77
Maulana Fazal-ur-Rahman 158
Mazdoor Kisan Party (MKP) 98, 125
Mboya, Joseph 3, 16n9
McKinley, William 10
McMahan, Colone 49
McMahan line 49
Mehrgarh sites 20
Mengal sardar 31, 130
Mengal, Sardar Ataullah see Sardar Ataullah Mengal
Menon, V.P. 76, 78
Merewether, Sir W. 44
military intervention myth: and forcible accession of Kalat 78
military operation, against Baloch insurgents 157–8
Milosevic: on occasion of anniversary of Battle of Kosovo 4–5; role in Bosnian conflict 4; speech (in 1987) 4; use of narrative based on collective memory of historical injustice 5
Ministry of Foreign Affairs (MFA) 74, 90n53
Mir Abdul Aziz Kurd 51–2
Mir Abdul Quddus Bizenjo 190
Mir Abdul Rehman Bugti 52
Mir Ahmad Khan 32
Mir Ahmad Yar Khan see Ahmad Yar Khan
Mir Ali Ahmed Talpur 99
Mir Alsam Khan Gichki 104
Mir Anwar Khan 52
Mir Azam Jan 52
Mir Azam Khan 50
Mir Chakar Rind 27
Mir Ghaus Bakhsh Bizenjo see Ghaus Bakhsh Bizenjo
Mir Gohram Lashari 27
Mir Habibullah Khan 74
Mir Hasil Bizenjo 156
Mir Hazar Khan 88, 104
Mir Hazar Ramkhani 114, 135
Mir Jafar Khan Jamali 67, 83

Mir Jalal Khan 24, 32
Mir Khuda Bux Bijrani Baloch 26
Mir Khudadad Khan 43, 45–6, 50–1
Mir Lashkari Raisani 163
Mir Mahmud Khan 50
Mir Mahmud Khan II 50
Mir Mehrab Khan 42
Mir Mohammad Habibullah Khan 72
Mir Nabi Bakhsh Zehri 138
Mir Nasir Khan 29, 39, 84
Mir Nasir Khan Nuri 39
Mir Umer Qambarani 27
Mir Yusuf Ali Magsi 51
Mir Zafarullah Khan Jamali 138, 152
Mirza Aslam Beg, General 126
Mirza, Iskander 83–5
missing and dead persons 168
Mithankot conference (1871) 44
Moinuddin Baloch 138
Moore, Thomas 133
Moscow 132, 135
motebars leadership system 34
Mountbatten, Lord Louis 65
Movement for the Restoration of
    Democracy (MRD) 124
Mufti Mahmud 97–8, 107
Mughals 28, 40
Muhammad Ali Talpur 105
Muhammad Arif Hasani 139
Muhammad Aslam Khan 64, 72, 74
Muhammad Hussain Unqa 52
Muhammad Khan Junejo 126
Muhammad Sardar Khan 25, 36n5
Mujib, Sheikh 102
Mujibur Rahman 95–7, 101–2
Mushahid Hussain Syed 152
Musharraf, General see General Pervez
    Musharraf
Muslim Central Asian Republics (CARs)
    140
Muslim League 16, 65–6, 94–5, 98, 124,
    127, 138–9, 165
Mutahida Majlis-e-Amal (MMA) 147

N-cadet scheme 166
Nabi Bakhsh Zehri 112, 138
Nadir Shah 24, 29–30
Najam Sethi 105–6, 168
narratives: defined 4, 48, 85, 164;
    description of; elements of 7–8;
    ethnic elite and 10–14; ethno-political
    conflict and 8–10; significance of
    5–6
Nasir Khan I 29–33, 43

National Awami Party (NAP) 94–5, 97,
    115, 124, 138; Bugti–NAP differences
    112; leadership's lack of political
    acumen 112
national elections: in Pakistan (2008) 161;
    and separation of East Pakistan (1970)
    95–6
Nauroz Khan: armed resistance against
    Pakistan Army 85–6
Nausherwan 27
Nawab Akbar Bugti see Akbar Bugti
Nawab Bai Khan 78–9
Nawab Bai Khan Gichki 78
Nawab Ghous Bakhsh Raisani 83
Nawab Khair Bakhsh Marri 83, 94, 99,
    104–5, 112, 128–31, 135, 146, 158
Nawab Magsi 139
Nawab Muhammad Aslam Raisani 163
Nawab Muhammad Khan Jogezai 67
Nawab Sir Mir Shams Shah 50
Nawab Zulfiqar Ali Magsi 163
Nawaz Sharif 126–7, 139–41, 147, 164–5,
    189; arrest of 147; PML-N 164; visit to
    China (2014) 189
Nehru, Jawaharlal 77
NFC (National Finance Commission)
    award 163–4, 178n93
Nimrod the Belus 25
9/11 terrorist attack 147
Nizam-e-Mustafa 123
Nurul Amin 117n13
NWFP (Khyber Pakhtunkhwa) 49, 66–7,
    83, 93, 95–8, 101–11, 113, 117n14,
    124–5, 132, 150
Omer ibn-ul-Khatab 27

One Belt One Road (OBOR) 188, 190
One Unit policy 64, 129, 183
Operation Fair Play 116, 122
Operation Searchlight (1971) 95
Oreitai group 27
other 2, 6, 10
Owais Ahmed Ghani 161, 163

Pakistan 13; Afghanistan relations and
    113; Central Asian Republics (CARs)
    140, 142, 187; China and 183–4;
    constitutional debate 97; CPEC and
    16, 187, 189–90; creation of 7, 47, 52,
    64, 73, 83–4, 95–6, 106, 109, 125, 133,
    163; decade of democracy (1988–99)
    in 121–2, 126, 128, 138, 141–2, 146,
    184–5; developments in 91; emerging
    trends in evolving political culture of

210   *Index*

127–8; under General Yahya Khan
94; government of 69, 77, 80, 103;
Islam in national integration 91n89,
123–4, 129, 134; issued white paper
on Balochistan 108, 117n36; Kalat
and 149, 167, 174, 181; martial laws
in 84; national elections (2008) in
156–7; Nauroz Khan's armed resistance
against 85; passing of 18th amendment
to constitution of 163–4; political
reconstruction 97; return of Gwadar to
84; security forces 12, 19n59, 78, 85–6,
100–1, 104, 106, 108, 125, 153, 157,
159–61, 167–8; solution to national
integration problem 135; state- and
nation-building challenges 65; USSR's
invasion of Afghanistan and x, 80,
121, 131–3, 140, 184; view on Indian
involvement in Balochistan 170; Zia and
x–xi, 15–16, 111, 116, 121–6, 128–38,
140–2, 146, 184
Pakistan Armed Forces 124, 132, 172
Pakistan Muslim League (Qayyum) 95
Pakistan National Alliance (PNA) 123
Pakistan National Party (PNP) 124, 134,
137–8
Pakistan Peoples Party (PPP) 94–5, 113,
124, 139, 162–3; Aghaz-e-Huqooq-
e-Balochistan package 163; all-party
conference on Balochistan 163;
government 161–2, 172
Palu Sherik (partners) 31
Pararis 104, 114
partition of Indian subcontinent 64–5
Pashtun Ghilazis 28
Pat Feeder incident 112
Patriotism 8, 136
peace interval, in Balochistan (1977–99)
121–2
Pervez Musharraf, General see General
Pervez Musharraf
Peter the Great 41
Phayre (Colonel) 43
political activities, in Balochistan during
decade of democracy 138, 142, 184
political culture of Pakistan, during decade
of democracy 122, 127, 155, 161
political legitimacy, gaining 3
Political Parties Amendment Act (1985)
125
Polo, Marco 26
Port of Singapore Authority (PSA) 188
Pottinger, Henry 33, 35, 38n64, 41
Princip, Gavrilo 1, 16n2

Public School in Sui 166
Punjab 9–10, 28, 41–2, 44, 46–7, 64–6,
79–80, 82–3, 95–6, 100, 104–5, 109,
111, 115, 123–5, 128–30, 132–7, 146–7,
150, 153, 165–8, 172–3, 178n99
Punjabi fascism 79
Punjabization of Pakistan 124–5

Qayyum Khan 98, 100, 110
Qayyum League 94
Qayyum Muslim League (QML) 98
Qazi Hussain Ahmad 158
Quaid-e-Azam Muhammad Ali Jinnah 14,
63–4, 66–7, 69, 71–4, 80, 88–90n53,
182–3
Quetta 30, 36n4–7n38, 42, 46, 49, 52, 55,
57–9n9, 67, 83, 100, 114, 131, 133, 136,
149, 161, 166–7, 172
Quetta Institute of Medical Sciences
(QIMS) 166
Quetta Municipal Committee 67

Radcliffe, Sir Cyril 65
Rahimuddin Khan, Lt. General 130
Rai Chach 27
Raja Ahmed Khan 130
Raja Tridev Roy 112n13
Ranjit Singh, Maharaja 41
Rashid Rehman 105
Rashomon (film by Kurosawa) 1
Rasul Baksh Talpur 117n14
Raza, Rafi 99, 17n32
Red Army 121, 184, 187
Redaelli, Riccardo 54
referendum, in British Balochistan 66–7
resentment against abadkars 83
revolution x, 85, 91n106, 106, 131
Rind tribe 24, 27
Rivaj (code of honour) 33–4, 73
road construction, in Balochistan 133–4
Roberson, Agneza 4, 17n17
Russia 41
Rwanda, ethnic conflicts in 1

Saan group 31
Saeed Sultan 30
Sajid Tareen 156
Saleem Khoso 156
Samad Khan 77
Sana Baloch 156
Sandeman, Robert 43–4, 46, 51, 57, 59n16,
184; policy towards Balochistan 46, 57,
88, 129–31, 133, 148, 173, 181, 183
Sandeman system 40, 48, 51, 55

Sarawan Brahui group 24, 31, 34
Sarbaz Baloch 162
Sardar Akhtar Mengal 128, 150, 156
Sardar Ataullah Mengal 9, 93–4, 99–100, 104, 109, 111–12, 125, 128–32, 136, 138, 150, 152
Sardar Behram Khan Leghari 51
Sardar Doda Khan Zehri Zarakzai 86
Sardar Ghous Bakhsh Raisani 112
Sardar Khan Baluch 36n5, 76, 90n61
sardar leadership system 34
Sardar Muhammad Khan Shahwani 51
Sardar Muhmmad Khan 51
Sardar Rasulbakhsh Zarakzai 51–2
Sardar Rasulbaskhsh Mengal 52
Sardar Sherbaz Khan Mazari see Sherbaz Mazari
Sardar Yar Muhammad Rind 163, 175n35–6n43
sardari system 34, 103, 106, 110, 115, 148, 177n68
sardars: and British government in India 41–5, 49, 51, 68; centrality of 32, 35, 47; and Khan of Kalat 14, 29, 31, 33, 36, 39–59, 63–4, 67–82, 84, 88, 90n71, 110, 115, 182, 184; Sandeman's policy towards 46, 48; supporting Ahmad Yar Khan 8–9, 14–15, 40, 52–6, 58–9n36, 63–4, 67–9, 71–86, 88–90n38, 103, 182–3
Sayyid Ali Khamenei 170
Scholz, Fred 32, 37n54
sectarian violence 146
Seleucus 27
senate committee on Balochistan 153, 155, 173
Serbian League of Communists 4
settlers see abadkars (settlers)
7th National Finance Commission Award 164
shadi-ghum 33
Shafiq Ahmed Khan 167
Shah of Iran 41, 84, 111–14
Shah, S.B. 74
Shah Shuja 38
Shahi Jirga 41–2
Shaikh Hasina Wajid 118n45
Shaukat Aziz 156, 159
Shazia Khalid 156
Sheikh Mujibur Rahman 97, 101–2
Sher Muhammad Marri 87
Sherbaz Mazari 83, 86, 94, 99, 112–14, 117n4
Sherpao, Aftab Ahmed Khan 168

shishak (agricultural tax) 34
Shivshankar Menon 170
Short Service Commission 166
Shuja Nawaz 84, 91n100
Shujaat Zamir Dar, Major General 157
Shujaat–Mushahid committee 150, 152
Siber, Ivan 2, 3, 16n7
Simla Accord 98
Sindh 27–8, 30, 41–4, 46, 48, 65, 79, 82, 96, 101–11, 117n14, 124–5, 151, 167
Sindhi–Baloch–Pashtun Front (SBPF) 125
Small, Andrew 189, 191n5–2n17
Smith, Joshua 12, 18n51–19n52
Soviet invasion of Afghanistan 121, 132–3, 140–1, 184; Balochistan in wake of 122, 132–3, 183–4
Special Development Plan for Balochistan 133
Squire, Frederick 53
Sri Lanka, ethnic conflicts in 1
standstill agreement: between Pakistan and Kalat 68, 72, 76
steam engine 40
Strayer, Joseph 66, 89n9
Sui gas field 172, 179n124
Sui Military College 166
Sui Northern Gas Pipeline Limited (SNGPL) 150
Suleman Baloch 24
Suliman Khan Ahmadzai 104
Sultan Muhammad Mengal 109
Sultan Saeed 84
Sultana Bibi 30
Sunni Muslims 26
surrender game 159
Swidler, Nina 29–30, 33, 37n34–8n61
Syed, G. M. 101
symbolic politics 6, 17n21

Tactical Support Division (TSD) 170
Tahreekh-e-Balochistan (History of Balochistan) 76
takkaris leadership system 34
Talal Bugti 162
Talbot, Ian x, 66, 96, 117n6
targeted killings, of Punjabi settlers 166
Tariq Ali 109, 119n90
Tariq Aziz 153, 155, 175n38
Tariq Masoori Bugti 158
Tate, G.P. 23
Tehreek-e-Taliban Pakistan (TTP) 171
Tehrik-i-Istiqlal 125
threats, types of 12
Tikka Khan 122, 172

212 Index

Tipu Sultan 40
Treaty of Fars 41
Treaty of Gandermak of 49
tribal areas 13, 49, 96, 127
tribal feuds 25, 93, 107, 112, 116, 131, 146, 183–4
Tsur, Nadir 9, 18
Tuman 32
Turkmenistan–Afghanistan–Pakistan pipeline (TAP) 141

Union of Soviet Socialist Republics (USSR) 1, 5; dissolution of 1, 9, 15, 82–3, 86; invasion of Afghanistan x, 121, 131–3, 140–1, 184
Unionist Party 66
United Arab Emirates (UAE) 125
USAID 134
Uzbekistan 140

Vara Pishin-anha (valley of Pishin) 26
viceregalism 66
victim complex 6
Vinod Bhatia 171
violation 87, 157, 165
violence x, 1–6, 9, 12, 15–16, 46, 44, 82, 87, 105, 108, 112, 122, 135, 142, 145–6, 149–50, 156–7, 159, 161, 166–7, 171, 180–1, 185; return of 144–56
V.K. Singh 170

Wadera Jumma Khan 159
Waheed Abdullah 114
Wakefield, Edward 51
Wali-i-Kalat (Governor of Kalat) 31

Wali Khan, Khan Abdul 97, 101, 125, 132
Western Baloch 24
white paper, on Balochistan 108, 117n36
Wirsing, Robert 83, 120n124, 174n1
Wolpert, Stanley 102, 119n80

Xi Jinping 189, 192n11

Yahya Khan, General 15, 93–4
Yugoslavia: disintegration of 4; ethnic conflict in 4–5

Zafar Khan 104
Zafarullah Khan 164, 173
Zafrullah Zehri 169
Zarakzai sardar 31, 110
Zardari, Asif Ali 162–3
Zia-ul-Haq x–xi, 121–2, 142n1; accommodation and reconciliation policy 137, 162; approach and policy towards Baloch issue 129, 153, 170; and Bhutto 117–18, 124–5; controlled democracy under 126; and decade of democracy (1988–99) 121, 126, 184; declared amnesty for Baloch insurgents 141, 184; finding other allies in Balochistan 131; his view of Pakistan and its politics 118–19; initial contacts with Baloch leaders 125–6; MQM created during his regime 128, 177n71; Operation Fair Play 116, 122; policies pursued by him 122; political opposition to his regime 123–4; releasing Baloch prisoners 130
Zikris x

Printed in the United States
By Bookmasters